The Teacher Credibility Codebook

How can you build a classroom environment that creates buy-in from students? Richard Young shows how teacher credibility goes beyond building relationships. He offers a practical framework centred on student perception, engagement, motivation, trust, and communication, resulting in improved learning outcomes.

With compelling visuals throughout, Young offers insights into how student motivation and social dynamics shape their perceptions. He also explains the nuances behind student inferences, social contagion, and cognitive alignment, so that you can learn how to proactively address misinterpretations, reinforce credibility, promote positive student perceptions, and create a more connected, cooperative learning environment. Each chapter offers actionable strategies and research-based tools to help you implement the ideas.

Teachers at the middle and high school levels, where social dynamics and student misperceptions frequently impact learning environments, will particularly benefit from the unique and effective ideas in this book.

Richard A. Young is an education consultant with the Western Quebec School Board, near Ottawa, Canada. He collaborates with administrators to analyse student voice, school climate, and engagement. Before transitioning into consultancy, he spent 27 years as a teacher and vice-principal, leading at both the elementary and high school levels.

Also Available from Routledge
Eye On Education
www.routledge.com

What Great Teachers Do Differently, Third Edition:
Nineteen Things That Matter Most
Todd Whitaker

Passionate Learners, Third Edition:
How to Engage and Empower Your Students
Pernille Ripp

Motivating Struggling Learners:
10 Ways to Build Student Success
Barbara R. Blackburn

The Student Motivation Handbook:
50 Ways to Boost an Intrinsic Desire to Learn
Larry Ferlazzo

A Lasting Impact in the Classroom and Beyond:
Knowledge and Insight for Brave Teachers
Larry Strauss

Classroom Management from the Ground Up
Todd Whitaker, Katherine Whitaker, Madeline Whitaker Good

The Teacher Credibility Codebook

Research-Based Tools for Improving Student Perception, Motivation, and Buy-In

Richard A. Young

NEW YORK AND LONDON

Designed cover image: Getty Images

First published 2026
by Routledge
605 Third Avenue, New York, NY 10158

and by Routledge
4 Park Square, Milton Park, Abingdon, Oxon, OX14 4RN

Routledge is an imprint of the Taylor & Francis Group, an informa business

© 2026 Richard A. Young

The right of Richard A. Young to be identified as author of this work has been asserted in accordance with sections 77 and 78 of the Copyright, Designs and Patents Act 1988.

All rights reserved. No part of this book may be reprinted or reproduced or utilised in any form or by any electronic, mechanical, or other means, now known or hereafter invented, including photocopying and recording, or in any information storage or retrieval system, without permission in writing from the publishers.

For Product Safety Concerns and Information please contact our EU representative GPSR@taylorandfrancis.com. Taylor & Francis Verlag GmbH, Kaufingerstraße 24, 80331 München, Germany.

Trademark notice: Product or corporate names may be trademarks or registered trademarks, and are used only for identification and explanation without intent to infringe.

ISBN: 978-1-041-08171-5 (hbk)
ISBN: 978-1-041-08170-8 (pbk)
ISBN: 978-1-003-64408-8 (ebk)

DOI: 10.4324/9781003644088

Typeset in Palatino
by codeMantra

This book is dedicated to the educators doing that quiet, credibility-building work every day—often unseen, but never unnoticed by the students who need it most.

Contents

Simplicity Mission — ix
Preface — x
Meet the Author — xv

Why This Book… An Introduction to the Ideas — 1

Part 1   How Students Interpret You — 5

1 Simplifying the Complexity of Your Classroom — 7

2 How Students Think about You and Why It Matters — 12

3 Student Perception: What's Real and What's Not — 24

4 Peer Influence and Social Contagion in Your Classroom — 46

5 Echo Chambers and Tribalism in Your Classroom — 59

6 Why Your Credibility Is So Critical — 67

Part 2   Beyond Contagion: Making Sense of Group Perceptions in Your Classroom — 87

7 What Most of Your Students Have in Common — 89

8 When Your Class Doesn't See You the Same Way — 94

9 The Two Classroom Profiles and What They Mean for You — 100

10 What You Can't See Can Still Hurt You — 107

Part 3   Activating the Codebook: Replacing Irrational Thinking and Inoculating Against Coercion and False Beliefs — 139

11 The Irrational Beliefs That Derail Student Thinking — 142

12	The One Core Irrational Belief That Destroys Your Credibility	158
13	How Rational Thinking Transforms Your Classroom	174
14	Code 1: Replacing Irrational Beliefs with Rational Ones	180
15	Code 2: Replacing Peer Coercion and Misinformation with Critical Thinking and Prosocial Behavior	219
16	Quick-Start Study Guide: Turning Codes into Classroom Practice	245

Simplicity Mission

The Teacher Credibility Codebook is designed with simplicity in mind, allowing you to quickly understand and apply its concepts. Through the extensive use of infographics and illustrations, complex ideas are broken down into accessible, practical insights that you can readily implement in your classroom.

Preface

Reflecting on my 30 years in education—as a teacher at both the elementary and high school levels, a varsity football and hockey coach, a school administrator, and now as an education consultant analyzing student voice, school climate, and engagement—I often return to a lesson I learned in my early years of teaching:

The Lesson: Part 1—Maslow's Hierarchy of Needs

Interestingly, this early lesson does not focus on teacher credibility, but on Maslow's Hierarchy of Needs. Throughout my teaching career, whether it was early elementary or senior high school, there were always students in my classes who approached school from the base of the hierarchy, while other students had access to the top levels.

That's an oversimplification, of course. It's much messier than that. But essentially, students at the base face real obstacles in accessing things like academic achievement, confidence, authentic respect from others, recognition, and status. These are the **Esteem** needs that other students in class can access. At the highest level, **Self-Actualization**, students at the base rarely experience helping other students with academic or extracurricular goals or pursuing their full potential in an area that truly motivates them. Some students at the base even struggle with a sense of **Belonging** in their class and school, while others access this essential psychological need.

At the start of the school year, I realized that some students face inequalities in accessing basic, psychological, and self-fulfilment needs. It occurred to me that some students may never experience what it feels like to achieve belonging, esteem, and self-actualization at school with their peers.

The Lesson: Part 2—"Survival Mode" Is Essential, But Not Enough

It's been my experience that students who need support with basic needs receive it. Without exception, teachers, support staff, and administrators who are deeply committed to student well-being go above and beyond to meet the needs of students at school. The collective will, effort, and limited resources of a school come together in what I would describe as a necessary **survival mode**—a relentless effort to ensure that students' most essential needs are met. For example, a student who needs adequate winter clothing receives it, a student who does not have snacks or lunch gets them, and a student who has behaviour and self-regulation difficulties receives additional resources.

In that first year, and which became apparent over the next 26 years, I observed that many students who come to school operating at base need levels, even after receiving essential help from the school, often continue to encounter obstacles and inequalities in accessing higher-order needs in the classroom, such as belonging, self-fulfilment, and self-actualization. For example, a student who received a winter coat still felt excluded. The winter coat or the snacks, though essential, didn't on their own help the student achieve academic success, receive authentic respect from others, recognition, or status. They were stuck, while their classmates were not. This, it turns out, presents a very serious problem for everyone.

The Lesson: Part 3—The Hierarchy Is Non-Linear

Something interesting happened later in the year as I saw the benefits of our collective "survival-mode" plateau. The return on our school's collective investment only went so far. Most of the students who received support in my class saw their access to higher-order needs stagnate. When this happens, you can find yourself in a relentless cycle, addressing immediate survival needs, only to face new ones the next day. When students remain stuck at the base of Maslow's hierarchy, the demands on teachers can become overwhelming.

The interesting part is that I attended a literacy workshop. Over several sessions, I did not hear a single "survival" technique—only teaching strategies focused on analysis, synthesis, graphic organizers, collaborative group work, levelled texts, and problem-solving. These strategies seemed to target exclusively students already accessing higher-order needs, not those struggling with basic ones. I believed that the students at the base of the pyramid wouldn't be served by this type of professional development; my understanding was that they needed strategies providing necessary incremental steps to help them move upwards.

It just so happens that in my class that same year, and in every other class I taught, the most effective way to pull students into the club of esteem and self-actualization, and dismantle inequity, is to use those same high-impact, higher-order teaching strategies with high expectations for students at the base. Success with higher-order learning often fulfils the base-level needs more effectively and sustainably than continuously addressing survival mode reactively. The paradox is that Maslow's hierarchy is non-linear in the classroom. That's the key I learned, as counterintuitive as it was. Teachers' needs function the same way, incidentally.

The Lesson: Part 4—Teacher Credibility Is the Way You Circumvent the Hierarchy

Now, success in higher-order learning—and the effective teaching strategies needed to support it—requires students to take chances and embrace academic risks. Risk-taking often involves falling down and getting back up, learning from failure along the way; it is both necessary and essential. Through this process, as students allow themselves to be vulnerable, they develop the insight, wisdom, and resilience that come exclusively from trial and error, from winning and losing. This is what it takes to reach higher-order needs such as esteem and self-actualization.

Additionally, working in groups requires both self-regulation and soft skills. And so, the list of prerequisites for successfully implementing high-impact strategies continues to grow. I learned that students at the base of Maslow's hierarchy usually have not yet developed the capacity to take risks or to fail in front of their peers; they're stuck. Why? You need to trust others and feel that they care for you and have your best interests at heart in order to risk failing. Without trust and care within your "tribe," your risk tolerance for ridicule, shame, loss of belonging, or exclusion in the event of failure is very low. That lies at the heart of being human.

My realization is that you can have a toolbox full of high-impact strategies, yet still encounter significant obstacles when deploying them successfully. John Hattie (2021) succinctly sums up this reality when he reminds us that "if a student believes that the teacher has no credibility, then the teacher is unlikely to have much impact—even if they are using all the desirable teacher strategies with great classroom climates." You see, the most powerful aspect of teacher credibility is the students' perception that the teacher cares for them, that they can trust the teacher, and that the teacher is competent in upholding fairness, justice, and protecting them. Without teacher credibility—the precursors of trust and caring—in my experience, both students and teachers remain stuck in survival mode. You can't move them up the hierarchy with instructional strategies alone. However, with a teacher whom students believe cares for them, whom they trust, and who will protect them, I have learned that this effectively circumvents the hierarchy—it becomes non-linear. Your credibility is the way you circumvent the ladder. You've set the stage for the strategies to work.

The Lesson: Part 5—The Cart and the Horse

In my classroom, teacher credibility is the horse, while high-impact teaching strategies and classroom management are the wagon. Without a strong horse, students at the base are the first to jump off the cart.

For me, this helps explain why teachers and schools can become stuck in a cycle of addressing only survival needs, directing most of their limited resources towards physiological and safety needs. As the number of students left behind by the cart and horse increases, so too does the demand for teachers and schools to prioritize those fundamental needs.

This has serious consequences: as students jump off, teacher self-efficacy, collective teacher efficacy, and teacher credibility also decline. Given that Hattie's meta-analysis identifies teacher credibility and collective teacher efficacy as two of the most impactful factors in student achievement, this decline can have profound implications for overall learning outcomes (Hattie, 2008).

It puts a heavy strain on the system because when no one is paying attention to the horse, what remains of the school's resources is funnelled into the cart—and I've realized that doesn't work. As you continue reading this book, you'll see that high teacher turnover, burnout, student misbehaviour, and even teacher misbehaviour are some of the unfortunate outcomes of poor teacher credibility—or, in this analogy, a horse that is neither strong nor healthy.

So, take care of the horse. That's the lesson.

Final Note

It should come as no surprise that caring, trust, and competence drive higher-order learning and support the essential needs for belonging, esteem, and self-actualization in the classroom.

As a parent myself—alongside my wife of 30 years, who is also a teacher—I am reminded of this lesson not only in my professional life but also through our four children. As my sons prepare to bring home a national lacrosse championship to their respective universities, and as my two daughters pursue degrees in communications and psychology away from home, they embody the idea that taking risks, pursuing their dreams, and mustering the courage to reach their potential all stem from one essential ingredient: their **belief** in our care, trust, and support.

In my experience, the same holds true for the students in our classrooms.

References

Hattie, J. (2008). *Visible learning: A synthesis of over 800 meta-analyses relating to achievement*. Routledge.

Hattie, J. (2021). Foreword. In W. Rollett, H. Bijlsma, & S. Röhl (Eds.), *Student feedback on teaching in schools: Using student perceptions for the development of teaching and teachers* (pp. v–viii). Springer. https://doi.org/10.1007/978-3-030-75150-0

Meet the Author

Richard Young is an educator, coach, and education consultant with over 27 years of classroom experience. He specializes in student engagement, school climate, and teacher credibility—helping schools turn student feedback and perceptual data into practical, high-impact strategies. Richard has worked with directors of education, principals, and senior leadership teams. He's known for making complex data simple, relevant, and actionable for busy schools.

He believes that a school's true credibility is revealed not just in the classroom, but in the everyday, unstructured moments—in hallways, during lunch, on buses, before and after school, and through extracurricular activities. These are the spaces where trust, care, and safety quietly shape how students perceive their teachers, their school, and their place within it.

As both a classroom teacher and varsity coach, Richard has spent decades building trust in the places where student character is shaped—on the football field, in the hockey arena, during daily supervision, on lunchtime 5K anti-bullying runs, and in the classroom, through shared struggle and support.

Why This Book... An Introduction to the Ideas

Below was a typical week in my life as a teacher: all 361 of my students visited me in 14 groups of about 25 for a 75-minute ethics class. Rinse and repeat for the next 36 weeks of school!

Figure 0.1 This image represents all the students I taught each week throughout the school year.

DOI: 10.4324/9781003644088-1

I taught Ethics to all Grade 7 and 8 students at our school for the entire year. Additionally, I coached the varsity football team, the varsity hockey team, the lunch hour running club, and the hockey academy. This meant I worked with every student, every profile, every behaviour, and every learning need—everybody. And I loved it.

My top priority as a teacher was communicating care, trustworthiness, and competence to all students. It just happens that these behaviours constitute the key dimensions of teacher credibility. If your students perceive that you care about them, have their best interests at heart, and see you as an effective teacher (assessment, instructional methods, classroom management, etc.), then you have high credibility. This positive perception students have of you, especially as a collective classroom narrative, is very important. It's a lifeline, actually.

So this brings up some interesting ideas about student perception that need to be discussed… particularly since I'm suggesting that they serve as the lifeline to a teaching career

Perception Influences Motivation Model: Students assess their teacher's effectiveness based on their interactions with the teacher and their classroom experiences, reflecting a classroom climate-driven perspective (Schenke et al., 2018).

Motivation Influences Perception Model: Students bring into the classroom pre-existing motivations, like past classroom experiences, that shape and influence how they perceive their interactions with the teacher, indicating a student-driven approach (Schenke et al., 2018).

Without Teacher Credibility, You're Lost

So here we go again with my high school workload… This time, we're covering the last 14 years (the first 13 years, I was mostly teaching grades 1 and 2). Out of the approximately 200 classes and almost 5000 students I've taught, I want to focus on just one classroom. Because that's what this book is about: one teacher, 25 students, and the unique dynamics within that single classroom. That's the scope.

Back to the two models about student perception. What model do you think this class predominantly operates under? Model 1 or model 2, or maybe a more equal distribution of both? The short answer is, you wouldn't know until you walked in.

Why This Book... An Introduction to the Ideas ◆ 3

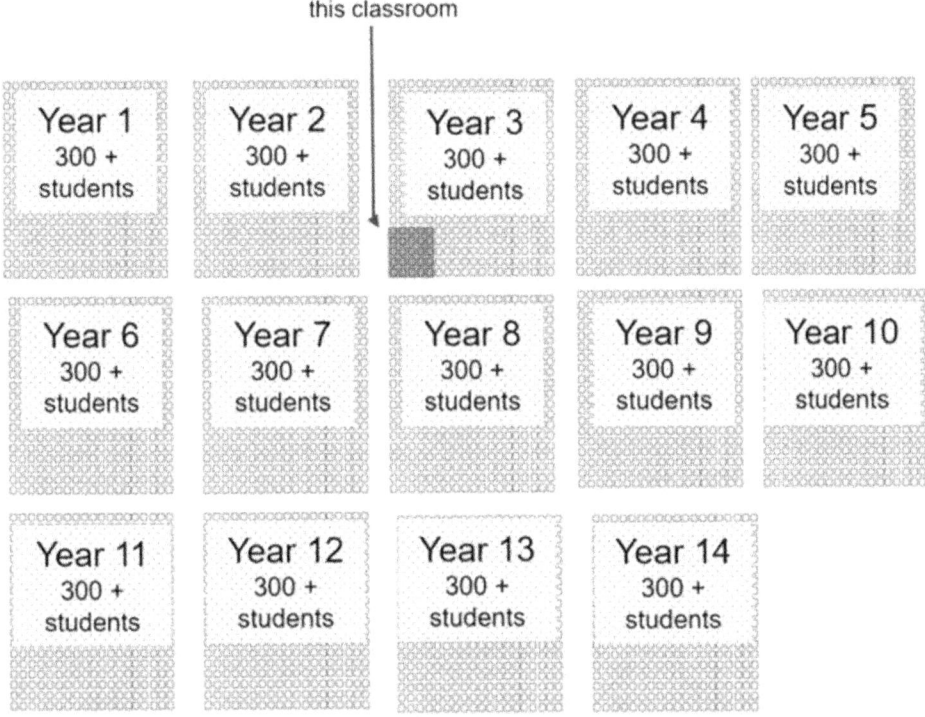

Figure 0.2 This image represents all the junior high and high school students I've taught. The highlighted classroom raises the question: what model of perception are these students using?

This book is about walking into any one of these 200 classrooms with me, and decoding student perception so you can differentiate which model your students are operating under. Having been in all of these classrooms for ten months at a time, I can tell you that the difference in student perception becomes obvious if you know what you're looking for.

Does it even matter? You might ask. Remember the lifeline I was referring to. Understanding (decoding) how students create their collective classroom narrative of you—that was my lifeline. The alternative, you'll learn, can be very ugly.

Why? Building and sustaining teacher credibility is a very different enterprise depending on what perceptual model your students are using. For students whose classroom perception is influenced by pre-existing elements within their psychological environment, many factors beyond merely their interactions with you influence their judgements. If only it were that easy if they did.

Like someone said... without teacher credibility, you're lost.

References

Hattie, J. (2021). Foreword. In W. Rollett, H. Bijlsma, & S. Röhl (Eds.), *Student feedback on teaching in schools: Using student perceptions for the development of teaching and teachers* (pp. v–viii). Springer. https://doi.org/10.1007/978-3-030-75150-0

Schenke, K., Ruzek, E. A., Lam, A. C., Karabenick, S. A., & Eccles, J. S. (2018). To the means and beyond: Understanding variation in students' perceptions of teacher emotional support. *Learning and Instruction, 55*, 13–21.

Part 1

How Students Interpret You

Overview

Part 1 lays the foundation for understanding how students perceive you and how those perceptions shape classroom behaviour. It introduces key models and frameworks that simplify the complex dynamics of teacher credibility, student inference-making, and peer influence—helping you recognize and respond to the hidden factors driving student behaviour.

Figure P.1 Illustration of the varied interpretations students may hold in a single classroom.

DOI: 10.4324/9781003644088-2

Chapter 1: Simplifying the Complexity of Your Classroom
Introduces the activating event, belief, consequence (ABC) model to help you understand student reactions to your behaviour and presents the concept of "codes" to reduce misinterpretations of your communication.

Chapter 2: How Students Think about You
Explores how students make inferences about your behaviour, forming beliefs that shape your perceived credibility, often without you realizing it.

Chapter 3: Student Perception: What's Real and What's Not
Introduces three types of cooperation: informative, material, and communicative, and explains how deception, antisocial actions, and false beliefs can take root when interpretations go wrong.

Chapter 4: Peer Influence and Social Contagion
Examines how peer dynamics influence student beliefs and behaviour, showing how social contagion can distort your credibility even when you're doing everything right.

Chapter 5: Echo Chambers and Tribalism
Analyzes how group loyalty and echo chambers form in classrooms, reinforcing false narratives and making it harder for students to see your true intent.

Chapter 6: Why Your Credibility Is So Critical
Defines teacher credibility: competence, caring, and trustworthiness, and explains how credibility loss can create a downward spiral of misbehaviour, disengagement, and burnout.

Together, these chapters provide a structured approach to understanding classroom interactions, offering a roadmap for teachers to navigate perception, communication, and social dynamics to foster a positive and productive learning environment.

1

Simplifying the Complexity of Your Classroom

Overview

Classrooms are busy, complex places where students are constantly interpreting your words and actions. This chapter introduces the ABC model (Activating Event, Beliefs, and Consequences) to help make sense of those interactions. You'll also learn about using "codes"—clear, consistent ways to guide how students understand your behaviour. These codes help create strong, reliable links between what you do and what students believe, making your communication clearer and your credibility stronger.

Figure 1.1 Illustration of the ABC model as a way to simplify the complexity of the classroom.

DOI: 10.4324/9781003644088-3

> *The interpersonal process of teaching is complex, difficult and demanding requiring enormous patience, empathy, higher order thinking, parallel processing of multiple sources of information in real time and the ability to relate to dozens of "clients" at once…. It is, in short, even for the most dedicated and "natural" teachers, a highly stressful occupation at least some of the time.*
>
> Lewis and Riley (2009)

The ABC Tool

Activating Event

When students enter your classroom, you begin the job of teaching, which involves assuming responsibilities and performing tasks throughout the period. Your behaviour is the primary tool for fulfilling these responsibilities and executing these tasks. This behaviour interacts with your students and generates typical classroom events. By using the ABC model as a framework, we can identify any of these interactions as an "Activating Event," represented as the "A" in the ABC model.

Belief

You can often assume that in any given interaction, now referred to as an "Activating Event," students accurately infer (interpret) the meaning of your message, behaviour, and intentions. I refer to the students' interpretation, perception, and inference of the teacher's behaviour as the "Belief," represented as the "B" in the ABC model.

Beliefs fall into two categories: those based on students' interactions with you and their classroom experiences (Classroom Climate-Driven Model), and those based on their pre-existing motivations and elements in their psychological environment (Student-Driven Model), like past classroom experiences and individual factors, that shape and influence how they perceive their interactions with you and their classmates.

Consequence

The impact these beliefs and inferences have on your students' behaviour, and the resulting perceptions of your teacher credibility, are identified as the "Consequence," represented as the "C" in the ABC model.

> **Quick Note: Adapting the ABC Model to the Classroom**
>
> Dr. William J. Knaus developed Rational Emotive Education to apply Albert Ellis's ABC model in schools, helping students think more rationally about challenges. Here, I use it to highlight how student perceptions and interpretations of teacher behaviour—the Belief—shape their reactions—the Consequence (Knaus, 1974).

1—ABC Example:

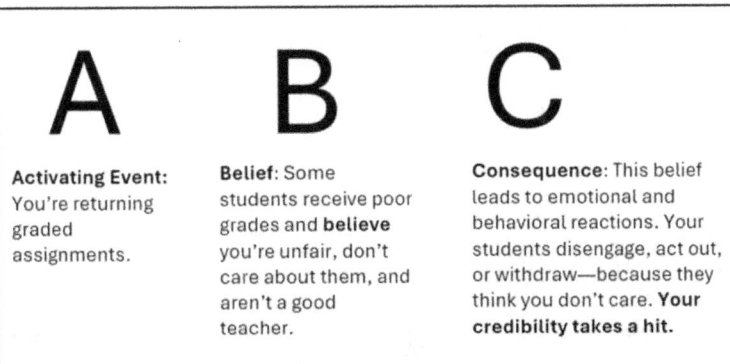

Figure 1.2 Illustration of the ABC model as a way to simplify the complexity of the classroom.

2—Why Codes?

In the example above, even when your teaching is caring, trustworthy, and competent, students may still form inaccurate beliefs about your intent based on activating events, leading to serious consequences.

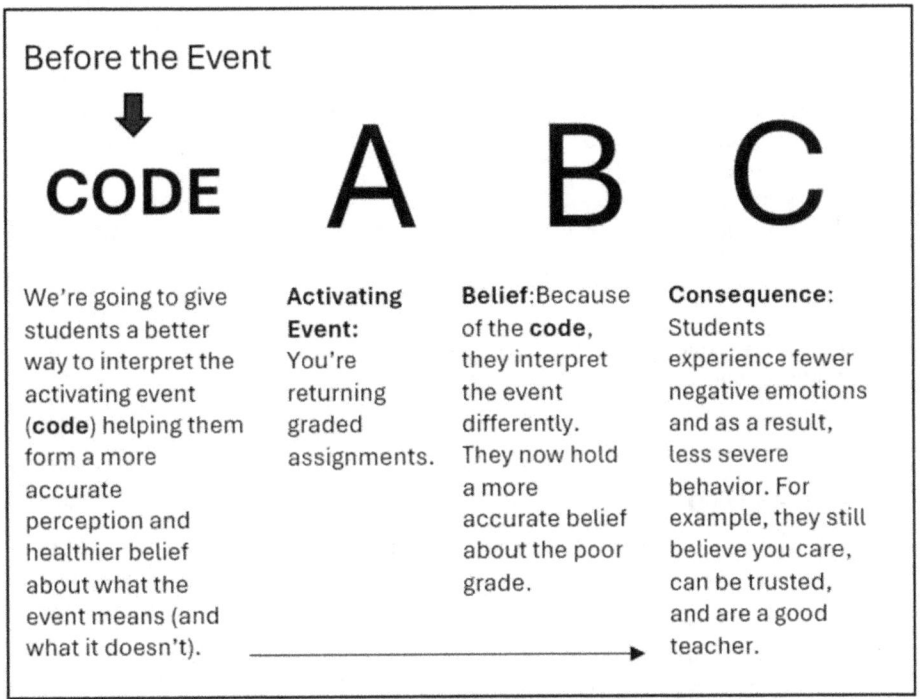

Figure 1.3 An example of grading an assignment as an activating event, showing the related belief and consequence.

3—Reducing Antisocial Behaviour and Deception

For the codebook to work, students need to communicate their inferences (beliefs) truthfully. By equipping them beforehand with a prosocial component to the code, you reduce both the likelihood, and the group's acceptance of, students making deceptive or misleading statements about your intentions. This helps prevent the spread of false narratives and minimizes antisocial behaviour in your classroom:

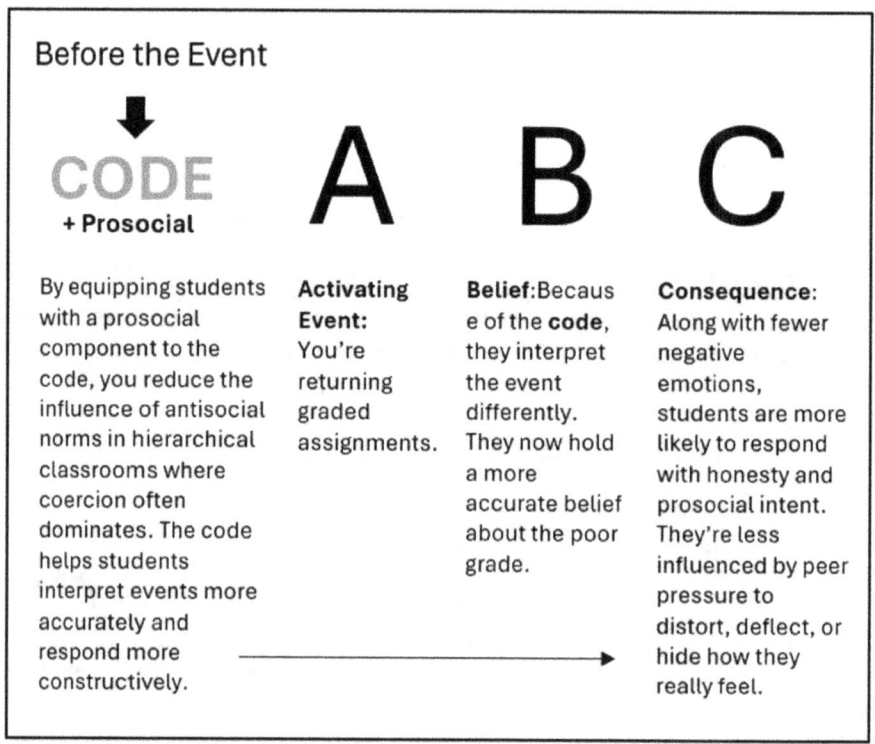

Figure 1.4 An example of inserting a code to provide students with a better way to interpret your behaviour.

Chapter Summary

- ★ This chapter introduced the **ABC model**—Activating Event, Beliefs, and Consequences—as a way to simplify how students interpret your behaviour.
- ★ Using codes before activating events helps students resist false beliefs and distorted thinking **before** they take hold.
- ★ By shaping beliefs at the point of interpretation, codes strengthen your credibility and reduce misunderstandings.

> **Key Takeaway:**
>
> The codebook is designed to reduce divergence, variance, and inaccuracies in student perception—and to minimize the chances that students will communicate interpretations of your behaviour deceptively. By providing a consistent framework for inference-making, the codebook helps students form more accurate beliefs, express those beliefs truthfully, and act in prosocial ways.
>
> When you consistently communicate care, trustworthiness, and competence, the codebook narrows the range of possible interpretations. It guides students towards rational, accurate inferences—ultimately strengthening your credibility in the classroom.

References

Knaus, W. J. (1974). *Rational-emotive education: A manual for elementary school teachers*. Institute for Rational Emotive Therapy, https://rebtnetwork.org/library/Rational_Emotive_Education.pdf

Lewis, R., & Riley, P. (2009). Teacher misbehaviour. In L. J. Saha & A. G. Dworkin (Eds.), *International handbook of research on teachers and teaching* (pp. 417–431). Springer. https://doi.org/10.1007/978-0-387-73317-3_27

2

How Students Think about You and Why It Matters

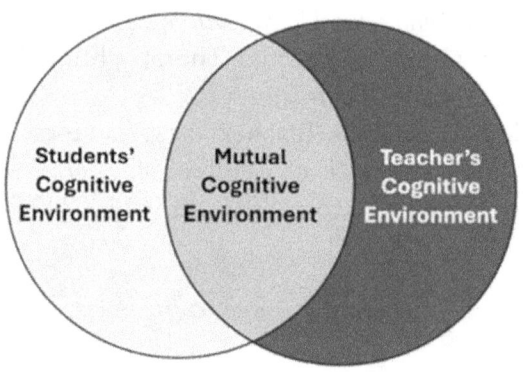

Figure 2.1 Venn diagram illustrating the alignment of the cognitive environment.

Overview

Effective communication in the classroom is essential for successful teaching and learning. As educators, our ability to communicate care, trustworthiness, and competence plays a crucial role in fostering an environment where both we and our students can thrive emotionally. One of the most powerful tools at our disposal for achieving this is the Inferential Model of Communication.

Rooted in cognitive psychology and communication theory, as outlined by Jessica Gasiorek and R. Kelly Aune in *Message Processing: The Science of*

Creating Understanding (2018), the Inferential Model provides a framework for understanding how we communicate and interpret meaning in interactions. At its core, this model highlights the processes by which individuals make inferences about each other's thoughts, intentions, and emotions during communication. It emphasizes the importance of mutual understanding and the creation of shared cognitive environments, where both teacher and student are aligned in their interpretations and expectations.

In this chapter, we take Gasiorek and Aune's insights and apply them directly to the classroom environment. We will explore how students perceive and interpret teacher's mental states and how these perceptions shape classroom communication and behaviour. Through this lens, you will gain a deeper understanding of how student perceptions of teacher credibility are complex, inherently social, and influenced by factors such as past experiences, motivations, and individual differences—many of which may be beyond the teacher's control.

Theory of Mind—Students

Having explored the Activating Event, Belief, and Consequence (ABC) framework's role in simplifying classroom communication by focusing on activating events and the beliefs students infer and attribute to these events, we can now look into how students **create meaning** through these classroom interactions. This is where Jessica Gasiorek and R. Kelly Aune's *Inferential Model of Human Communication* (2018) becomes crucial.

If we apply the Inferential Model to your classroom, it suggests that students instinctively interpret your behaviour in terms of intentions and mental states, rather than your objective teaching actions. A mental state can be what students believe about the emotions you're feeling, a belief you're holding, a memory you're accessing, a goal you're trying to achieve, and so on. Accordingly, your students can believe that these mental states guide your classroom behaviour and are reflected in your actions. For example, they might think, "Ms. Smith is in a bad mood today, so we're probably going to have a boring class, her favourites will just love it like usual."

Since students can't directly know what your thinking is, **Theory of Mind** enables them to attribute thoughts, desires, and intentions to you using available evidence to make informed guesses. In the example above, students don't know what Ms. Smith is feeling or planning, but they can attribute a mental state to her based on their own past experiences, motivations, and personal perspectives to help predict or explain her actions and figure out her intentions.

Theory of Mind allows students to understand that Ms. Smith's mental state can be the cause of—and can be used to explain—her classroom behaviour.

However, this process of inference-making, while natural, can easily lead to mistakes, both intentional and unintentional. Correctly inferring your intentions, beliefs, and goals requires advanced social cognitive abilities in your students.

Teacher Credibility

Before we dive into the Inferential Model, let's first control for the variable of teacher behaviour. This step is crucial in simplifying how the Inferential Model applies to the real-life complexity of your social classroom. To do this, let's establish that both your teaching behaviour and Ms. Smith's have been assessed by a trained observer as competent, caring, and trustworthy. In other words, your teacher credibility and Ms. Smith's are consistently positive in the classroom scenarios that follow:

Correcting Misbehaviour: Applying the Inferential Model

Figure 2.2 Example of a teacher's intention.

Your Intentions

Notice that it's just an internal thought, a goal: for students to be on task so they can prepare for an important exam. It's what you want to achieve—to activate in students' minds so they understand your message: **get to work so you can be successful—I care about you.** Your intention is the purpose or desired outcome behind your communication, it just hasn't been communicated in your words or actions yet.

Your Behaviour

Your behaviour is the outward communication of your intention, it's both verbal and nonverbal: voice, tone, gestures, proximity, etc. By engaging with students, providing feedback, demonstrating immediacy, enthusiasm, and consistently applying classroom management strategies, you communicate your intention. Your behaviour is intended to emphasize to students the importance of being on task and engaged in the review because, beyond the academic goal, you care and have their best interests at heart. In this context, correcting misbehaviour equals caring.

Figure 2.3 Example of a teacher's behaviour during classroom management.

Collateral Stimuli

It's a hot June day without air-conditioning, there's construction noise outside and open windows, Wi-Fi is intermittent but necessary for the review, and there are personal distractions and conflicts among students. There's a lot going on in this classroom!

According to the Inferential Model, these are all examples of collateral stimuli—unintended environmental factors or background elements present during communication in the classroom that can influence your students' interpretation of your intended message. Teaching is easy... said no one!

Your Students' Beliefs vs. Objective Reality

Now let's go back to Ms. Smith and her apparent poor humour. Poor Ms. Smith, look what she has to deal with! Let us consider that her students feel that she is having a bad day, a bad mood, and that's why she's "cracking down" on their behaviour more than usual. Whether she's in a bad mood or not, what matters is that her students **believe** that she is and that her teaching and decision-making today will be influenced by her perceived mental state. You see, by applying the Inferential Model to classroom communication, you can begin to understand that even if students' inferences of Ms. Smith's mental state and intentions are **inaccurate**, they can still attribute the outcome of the class on her supposed bad mood, favouritism and corresponding behaviour.

To further complicate matters, students also tend to see teachers as the ones in charge, actively making things happen, or as passive and not in control. According to our model of human communication, people naturally interpret others' actions as goal-driven. Applied to the classroom, this means students often view your actions as purposeful attempts to achieve specific objectives. For example, students might infer that Ms. Smith's goal was to get through the class with the least amount of effort because she was in a bad mood, tired, stressed, and not enjoying her job.

Thus, **theory of mind** shapes students' perspectives of you: they instinctively perceive and interpret your behaviour in terms of mental states and intentions, rather than objective actions. So accurate student inferences are very important for you and your teacher credibility.

Mind Reading – It Needs to Be Accurate

According to the Inferential Model, communication essentially consists of successful mindreading based on your social stimuli. Social stimuli refer to your verbal and nonverbal behaviour, such as your tone of voice, facial expression, body posture, demeanour, classroom management, etc.

Mindreading in the classroom is the process of students inferring what you're thinking, and **you** trying to figure out what your students are thinking. When your students enter the class, they begin a complex social interaction with you and each other, generally perceiving and thinking about you and each other (yes, you got it) in terms of **intentions** and **mental states**, like a high-stakes game of social guessing. That's what the Inferential Model is trying to tell us.

So, your students do not necessarily "see" or interpret social stimuli objectively as actions (e.g., teacher collecting term assignments, voicing disappointment in some student excuses). Rather, they experience these as pieces of evidence, indications, or reflections of what is going on in the teacher's mind… in your mind. For communication to be successful, this mindreading needs to be accurate. For example, understanding that you are correcting behaviour in some groups and offering positive feedback to others because you care about all of them equally—rather than believing you have favourites and are openly praising "your favourites" while embarrassing your less-liked students in the classroom. That is an important distinction with profound consequences for you depending on which one of these narratives your students **believe**.

Your behaviour activates and/or creates ideas or messages for students. These ideas in students' minds, whether accurate or not, form their inferences about your intentions and mental states. This process is essentially mindreading. To successfully communicate teacher credibility, students need to make **accurate inferences**.

Ms. Smith Correcting Misbehaviour: The Case of the Accurate Beliefs—Accurate Inferences

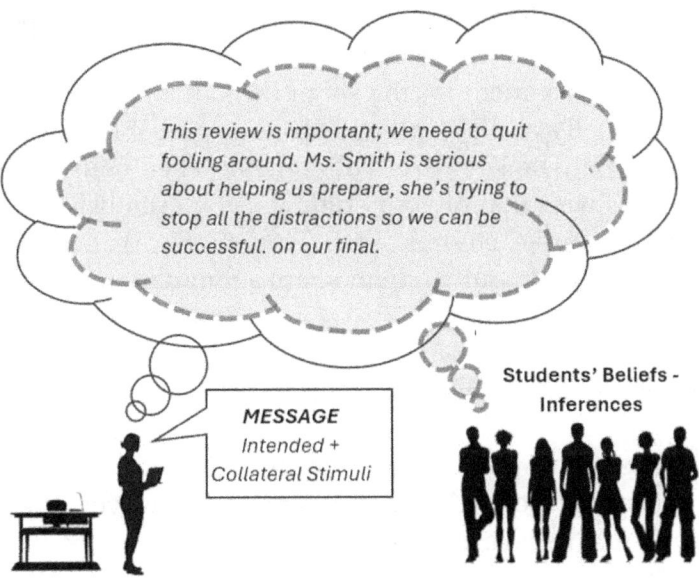

Figure 2.4 Example of cognitive alignment between a teacher's message and students' inferences.

Ms. Smith Is Awesome!

Despite the many distractions (collateral stimuli), most students in this scenario correctly infer Ms. Smith's intentions. The overlap between student inference and the teacher's intention demonstrate a **shared understanding**. Here, perceptions among the teacher and students align, signifying agreement. Ms. Smith's intention, communicated through her behaviour, activated the intended message in the students' minds.

Do you see how important it is that they **trust** Ms. Smith? That they believe she has their best interests at heart? That they feel she cares, even when she is disciplining some of them? It's crucial they receive the right message, isn't it?

This alignment indicates effective communication. Successful inference-making (student belief) results from the joint attention and effort between the teacher and her students.

Consequence (Remember the ABC Model?)

When Ms. Smith, or you in your classroom, corrects student misbehaviour, the ideal consequence is that students perceive it as the act of a caring, competent, and trustworthy teacher—not as a reaction stemming from stress, poor humour, or favouritism. This positive interpretation ultimately enhances Ms. Smith's credibility. In this scenario, the students choose to believe Ms. Smith's intended message. Yes! Great job, Ms. Smith!

The Credibility Power of Cognitive Environments

For you and your students to make the necessary inferences for effective communication—just like Ms. Smith did—you both need to pay attention to what each other knows and believes. In other words, as the teacher, you need to understand what exists within your students' cognitive environments.

A cognitive environment is "the set of facts that a person is capable of representing mentally and accepting as true or probably true" (Sperber & Wilson, 1986, p. 39). The key here is alignment: when your cognitive environment overlaps with that of your students, you establish what is known as the mutual cognitive environment. This overlap is where credibility thrives, as both you and your students share a foundation of understanding and belief.

Two Important Things You Need to Know About Your Students

1. The content of your students' cognitive environment (what they believe) may be objectively incorrect or false. However, as long as they perceive and believe that content to be true, it remains a part of their cognitive environment.

2. Each student's cognitive environment is shaped by their unique life experiences, psychological characteristics, and motivations. Teachers are no different—we also bring our own interpretations and life experiences into the classroom.

Additionally, social and cultural backgrounds significantly influence both your and your students' cognitive environments. An important aspect of the classroom dynamic is that students' beliefs are not static; they evolve as they gain new experiences and knowledge.

Why Did Students Trust and Believe Ms. Smith's Discipline Was Caring?

Simply put, understanding what students believe is true helps the teacher decide how to communicate effectively. This awareness makes it more likely that students will interpret your message the way that you intend, rather than misinterpret the meaning or intention.

In this case, the overlap indicates that students and Ms. Smith share similar beliefs about why and how the teacher corrects misbehaviour. By holding students accountable, she demonstrates caring. That's the power of the mutual cognitive environment, especially for the students who received her disciplinary prompt! Remember, they were singled out in front of their peers. To communicate effectively, you need to determine what your students **also** think is in their mutual cognitive environment. This recursive knowledge (i.e., I know that you know that I know) shapes and constrains your choices when constructing messages that will activate your intended ideas in students' minds, as well as the possible inferences that they make based on your behaviour. Ms. Smith understood what students would believe is true when

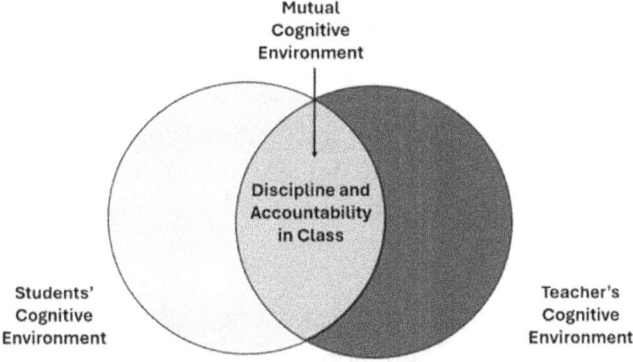

Figure 2.5 Venn diagram illustrating the alignment of discipline and accountability between teacher and students.

enforcing consequences they would infer: "She cares." This alignment can have a substantial and powerful impact on your credibility.

Uh-Oh, It's Not Nearly That Easy (Unfortunately)

Ms. Smith makes it look so easy, but is it really? Your classroom messages often comprise multiple stimuli, such as facial expressions, spoken words, tone, body language, and immediacy. According to the Inferential Model, altering a single element of this message "packet" can activate a different meaning in your students' minds. Furthermore, students do not always attend to the entire message or are aware of the social context in which it occurs. The message packet sent by you and Ms. Smith can be received by your students with missing or altered elements, leading to meanings that compete with what you intended. Students might omit something you wanted them to hear or see, include something else you did not intend, or attribute intentions based on insufficient understanding or an incomplete picture. Has that ever happened to you?

Your students can also selectively perceive messages and the social environment in ways that don't always align with your intentions. Motivation, past experiences, and individual factors all influence how they interpret what you say and do.

Surprise: students aren't always paying attention. Sometimes they catch only part of the picture—or choose to interpret it in a way that best serves their interests. It happens. These perception-disconnects often arise from an insufficient overlap in the mutual cognitive environment.

The Inferential Model helps explain how these situations occur, revealing the processes that lead to disconnects in inference-making, misunderstanding intentions, and ultimately impacting teacher credibility.

So, What Could Go Wrong?

As you can see, teachers face significant challenges when communicating effectively in their classrooms. Below is an example of a disconnect in perception. Now that you understand cognitive environments, you can see how, in this second scenario, Ms. Smith and her students—particularly when it comes to correcting behaviour—are not aligned. In this context, there's nothing mutual about their interpretations or the inferences they make from one another's actions.

Students Beliefs and Your Intentions—Not Always Aligned

Students' knowledge and beliefs about you—or in this case, Ms. Smith—can be objectively incorrect or false. However, as long as they perceive and believe that content to be true, it becomes part of their cognitive environment. This disconnect can lead students to interpret your corrective behaviour (or

How Students Think about You and Why It Matters ◆ 21

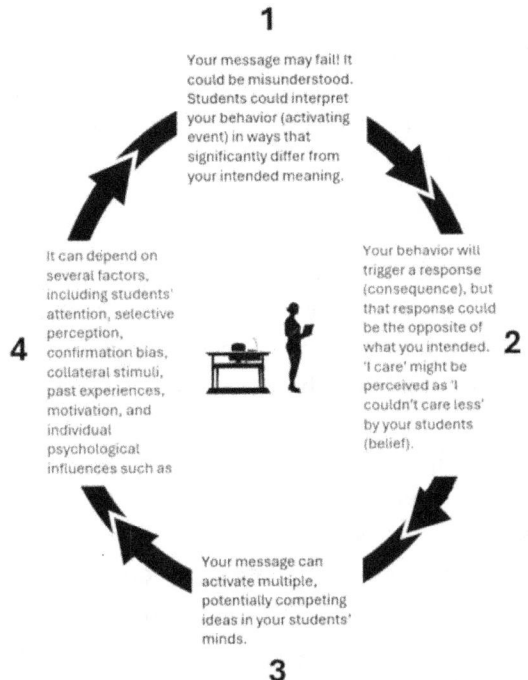

Figure 2.6 Flowchart illustrating how students can misunderstand teacher behaviour.

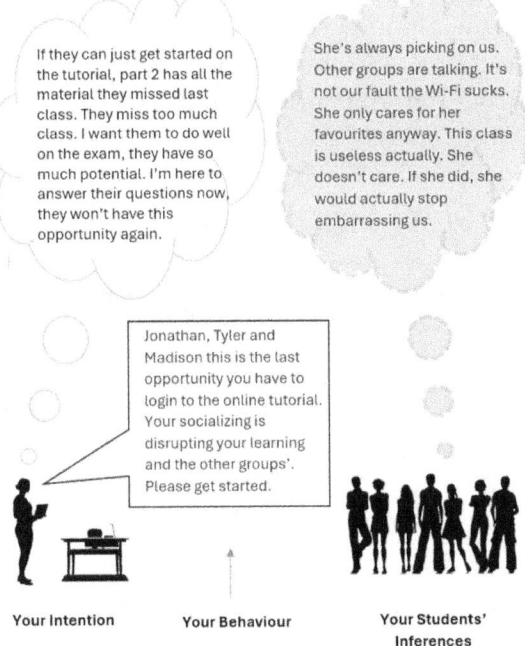

Figure 2.7 Example of how a teacher's intention, behaviour, and student inferences can differ in the classroom.

any activating event) in ways that differ significantly from your intentions, shaping a narrative that neither you nor an outside observer may recognize.

In this scenario, it's not teacher behaviour that's responsible for students' inaccurate inferences and beliefs. Instead, student motivations, past experiences, and individual factors—often unknown to the teacher—play a significant role in shaping perceptions.

Consequence: More Than Just a Small Thing

When it comes to correcting behaviour—or any activating event—the problem often lies in the gap between the teacher's and students' cognitive environments. They can often occupy distinctly different mental spaces with little or no overlap.

If you, or Ms. Smith, aren't aware of the hidden factors shaping student perceptions (later referred to as hidden attributes), it's easy to misread behaviour and assume it's rooted in defiance, disrespect, or irrationality. When false beliefs go unchallenged, they can create a disconnect and feed into a broader classroom narrative that undermines teacher credibility.

The Inferential Model helps explain how our students' perceptions and interpretations can be shaped by selective perception, perception bias, and social contagion. This may lead to inaccurate inferences and false beliefs spreading within the group. Over time, the students' cognitive environment can turn into an echo chamber, isolating itself from the perspectives of the teacher, school administration, and parents. This not only affects Ms. Smith but could also impact others in the school community, impacting collective teacher efficacy, teacher burnout and turnover…

The Question Is How Do We Align the Two?

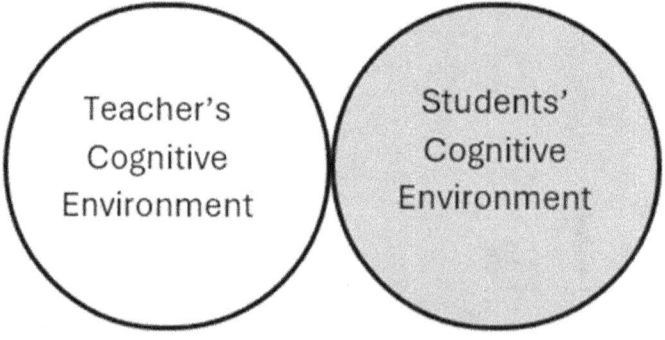

Figure 2.8 Venn diagram illustrating divergent cognitive environments.

Chapter Review

★ Students can't access your thoughts directly, so they rely on **Theory of Mind**—using available cues to guess your intentions, desires, and beliefs.

★ A student's **cognitive environment** (what they believe) may be objectively false, but if it feels true to them, it shapes how they interpret your behaviour.

★ Students often **selectively perceive** your actions and classroom cues. Motivation, past experiences, and personal factors all influence how your messages are received.

★ When correcting behaviour—or during any activating event—the issue often lies in the **gap between your cognitive environment and theirs**. You may be in completely different mental spaces, with little overlap.

★ What looks like defiance or disrespect may actually be driven by **false, unchallenged beliefs**. Left unaddressed, these beliefs can widen the disconnect and feed a narrative that quietly erodes your credibility.

 Key Takeaway:

When students interpret your actions through inaccurate beliefs, the real issue isn't misbehaviour—it's misperception. Unless that gap is addressed, your credibility will quietly erode.

References

Gasiorek, J., & Aune, R. K. (2018). *Message processing: The science of creating understanding*. University of Hawaii Press. Retrieved from https://pressbooks.oer.hawaii.edu/messageprocessing/

Sperber, D., & Wilson, D. (1986). *Relevance: Communication and cognition*. Blackwell.

3

Student Perception
What's Real and What's Not

Overview

This chapter explores the complex task of communicating teacher credibility in classrooms where students can interpret your actions—and share their interpretations—in multiple, often inaccurate or even deceptive ways. Every interaction, or *activating event*, carries the potential for misinterpretation, highlighting just how difficult it can be to ensure your intentions are understood as you meant them.

Drawing on the Inferential Model, we examine how student behaviour—ranging from honest communication to intentional deception, and from prosocial to antisocial actions—shapes the classroom environment. When inaccurate inferences, false narratives, or harmful behaviours go unaddressed, they can harden into a shared perception that diminishes your credibility. This "echo chamber" effect doesn't just skew how students see your competence and intentions—it can produce real, lasting consequences for both you and your classroom.

> *"It is essential for prospective teachers, educators, and administrators to grasp an understanding of the pervasive role teacher credibility plays in the classroom."*
>
> (Myers & Martin, 2006)

DOI: 10.4324/9781003644088-5

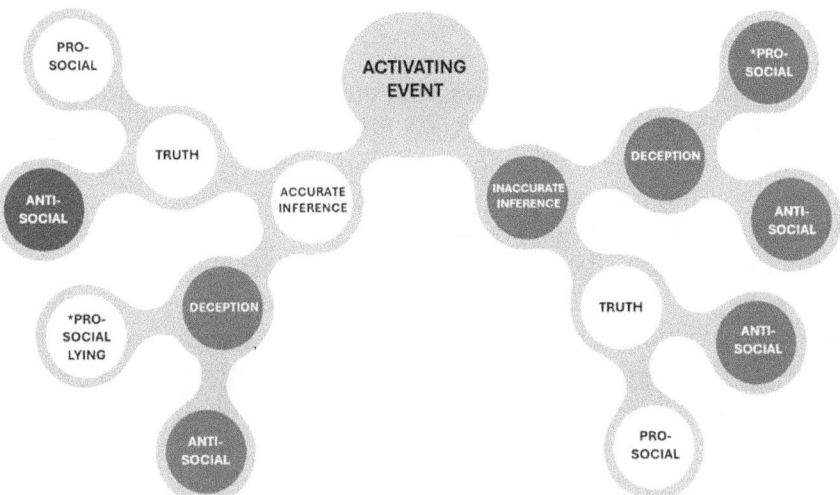

Figure 3.1 Illustration of informative, material, and communicative cooperation and uncooperative behaviour.

So, What Does It Take to Successfully Communicate Teacher Credibility?

In *Message Processing: The Science of Creating Understanding* (Gasiorek & Aune, 2018), Scott Phillips (2015) is cited for identifying three distinct types of cooperation that underlie human interaction:

1. Communicative cooperation
2. Informative cooperation
3. Material cooperation

These categories provide a useful lens through which to understand how students interpret teacher behaviour—and why teacher credibility can succeed or fail depending on which type of cooperation is present, absent, or misaligned.

1. Communicative Cooperation: Simply put, communicative cooperation happens when you use language that students can understand, paired with clear explanations, examples, and context. It also includes nonverbal behaviours—like immediacy, enthusiasm, and clarity—that help reinforce your message and behaviour. Basically, you're acting in ways students can easily interpret. In this—and in all upcoming classroom scenarios—you provide information in a way that allows students to make reasonable inferences about your intentions (competence, caring, trust).

> **Quick Note**
>
> In all classroom scenarios so far, your teacher credibility (a concept we'll revisit later) is reflected through consistent demonstrations of care, trustworthiness, and competence—as a trained observer would recognize and assess. From this perspective, your communication is credible: your words, instructions, and behaviours align with what reasonable students interpret as signals of a caring, trustworthy, and capable teacher.
>
> At this point in the process—the **Activating Event**—your message has been delivered, and students have already interpreted its meaning and intent **(the Belief)**. What follows now hinges on student cooperation, specifically how they choose to respond through their own communication and behaviour.

The Critical Role of Student Behaviour: Truth and Prosocial Actions

2. Informative Cooperation happens when students truthfully communicate their understanding of your behaviour—to you or to their peers. They share honest verbal and nonverbal messages that accurately reflect their interpretation of your intentions, without attempting to deceive or distort their message.

In the previous scenario, where Ms. Smith addressed student misbehaviour and where cognitive environments were aligned, students correctly inferred her intentions—recognizing her actions as credible. Here's what matters: those students didn't just interpret correctly; they also shared their understanding truthfully. This is **informative cooperation** in action.

For example, instead of spreading a false narrative, students say, *"Ms. Smith is cracking down because she wants us to succeed."* Their statements reflect their sincere understanding of her behaviour. Their communicative behaviour reflects their truth. This is what they tell you, their friends and their parents.

3. Material Cooperation: This involves students acting in ways that promote or pursue **prosocial** goals. When students share their interpretation of your behaviour—whether with you, their classmates, parents, or other teachers—they do so in a way that is constructive and considerate.

In other words, even if they don't fully agree with your decision, they express their experience honestly while behaving in a way that contributes to the classroom community and respectful relationships. Their words and actions reflect a desire to be fair, helpful, or understanding—something others can appreciate and build on.

Bringing It All Together

So, the cumulative result of accurate student inferences, beliefs communicated honestly, and resulting prosocial behaviour is an enhanced perception of teacher credibility—what we identify as the *Consequence* in the ABC model.

When students interpret your behaviour accurately (Belief) share their understanding truthfully (Informative Cooperation), and act in prosocial ways that support the classroom community (Material Cooperation), the conditions are set for a positive, trust-filled learning environment. Credibility isn't just built through what you say and do—it's co-constructed through how students perceive, communicate, and behave in response:

The Complex Task of Communicating Teacher Credibility: Navigating Student Behaviour and Interpretation

Each pathway—**The Good, the Bad, and the Ugly**—will be explored in detail on the following pages. As illustrated, the three types of cooperation—Communicative, Informative, and Material—can combine in various ways. In the example used to illustrate Phillips' Three Types of Cooperation, the teacher demonstrates communicative cooperation; the activating event provides enough clarity for a reasonable observer to infer your competence, caring, and trustworthiness. Yet not all students will interpret your intentions accurately.

What becomes especially intriguing is the range of student responses and behaviour that can follow this initial inference. While truthfulness and prosocial behaviour are the ideal outcomes, certain conditions such as peer influences may lead some students to choose deception and/or engage in antisocial behaviours instead.

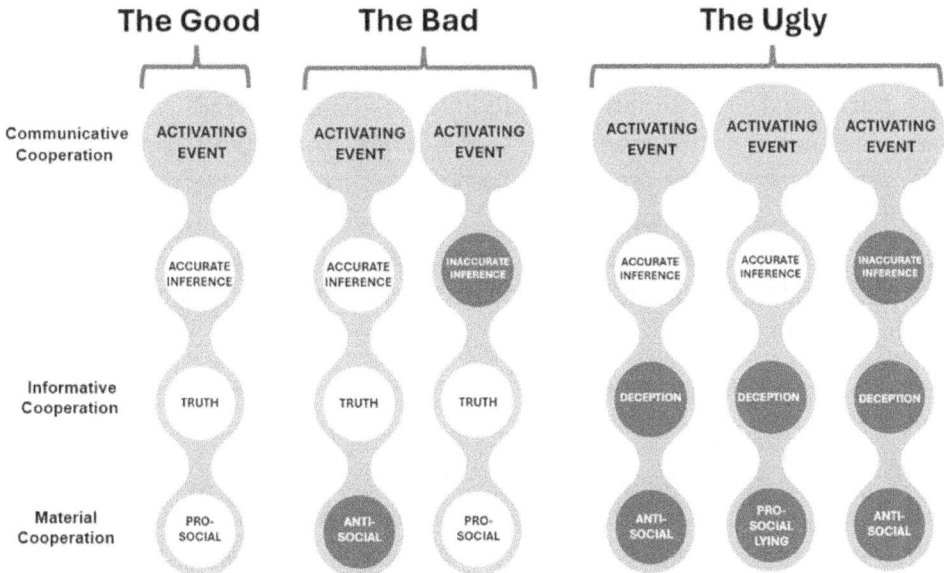

Figure 3.2 Illustration of the three communicative pathways: the good, the bad, and the ugly.

> Before you delve deeper, take a moment to reflect: *How might each of these pathways manifest in your own classroom?* Consider how different types of student responses—both cooperative and uncooperative—could impact your credibility and shape the overall learning environment.

Communicating Truth with Accurate Inferences and Prosocial Behaviour

Figure 3.3 The good, the first of three pathways.

New Activating Event

In this next classroom scenario, the teacher begins class by calling for oral presentations of a term assignment. Several students, however, decline to present, stating that they are not prepared. The teacher responds by reminding them of the penalty for late submissions, referring to both the class outline and the assignment description—each of which clearly communicated the deadline and consequences.

However, not all students are treated identically: some who do not present were granted extensions and receive no penalty, while others have marks deducted immediately in front of their peers.

> **Quick Note**
> Assessment and evaluation are among the most powerful activating events in your classroom. These moments often carry significant weight in shaping how students perceive your fairness, competence, and overall credibility.

Student Perception: What's Real and What's Not ◆ 29

The Good: Communicating Truth with Accurate Inferences and Prosocial Behaviour

Communicative Cooperation

You express caring, trust, and competence in ways that reasonable students interpret accurately.

Informative Cooperation

When students share their perceptions of your behavior—with each other, with you, or with parents—they do so honestly and truthfully.

Material Cooperation

Students communicate their beliefs through prosocial actions, even in disagreement—driven by honesty, respect, and a willingness to cooperate.

Perception Check
- ✓ Classroom Climate Driven
- ✓ Student Driven

ACTIVATING EVENT

ACCURATE INFERENCE

TRUTH

PRO-SOCIAL

Activating Event- In the classroom, activating events are the everyday moments that prompt students to interpret your behavior—sometimes accurately, sometimes not. These events can be as simple as asking the class to quiet down or as complex as managing a conflict. Each one becomes a moment where students form inferences about your intentions.

Belief- Students form inferences about your intentions and mental states based on the evidence available to them. These inferences shape their perception of your credibility. Whether they interpret your behavior accurately or not directly affects what they believe about you. In this scenario, students correctly interpret your intentions.

Consequence- As a result, students consistently interpret your everyday actions (activating events) accurately, reinforcing positive perceptions of your credibility. They communicate their beliefs truthfully and behave in prosocial ways. Whether their perception is shaped by classroom interactions (*classroom climate-driven*) or by their internal context (*student-driven*), you share a mutual cognitive environment around expectations for behavior. In this case, even students who received a deduction understand the rationale, express that understanding honestly, and respond respectfully—such as listening attentively to other presentations.

Figure 3.4 Illustration of the good: communicating truth with accurate inferences and prosocial behaviour.

Communicating Truth but with a Hitch

Figure 3.5 The bad, the second of three pathways.

Fun Facts about Truth

What constitutes "truth" is grounded in your students' perspectives. If a student expresses something they genuinely believe to be true—even if it is objectively incorrect—their behaviour is still considered **informatively cooperative**.

For example, if a student tells you or a peer, *"You have favorites and you're not fair,"* they may be mistaken in their judgement. However, as long as they are expressing what they genuinely believe, their behaviour remains informatively cooperative—even if, in reality, the teacher is being polite, fair, reasonable, and professional, without showing favouritism.

In the current scenario (*the activating event*), the teacher is **communicatively cooperative**, clearly demonstrating positive teacher credibility. Still, the example shows how both accurate and inaccurate student inferences can give rise to different combinations of **informative** and **material** cooperation.

The concept of "truth" here becomes complex and subjective: if students' inferences don't align with objective reality, their actions may still reflect their personal *truth*. As a result, you may wrongly attribute misbehaviour or task avoidance to students—when, in fact, their actions are based on sincere (albeit inaccurate) beliefs about your intentions and a sense of justification for their own behaviour.

The Bad: Communicating Truth with Inaccurate Inferences and Prosocial Behaviour – The Erosion of Teacher Credibility

Communicative Cooperation
You express caring, trust, and competence in ways that reasonable students interpret accurately.

Informative Cooperation
When students share their perceptions of your behavior—with each other, with you, or with parents—they do so honestly and truthfully.

Material Cooperation
Students communicate their beliefs through prosocial actions, even in disagreement—driven by honesty, respect, and a willingness to cooperate.

Perception Check
- ✓ Classroom Climate Driven
- ✓ Student Driven

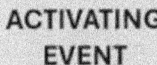

Activating Event- A key consideration here is how students *perceive* your handling of late assignments and grade deductions. Rather than simply observing your actions, they infer your *intentions* based on limited or incomplete evidence. In this case, serious gaps in their understanding lead to misinterpretations of your behaviour.

Belief- Some students believe they're being treated unfairly. They compare themselves to peers who received extensions and see you as less caring or even playing favorites. But they're missing key context: those extensions were requested before the deadline. Their inference about your intentions is based on assumptions, not facts.

Consequence- Communicating credibility isn't just about what you do—it's about what students *infer*. They need to see your actions as caring, trustworthy, and competent. If their inferences are off but they still act prosocially, there's room for honest discussion and growth. In these moments, a shared understanding can still form.

But if inaccurate inferences spread or become socially contagious, your credibility can erode over time. You can't always explain every decision—like who got an extension and why—so students need to trust that your actions are fair. In these cases, prosocial behavior and mutual trust are essential to realign perception and protect your credibility.

Figure 3.6 Illustration of the bad: communicating truth but with inaccurate inferences and prosocial behaviour.

The Bad: Communicating Truth with Accurate Inferences and Antisocial Behaviour – The Erosion of Teacher Credibility

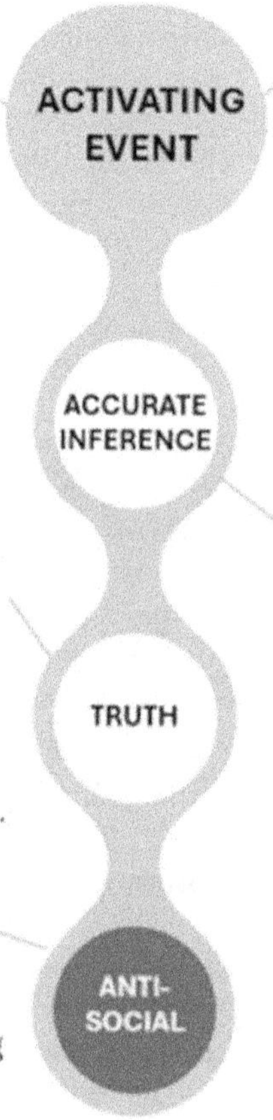

Communicative Cooperation

The teacher communicates caring, trust, and competence in a way reasonable students would understand.

Informative Cooperation

When students communicate their perception of the teacher's behavior to each other, the teacher, and parents, they are honest and truthful.

Materially Uncooperative

Students express their understanding through antisocial actions—such as shaming, blaming, or undermining others—in this case hijacking the teacher's message to serve their social goals.

Perception Check

✓ Classroom Climate Driven
✓ Student Driven

ACTIVATING EVENT

ACCURATE INFERENCE

TRUTH

ANTI-SOCIAL

Activating Event- While students who met the deadline accurately interpret your intentions behind the late penalty, they use that understanding to judge or undermine peers who received it. This creates tension within the student group—despite the accuracy of their inferences—and complicates the social impact of an otherwise fair decision.

Belief- Students infer your intentions accurately: you're acting fairly by upholding consequences and respecting those who met the deadline. But for those being judged, you remain the reference point for fairness, trust, and competence. How you respond now carries serious implications for your credibility with all students.

Consequence- Although students interpret your message accurately, their materially uncooperative behavior—using that understanding to shame or judge others—undermines your credibility. Even truthful perceptions can erode trust when paired with antisocial actions. Your message, *"I'm upholding fair and justifiable consequences,"* is being hijacked by students whose behavior is harmful to others. To stop this distortion, you must address the conduct—not the inference—before it further compromises your credibility and the shared understanding in your classroom.

Figure 3.7 Illustration of the bad: communicating truth but with accurate inferences and antisocial behaviour.

Accurate Inferences, Yet Deliberately Misleading Others to Believe Otherwise

Figure 3.8 The ugly, the third of three pathways.

Fun Facts about Truth (Part 2)

In the previous scenarios, students' inferences—whether accurate or not—were communicated truthfully. Students also provided evidence for their beliefs in an honest and transparent way. As a result, you had an opportunity to identify misperceptions related to the activating event and, through prosocial collaboration, work toward resolution. In this context, you had a fighting chance to maintain positive credibility.

In the upcoming scenarios, however, the dynamic changes. Students' beliefs about you remain accurate—they recognize your credibility. Internally, their understanding is not distorted. Yet externally, their communication becomes **deceptive** (*informatively uncooperative*), as they deliberately present a negative narrative.

This creates a clear divide between **internal belief** and **external communication**—while students perceive you as competent, caring, or fair, they intentionally misrepresent those beliefs due to social pressure, past experiences, peer alignment, avoidance of responsibility, or other personal motivations. In essence, their perception of you is accurate, but they choose to suppress or distort that truth in favour of a different message that serves their immediate interests.

As Mike Tyson famously said, *"Everyone has a plan until they get punched in the face."* Informatively uncooperative students can feel like that punch—an unexpected hit to your credibility, even when you're doing everything right.

> **Quick Note**
>
> What comes next in "The Ugly" may not paint a pretty picture of typical classroom behaviour or climate. But trust me—what you're about to read happens all the time. These scenarios aren't rare exceptions—they're part of the everyday human dynamics of school life. Keep in mind: because of the inherent power imbalance in the classroom, teachers often become targets of misrepresentation or deception.
>
> Much of what follows has been a regular part of my own teaching days and weeks. It may be hard to believe, but it's human nature. When you understand that **informative and material uncooperative behaviour** is not only natural but also influenced by student motivation and perception, you can begin to treat these behaviours as elements of the job—things you can anticipate, respond to, and ultimately influence.
>
> That's where the **Codebook** comes in. By applying its tools, you can provide leadership, offer guidance, and yes—especially in these messy moments—enhance your credibility with your students.

If They Understand Your Intentions: Why Do Students Choose Not to Tell the Truth About It?

Your students—individually or as a group—may intentionally engage in deception (deliberately misleading you, their parents, and other students) when communicating about your credibility, even when they have accurately understood your behaviour. Based on my personal teaching experience, students often choose to deceive for several reasons:

Common Motivations behind Student Deception

1. **Peer Influence and Social Dynamics**

   Students might deceive to align with the views of their social group. If a group of students dislikes you or sees you as an authority figure to challenge, individual students may misrepresent their perceptions of your credibility to fit in or avoid social isolation (See Chapter: Logic of False Beliefs).

2. **Revenge or Retaliation**

   Students may purposefully misrepresent your credibility out of resentment, using deception as a way to "get back" at the teacher. This could stem from feeling wronged by a specific action, such as being disciplined, or witnessing a friend or peer group being disciplined. They may also feel singled out or embarrassed and use deception to target your actions or to defend classmates.

3. **Deflecting Accountability**

   To avoid personal responsibility for their actions (e.g., poor academic performance or misbehaviour), students might misrepresent their understanding of your credibility. By portraying you as unfair or incompetent, they shift the blame from themselves to the teacher to avoid effort or to justify their behaviour or lack of effort.

4. **Gaining Favour with Other Teachers or Parents**
   Students may deceive when communicating about your credibility to influence how they are viewed by other authority figures, such as parents or other teachers. By painting you in a negative light, they may hope to gain favour or support from these figures or avoid responsibility for the incident in question.

5. **Seeking Sympathy or Leniency**
   Some students may deceive by exaggerating the teacher's perceived flaws to gain sympathy from peers, parents, or other authority figures. This may be done to seek leniency, extensions on assignments, or to avoid disciplinary actions, portraying you as the perpetrator and themselves and friends as the victim.

6. **Power Dynamics and Rebellion**
   Deception can be a tool for students to intentionally undermine your credibility as a form of rebellion or to challenge authority. In this case, deception serves as a way to weaken your authority and influence within the classroom.

Simple Methods of Deception

So, you've concluded that your students may still choose to be informatively uncooperative when communicating their beliefs. While recognizing deception is important, it's equally crucial to understand the **specific methods** students use to manipulate perceptions, often for personal or social gain.

Before we explore these methods, it's helpful to consider findings from a meta-analysis by Lee and Imuta (2021) on children, deception, and Theory of Mind (ToM). Their study found that ToM—the ability to understand others' mental states, such as thoughts, beliefs, emotions, and goals—is foundational to effective lying. In your classroom, this means students with a well-developed Theory of Mind are better able to anticipate how you and their peers will interpret behaviours and statements—and can therefore deceive more effectively when **motivated**.

The study also revealed that mental state understanding is critical not just for lying, but for lie maintenance—keeping a deception consistent over time. More sophisticated deception (avoiding detection) relies heavily on students' ability to track and manage what others **believe**.

However, the decision to engage in deception isn't purely cognitive. Lee and Imuta emphasized that **motivational and social factors**—like the desire to avoid punishment, gain approval, or fit in with peers—are **stronger determinants** of whether students choose to lie in the first place. Even students who have the capacity to deceive must weigh the perceived costs and benefits before deciding to act deceptively. In my teaching experience, these are the most frequent and best used methods students use... I've seen all of them used in a single day of teaching:

1. **Manipulation:**
   Students might twist or selectively interpret events to cast you in a negative light, often using emotional tactics or exaggerations to influence others' perceptions. This includes framing situations in a way that distorts the teacher's credibility for personal gain or to align with peer dynamics.
2. **Lies of Omission:**
   Students may deliberately leave out key facts or context, allowing others (peers, parents, other teachers) to believe something false about you. For example, they might omit the fact that they failed to ask for an extension on time when accusing you of being unfair.
3. **Exaggeration:**
   Students may embellish or blow small issues out of proportion. For example, a minor mistake by the teacher might be exaggerated into a much bigger issue to undermine credibility. This could include portraying you as consistently unfair based on a single incident.
4. **False Consensus:**
   Students might falsely claim that "everyone" feels a certain way about the teacher, when in reality, only a few students hold that opinion. By exaggerating the extent of discontent, they manipulate others into believing your credibility is more widely questioned than it actually is.
5. **Selective Reporting:**
   Students could choose to report only specific aspects of an event that support their negative portrayal of the teacher, while omitting or downplaying positive aspects. For example, they might report a strict rule enforcement but leave out the part where you clearly explained the rule beforehand.
6. **Deflection:**
   When confronted, students might shift the conversation away from their own behaviour by focusing on perceived flaws in the teacher. This method deflects attention from their actions and places your credibility in question. For instance, when questioned about poor grades, students might argue that its your teaching style that's the problem rather than their lack of effort.
7. **False Attribution:**
   Students might attribute motives or intentions to you that aren't accurate. For instance, they might claim the teacher "doesn't care about

students" or "is just picking favorites" even when your actions are neutral or positive. This method influences how others interpret your behaviour without outright lying.

These methods help students control the narrative around your credibility and often serve the various motives mentioned earlier, like deflecting responsibility or gaining sympathy. Each method undermines teacher credibility in different ways, creating challenges for you in maintaining authority (competence), trust and caring.

Perception Check: What Explains Student Deception—Motivation or Perception?
Up until now, whether students' inferences have been accurate or inaccurate—but communicated truthfully—could be explained by either of the two perceptual models.

Both Perception Influences Motivation and Motivation Influences Perception can account for these classroom scenarios.

However, when students begin to use deception, the explanation shifts: deceptive communication is best understood through the Motivation Influences Perception model, where internal motives drive students to misrepresent their perceptions:

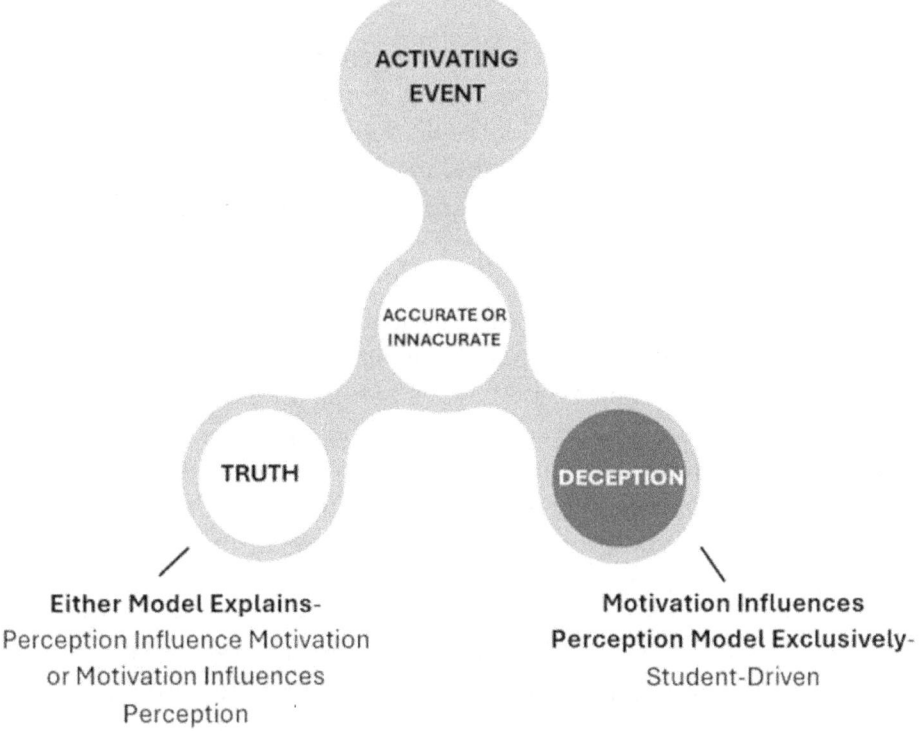

Figure 3.9 Illustration of truth versus deception: perception influences motivation or motivation influences perception.

Accurate Inference—But Students Choose Deception?
Sometimes, students move away from informative cooperation and use deception—even though they have accurately perceived your behaviour. This isn't a case of misunderstanding.

Instead, it's deliberate manipulation. Students accurately assess your credibility but choose to misrepresent it—usually due to social pressure, peer dynamics, or personal gain.

Here, there's a clear disconnect between what they believe internally and what they communicate externally. Their perception of you is accurate—but their outward behaviour is intentionally dishonest, shaped by motivations beyond your control.

Motivation as the Driving Force
When students deceive, it's not about your teaching—it's about their own motivations. Peer pressure, social dynamics, and personal gain often drive dishonest behaviour, not a failure in credibility.

It might sound convenient, but research backs it up (Part 2). This is why deception fits **Model 2: Motivation Influences Perception (Student-Driven)**—where internal motives, not teacher behaviour, shape your students' behaviour.

Why Is It Important for Teachers to Decode This Perceptual Model?
Decoding this model is crucial because it shifts responsibility for negative perceptions onto the students—not the teacher.

There are several reasons why this understanding is vital, but the foremost is that it allows teachers to engage in **cognitive reappraisal** of their working environment.

Teachers can recognize that students who communicate false beliefs are being shaped by **their own motivations**—such as social pressures or personal biases—rather than by the teacher's actual behaviour or credibility.

Your actions (activating events), when assessed positively by an outside observer, confirm that your teaching is not the source of negative perceptions. Instead, **students' internal motivations** drive deceptive communication, resulting in a **person-driven rather than situation-driven** dynamic (see "To the means and beyond: Understanding variation in students' perceptions of teacher emotional support.").

If left unchallenged, these false narratives can become contagious.

Other students may begin deriving their perceptual cues from peers who are **motivated** to communicate inaccurate beliefs. Over time, these false perceptions can harden into a shared "truth," forming the basis for further inaccurate inferences—and steadily undermining the teacher's credibility:

How False Narratives Spread

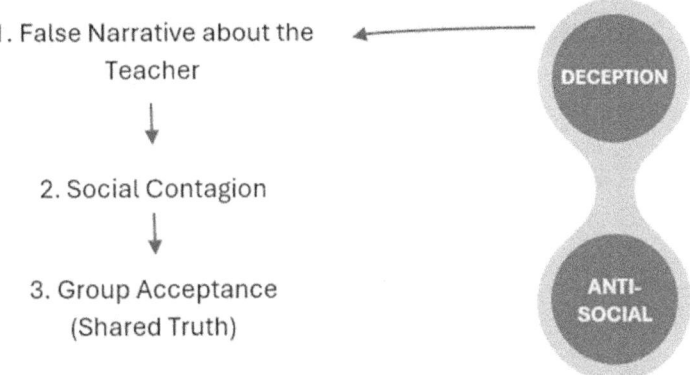

1. False Narrative about the Teacher
2. Social Contagion
3. Group Acceptance (Shared Truth)

Figure 3.10 Illustration of false narratives, social contagion, and group acceptance.

Negative Teacher Credibility and Resistance to Change

The issue here is not with your credibility. You may consistently demonstrate credible behaviours—such as care, competence, and trustworthiness—but when students' motivations are driven by external factors like social pressure, their deceptive communication, and the negative perceptions they convey can become resistant to change and spread rapidly.

This resistance is often reinforced through mechanisms like **social contagion, tribalism, and echo chambers**, where peer dynamics and groupthink further entrench false perceptions (see Chapters 4 and 5).

In such cases, even a highly credible teacher may struggle to alter students' perceptions, inferences, and false beliefs.

The problem lies not in your behaviour, but in students' motivations taking the front seat—while accurate inference and truthful communication are pushed into the backseat.

In summary, students' informatively uncooperative behaviour is driven by internal factors largely independent of the teacher's influence within the classroom. Recognizing when motivations—not your teaching—drive negative perceptions is key to safeguarding your credibility and addressing false narratives early.

> Reflection: Have you ever noticed negative perceptions spreading for reasons unrelated to your actual teaching? How did you respond—or how might you respond differently now?

The Ugly: Communicating Deception Despite Accurate Inferences with Antisocial Behaviour – The Undermining of Teacher Credibility

Communicative Cooperation

You express caring, trust, and competence in ways that reasonable students interpret accurately.

Informatively Uncooperative

When students say, "The teacher isn't fair," despite knowing the teacher's actions are justified, they engage in informative uncooperation by making deceptive or knowingly untruthful statements.

Materially Uncooperative

Students express their understanding through antisocial actions that undermine the teacher's message or disrupt the learning environment.

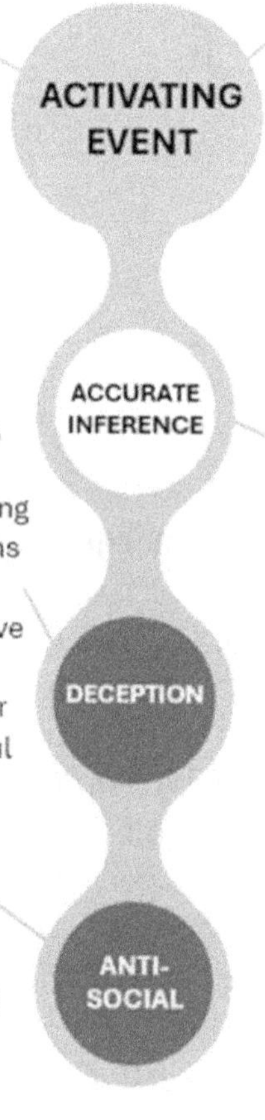

Perception Check

✓ Student Driven

Activating Event- This situation—a disagreement over fairness, policy, or being treated unfairly with a late penalty—isn't new. The same students have raised similar complaints in other classes, where teachers have often backed down. Most students know you're right to enforce the assignment rules, but they're also aware you don't know about this pattern.

Belief- Most of your students know the complaints aren't true. They understand your decision is fair and that the extension deadline was met properly—it's not favoritism. Yet despite that, they communicate—verbally and non-verbally—that your actions are unfair, especially toward students who aren't well-liked. Their behavior doesn't reflect confusion, but a choice to align socially, even when they know the facts.

Consequence-Many students communicate—verbally and non-verbally—that your decision was unfair. Even though they know your actions were justified, they continue to support a false narrative. By claiming, *"The teacher isn't fair,"* despite knowing the truth, students engage in **informatively uncooperative behaviour**, promoting a deceptive perspective.

Some who met the deadline also engage in **materially uncooperative behaviour**—using the false claims to delay presentations, gain extra time, or challenge your assessment. These antisocial actions are not about perception, inferences or misunderstanding but about securing personal advantage and reinforcing peer status by undermining your credibility (Student Driven).

Figure 3.11 Illustration of the ugly: communicating accurate inferences with deception and antisocial behaviour.

The Ugly: Communicating Deception Despite Accurate Inferences with Pro-Social Lying – The Undermining of Teacher Credibility

Communicative Cooperation

You express caring, trust, and competence in ways that reasonable students interpret accurately.

Informatively Uncooperative

Despite accurately inferring your actions, students claim you're unjust—justifying their behavior through false logic that serves their group, even though it promotes deception in your classroom.

Materially Cooperative*

Students lie to protect their peers from consequences, reinforcing trust within the group and framing your actions as unfair. Although rooted in prosocial intent, the cooperation is based on deception undermining your credibility

ACTIVATING EVENT

ACCURATE INFERENCE

DECEPTION

PRO-SOCIAL LYING

Perception
Student Driven

Activating Event- On the assignment due date, a group of students who collaborated on the project requests an extension. You deny the request and enforce both the policy and its penalty. Now, two groups push back: one consists of friends who accurately understand the policy but still reject your decision; the other includes students who misunderstand the policy but are influenced and empowered by the first group—who are academically successful and socially persuasive

Belief- Students who understand the policy believe that by lying, they're protecting their friends from negative consequences. In their view, their actions are prosocial—an act of loyalty and support. This creates a paradox: they see themselves as materially cooperative within their peer group, while being informatively uncooperative in the broader classroom context. Meanwhile, the second group protesting accepts the false narrative as genuine truth. This nuance is critical for teachers to recognize when interpreting student behavior and credibility dynamics.

Consequence- This kind of group loyalty can foster peer solidarity by casting you as a common enemy. In doing so, it normalizes deceptive behavior and increases resistance to classroom policies. As the false narrative spreads, a cognitive bias emerges—students begin viewing your decisions through a lens of mistrust, reinforcing perceptions of injustice, regardless of the policy's fairness. Over time, these dynamics can erode your credibility, making students more likely to interpret future interactions with suspicion or negativity.

Figure 3.12 Illustration of the ugly: communicating accurate inferences with deception and prosocial lying.

Inaccurate Inferences and Deliberately Misleading Others

Figure 3.13 The ugly, part 2: inaccurate inference and deliberate misleading.

Justification for Flawed Perceptions

In The Ugly: Part 2, we turn to students who misunderstand your actions. For example, some students wrongly believe you're showing favouritism. These students selectively share incidents that reinforce this false belief by purposely omitting contradictory evidence. This inaccurate-deceptive-antisocial pathway also affects other students. These students derive their perceptual cues from the first group. To them, the activating event and your behaviour are secondary. Their inference-making, deceptive communication, and antisocial behaviour stem from the influence of the first group. This is the "Just Plain Ugly Pathway." Don't take it personally; it has very little to do with you.

Navigating the Complex Pathways of Teacher Credibility: The Challenges of Successful Communication in the Classroom

The complexity of the branching pathways in this diagram highlights just how challenging it can be to successfully communicate your credibility in the classroom. With so many opportunities for inaccurate interpretations—and relatively few pathways leading directly to truthful, prosocial communication—it becomes clear how difficult it is to ensure your intentions are accurately understood.

Each activating event opens multiple possibilities for misinterpretation.

Achieving accurate inferences and reinforcing credibility requires **careful, intentional communication,** and a **continuous effort** to align with students' cognitive environments.

Just Plain Ugly

Communicative Cooperation
You express caring, trust, and competence in ways that reasonable students interpret accurately.

Informatively Uncooperative
Students shift blame onto you by selectively reporting details that support a negative narrative. They may falsely claim that "everyone" thinks your unfair, creating a false consensus as a form of retaliation or revenge.

Materially Cooperative
Genuinely believing they're being treated unfairly; their actions go beyond seeking resolution. Instead, they aim to damage your reputation through deception to gain sympathy by manipulating the narrative.

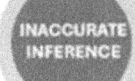

Perception

Student Driven

Activating Event- One group of students affected by the late submission policy argue they should receive the same extension granted to others in the class. They believe the penalty is unfair, especially since some of their group members missed the previous class for valid reasons. They claim this justifies a reconsideration of the deadline. However, the syllabus clearly states that students who miss class are responsible for catching up on missed notes, homework, and assignments.

Belief- These students believe they're being treated unfairly. Unlike those who received extensions, they feel their absences justify the same consideration—rather than a penalty. As a result, they perceive you as uncaring or unprofessional, and assume you favor other students. Their belief is distorted: you're applying the same policy consistently, including in identical situations across your other classes. Still, they view the deduction on a project worth 25% of their final grade as too punitive, regardless of the stated syllabus expectations.

Consequence- When part of your class makes inaccurate inferences and engages in antisocial behavior, your credibility can quickly erode, leading to a loss of authority and respect. This may create a negative classroom climate where disengagement, disruption, and management challenges increase. You may also experience added stress, frustration, and even administrative pressure if complaints escalate. As discussed, inaccurate inferences often spread through social contagion—where even **uninvolved students adopt the dominant negative narrative**. Once trust is broken, re-establishing credibility and classroom culture becomes significantly harder.

Figure 3.14 Illustration of just plain ugly: communicating inaccurate inferences with deception and antisocial behaviour.

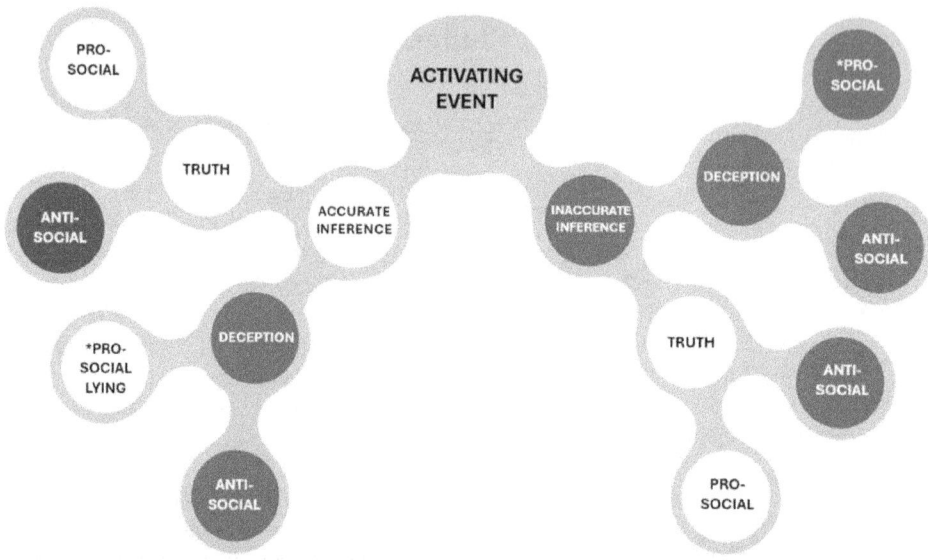

Figure 3.15 Illustration of informative, material, and communicative cooperation and uncooperative behaviour.

In your classroom, when students consistently make inaccurate inferences—such as interpreting your discipline as unfair or instruction as unclear—these misperceptions can solidify into a collective narrative that resists change. Unless intentional efforts are made to **expand the overlap between you and students' cognitive environments** (*mutual cognitive environment*), these false beliefs can harden over time. The diagram also illustrates how communication can flow in two directions: towards **truthful understanding**, or towards **deception and miscommunication**. Deception here refers to students developing or spreading misconceptions about your competence or intentions, which can create an **echo chamber effect**—where false perceptions are amplified and reinforced within your classroom

> **Chapter Review**
> ★ Classroom communication rests on three forms of cooperation: **communicative**, **informative**, and **material**. But students don't always engage in good faith. Sometimes, even when they understand your behaviour clearly, they may choose to **deceive**—misleading you, peers, or parents about your credibility.
> ★ This isn't usually about confusion—it's about **motivation**. As Lee and Imuta note, students often lie or distort the truth for social reasons: to avoid consequences, gain approval, or fit in with peers. In these cases, credibility isn't the problem—**social dynamics are.**

Key Takeaway:

Effective communication isn't just about clarity—it's about expanding the shared cognitive environment so that students can correctly infer your intentions. When students misrepresent your credibility, the issue isn't always misunderstanding—it's motivation. Peer influence and personal gain often drive deception, not failure in your teaching.

References

Gasiorek, J., & Aune, R. K. (2018). *Message processing: The science of creating understanding*. University of Hawaii Press. Retrieved from https://pressbooks.oer.hawaii.edu/messageprocessing

Lee, J. Y. S., & Imuta, K. (2021, March) Lying and theory of mind: A meta-analysis. *Child Development, 92*(2), 536–553. https://doi.org/10.1111/cdev.13535. Epub 2021 Jan 18. PMID: 33462865.

Myers, S. A., & Martin, M. M. (2006). Understanding the source: Teacher credibility and aggressive communication traits. In T. P. Mottet, V. P. Richmond, & J. C. McCroskey (Eds.), *Handbook of instructional communication: Rhetorical and relational perspectives* (p. 67–88). Pearson.

Scott-Phillips, T. (2015). *Speaking our minds*. Palgrave Macmillan.

4

Peer Influence and Social Contagion in Your Classroom

Overview

In this chapter, we explore the role of social contagion across relationships—among students, between students and teachers, among teachers, and between teachers and administrators. As with each chapter, we focus on applying education research and integrating findings directly into your classroom reality. Drawing on Laura Burgess's article, "The Influence of Social Contagion Within Education: A Motivational Perspective," we connect the concept of social contagion to the ABC model—examining how communication pathways can involve both accurate and inaccurate inferences, as well as material and informative cooperation. By understanding contagion effects, teachers can gain a new cognitive perspective on student inference-making, behaviour, and the deep motivational drive to connect with others—even when it leads to distorted or antisocial outcomes.

Remember Ms. Smith? Her students believed that she was bored, tired, and in bad humour—which was not true. Over time, these perceptions became their reality, shaping how they interpreted everything she did.

Research into social contagion highlights just how powerful—and contagious—these kinds of perceptions can become in a classroom:

> *Teacher contagion effects can also be considered as a version of social learning process—if students think that their teacher is feeling stressed and*

DOI: 10.4324/9781003644088-6

incompetent, students are likely to catch that feeling by inferring that they are learning something boring and difficult.

(Burgess et al., 2018)

Psychological research on motivation has long indicated the importance of social relationships in students' motivated behavior. These lines of work suggest that many, if not all, of the social contagion phenomena observed in education could be explained by motivational mechanisms.

(Burgess et al., 2018)

Social Contagion in the Classroom

In their article "The Influence of Social Contagion within Education: A Motivational Perspective," Burgess and colleagues (2018) discuss research on how behaviours, emotions, and beliefs can spread unconsciously through social networks like classrooms. Students often infer and "catch" attitudes from peers, significantly shaping their academic engagement, subject interest, and classroom behaviour. Peer influence emerges as a key mechanism of social contagion, strongly impacting classroom behaviour and dynamics.

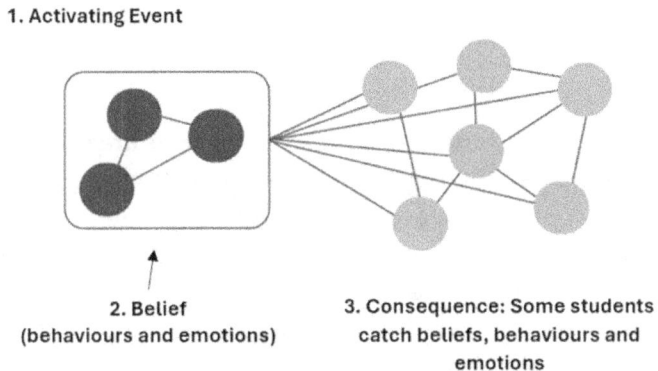

Figure 4.1 Illustration of social contagion in the classroom, shown through the ABC model (activating event, belief, and consequence).

On the next page, we see how some students make inferences about the teacher's intentions, and form beliefs that are expressed through behaviour and emotions (informative and material cooperation). Through social contagion these beliefs—whether accurate or inaccurate—can quickly spread throughout your classroom. Students, particularly those motivated by social connections, are likely to catch these beliefs and adopt similar behaviours and

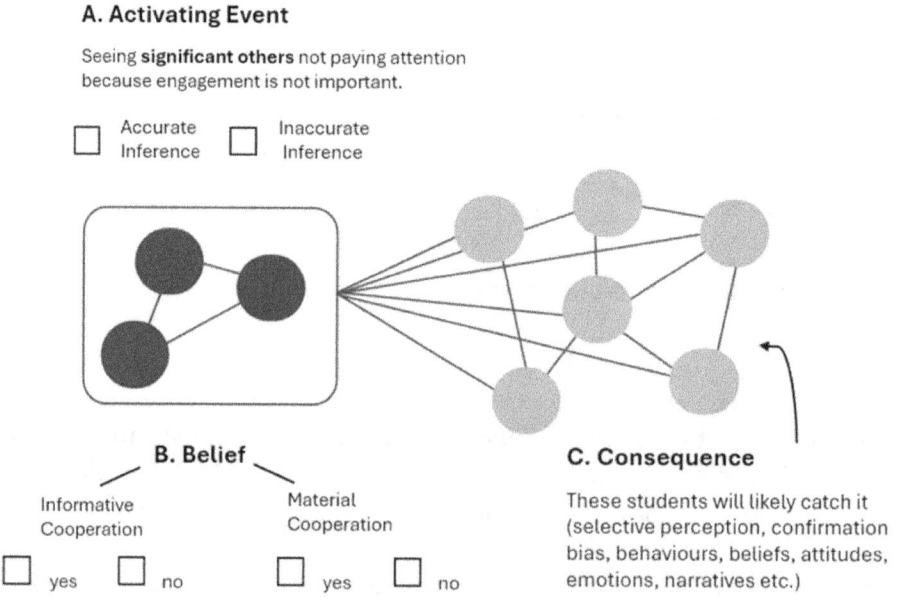

Figure 4.2 Illustration of how student beliefs and behaviours spread: the ABC–inference–contagion pathway.

attitudes about you or the lesson. As a result, students are not merely mimicking actions but are internalizing them based on inferences they make about what is socially acceptable or rewarding within the group.

According to research on social contagion in educational settings (Burgess et al., 2018), if some students see "significant peers" not paying attention in your class, they may infer paying attention is not important even though you said so. By applying inferential communication to social contagion, we can see how different types of motivation and cooperation (informative and material) impact the spread of beliefs, behaviours and attitudes.

The Motivational Basis for Social Contagion

In Burgess's exploration of social contagion within the classroom, she introduces a methodology for mapping behaviour change to networks that directly represent school cohorts. The authors argue that these various lines of research can be clearly interpreted through a **motivation** perspective, emphasizing the critical role of motivation in social contagion within education. Specifically, in classroom environments, students are motivated by a need to maintain social connections, which explains why they adopt the behaviours and attitudes of their peers.

This drive for **social connection** explains phenomena such as **peer influence** on academic engagement, where students imitate their friends' motivation and performance (Sacerdote, 2011). Similarly, Vania Martinez, in her study of social contagion in adolescents, highlights that adolescents are especially prone to social contagion due to both their developmental stage and the influence of social media, along with their peers. It is clear that **social connectedness** and an overwhelming need to **belong** are integral to understanding inference-making, communication, and student behaviour—whether that behaviour is prosocial or antisocial.

The Good, the Bad, and the Ugly—The Inferential Model

So when students "catch" beliefs, behaviours, and attitudes from one another in your classroom, and peer influence is the central element in shaping classroom dynamics, what kind of teacher credibility inferences would you prefer to be most contagious and spread through your students? The Good, The Bad or the Ugly? Obviously, we all aim for this.

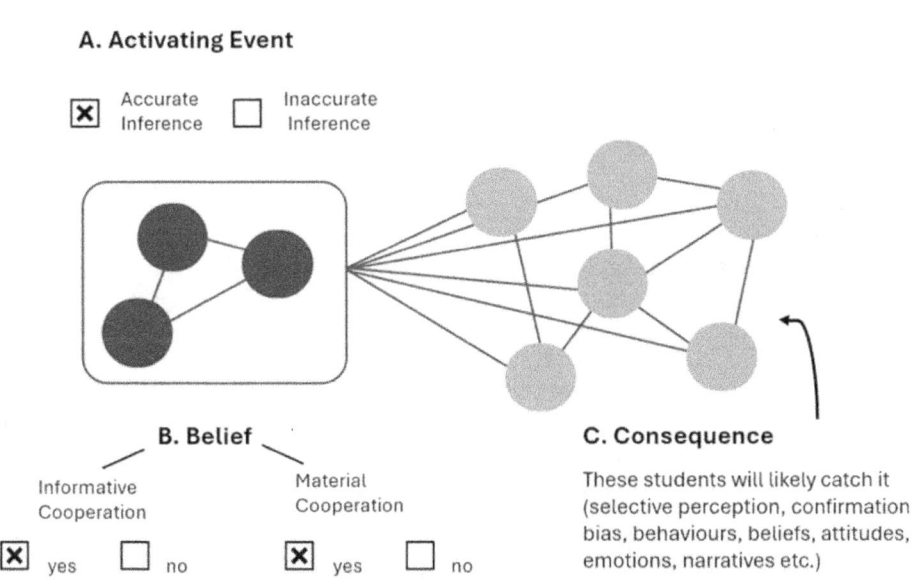

Figure 4.3 Illustration of catching beliefs: the good communicative pathway.

The effective communication of teacher credibility requires more than good intentions—it is a **shared, cooperative effort** between you and your students. Applying the Inferential Model to social contagion highlights the complexity of communicating caring, trust, and competence, and reveals the powerful role of social influence in shaping how students perceive you and your classroom climate.

The Ugly—Social Contagion: Peer Influence, Deception, and the Challenge to Teacher Credibility

But what happens if, in your classroom, students, motivated by their need to maintain social connections, adopt the behaviours and attitudes of their peers—but unlike The Good, their beliefs about your credibility are spread through inferences, both accurate and inaccurate, that are **deceptive and antisocial**? Meaning, the all-consuming drive for social connection, where students imitate significant peers' motivation and performance, is driven by peer influence derived from:

- Revenge or retaliation
- Deflecting accountability
- Gaining favour from other teachers or parents
- Seeking sympathy or leniency
- Power dynamics and rebellion

And essential social connection is reinforced by the use of:

- Manipulation
- Lies of omission
- Exaggeration
- False consensus
- Selective reporting
- Deflection
- False attribution

Social contagion in this classroom—the same unconscious spread of behaviours, emotions, and beliefs seen in *The Good*—now drives a **toxic dynamic**. In *The Ugly*, students "catch" negative attitudes, distorted narratives, and antisocial behaviours from peers, which can significantly undermine their motivation, disrupt engagement, and erode overall classroom behaviour.

When inaccurate inferences are reinforced through deception and peer influence, the result is a group dynamic that not only resists correction but also challenges the teacher's credibility at every turn.

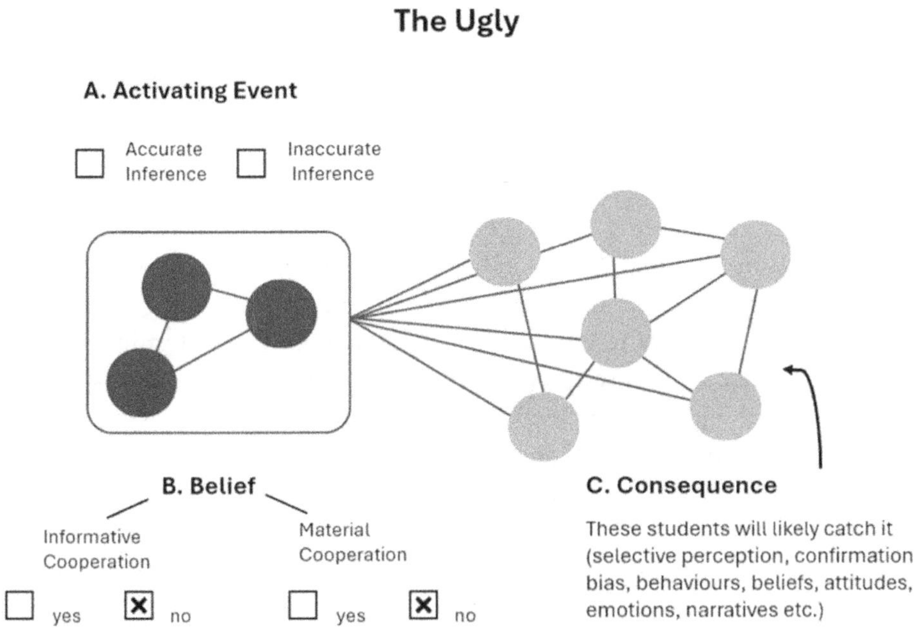

The Ugly

A. Activating Event

☐ Accurate Inference   ☐ Inaccurate Inference

B. Belief

Informative Cooperation
☐ yes ☒ no

Material Cooperation
☐ yes ☒ no

C. Consequence

These students will likely catch it (selective perception, confirmation bias, behaviours, beliefs, attitudes, emotions, narratives etc.)

Figure 4.4 Illustration of catching beliefs: the ugly communicative pathway.

The Logic of False Beliefs

The insights from James Clear's *Why Facts Don't Change Our Minds* provide a compelling framework for understanding the spread of **informatively and materially uncooperative behaviour** in the classroom. His work shows how social contagion operates through deep motivational pathways: students' beliefs—accurate or not—are often shaped by an instinctual drive to belong.

Clear explains that throughout human evolutionary history, being cast out of a tightly knit tribe could mean death. In today's classrooms, the same need to fit in, bond with peers, and earn social approval can lead students to adopt and spread false beliefs as a form of social survival. Even when something is objectively untrue—such as a negative inference about your credibility—students may mimic social behaviours, emotions, and beliefs to signal alignment with their peer group. These acts maintain social connectedness, especially when it feels threatened.

Clear quotes psychologist Steven Pinker, who observes:

People are embraced or condemned according to their beliefs, so one function of the mind may be to hold beliefs that bring the belief-holder the greatest number of allies, protectors, or disciples, rather than beliefs that are most likely to be true.

He also cites Kevin Simler:

> *If a brain anticipates that it will be rewarded for adopting a particular belief, it's perfectly happy to do so, and doesn't much care where the reward comes from—whether it's pragmatic (better outcomes resulting from better decisions), social (better treatment from one's peers), or a mix of the two.*

This phenomenon—what Clear calls *"factually false but socially accurate"*—offers a powerful lens through which to view student inference-making and classroom behaviour. When faced with a choice between aligning with the truth or with their social group, students will often prioritize **belonging over accuracy**—choosing their connections over the facts in your classroom.

This logic explains how negative peer narratives can take root and spread—even when they directly contradict your own observable classroom behaviour

Contagion Effects beyond Students

Social contagion doesn't just occur between students in your classroom. As Laura Burgess discusses in her article, contagion can spread from you to your students, between you and your teaching colleagues, and even from your principal to you. For instance, research cited by Burgess shows that teacher burnout has been shown to increase stress levels in students (Oberle & Schonert-Reichl, 2016). For example, when teachers are feeling burnt out or stressed, their students can pick up on that stress and feel more anxious themselves and are likely to catch that feeling by inferring that they are learning something boring and difficult.

Furthermore, **your own perceived motivation** has been shown to directly impact your students' engagement in your teaching. In a study cited by Burgess, students were less interested in lessons when they thought their teacher was being paid to teach rather than doing it because they wanted to—or because they were intrinsically motivated (Radel et al., 2010). Students **inferred** the teacher's lack of passion from the situation, which shaped their own engagement and **perception** of the class. This shows how your own motivations as interpreted by students and the cues you give off can impact how much they care about learning.

Burgess also examined teacher–to–teacher contagion, which occurs when stress, burnout, and emotional exhaustion can spread among staff members, potentially impacting overall school climate. She cites research showing that stress can also pass from school principals to you, showing how emotions in a workplace can spread and affect everyone (Westman & Etzion, 1999). Just one example of job-induced tension can pass from school principals to teachers, highlighting a "crossover effect" in workplace stress. For example, if you perceive you're your principal doesn't value your work, you might feel demotivated, which in turn affects how students infer your low energy as a sign that learning doesn't matter.

Exploring the spread of contagion beyond students highlights the interconnectedness of the school environment. What happens in other classrooms in your school—where beliefs influenced by materially and informatively uncooperative behaviour spread—can ripple through the entire school, impacting organizational dynamics and even your own classroom. For example, negative credibility in one classroom can spread and affect collective efficacy across your school, illustrating just how deeply contagion can influence the broader school environment.

Social Contagion and Teacher Self-Efficacy: Making Sense of Student Behaviour

> *It involves evaluating an emotionally charged situation from a different perspective than what comes automatically to mind. Cognitive reappraisal is used to counter habitual—and often negative—interpretations of events that can lead to getting stuck… or interfere with goal pursuits.*
> (Psychology Today, 2023)

> *Understanding alternative causes of misbehavior from the student perspective could promote cognitive reappraisal and consequently, elicit positive emotions even when teachers are dealing with challenging students.*
> (Aldrup et al., 2018)

When your students form negative inferences about your intentions in order to maintain social connection with peers who perpetuate these beliefs, they may also communicate these inferences through deceptive and antisocial behaviour. The spread of this false narrative through social contagion can significantly harm your teacher credibility, classroom behaviour, and your sense of **self-efficacy**—the belief in your own ability to manage the classroom and foster student success. As this false narrative persists, it can seriously erode your confidence, making you more vulnerable to burnout. However, there is a critical and potentially career-saving silver lining: Reframing Your Interpretation of Student Behaviour—Cognitive Reappraisal:

1. **Recognizing Alternative Causes**: Understanding that there are alternative reasons for negative student perceptions of teacher credibility other than you're your own teaching behaviour.
2. **Understanding Social Contagion**: Recognizing that the negative social contagion observed in your classroom can be explained by motivational mechanisms. Student motivation can very well be the underlying cause, and you can therefore make accurate inferences (decode) your students' behaviour.
3. **Changing Student Perception**: The solution is to shift student perceptions of your behaviour, so students make and truthfully communicate accurate inferences about your teaching using prosocial behaviour. This aligns the mutual cognitive environment shared between you and your students.

A Cognitive Reappraisal: Changing Students' Beliefs Means Changing Their Social Identity

Changing students' perceptions can be challenging and risky. As James Clear puts it, "convincing someone to change their mind is the process of convincing them to change their tribe." This dynamic is deeply rooted in our evolutionary need to belong. Abandoning their current beliefs means risking the loss of social ties with their peers—an especially difficult and unreasonable request during adolescence. The need for social acceptance often drives students to align with the beliefs of their peer group, even when those beliefs are irrational or inaccurate.

However, challenging this social identity can lead to disproportionate responses, where students' reactions are far more severe than your initial attempt to correct them. This escalation can reinforce perceptual biases like confirmation bias, leading to a reaction that doesn't fit the action, that amplifies the disconnect between your professional teaching behaviour and an overly negative student reaction.

Concepts such as Peer Orientation, Karpman's Drama Triangle, Anti-School Subcultures, and social hierarchies will be discussed later to explore these disproportionate responses further. Students heavily rely on inferring intention to understand communication, drawing conclusions not just from the content of the teacher's message (your behaviour) but from how they perceive that message in relation to the social dynamics of their peer group. In this case, beliefs that undermine your credibility serve as essential tools for maintaining social connectedness.

As Clear also notes, "nobody wants their worldview torn apart if the result is loneliness." Consequently, negative inferences, perceptions, and ideas about you can often be repeated and reinforced. This creates a disconnect between your rational, objective reality and what appears as irrational, deceptive, disrespectful, or antisocial motivations from your students. Considering what you now know about social connectedness and identity, it's important to understand how to shift student perception without threatening either their identity or social bonds. To do this, you need to invite students to join a new tribe—yours. As Clear wisely states, "Be kind first, be right later."

The Power of Cognitive Reappraisal: Accurate Mind Reading of Students to Help Bridge the Disconnect

To communicate effectively in order to bridge the disconnect between you and your students, teachers need to identify what is in the **mutual cognitive environment** they share with their students and—critically—what the students also **think** is in that shared environment. This recursive understanding (i.e., "I know that you know that I know") through cognitive reappraisal is essential for accurate **mindreading**. Here's how it works.

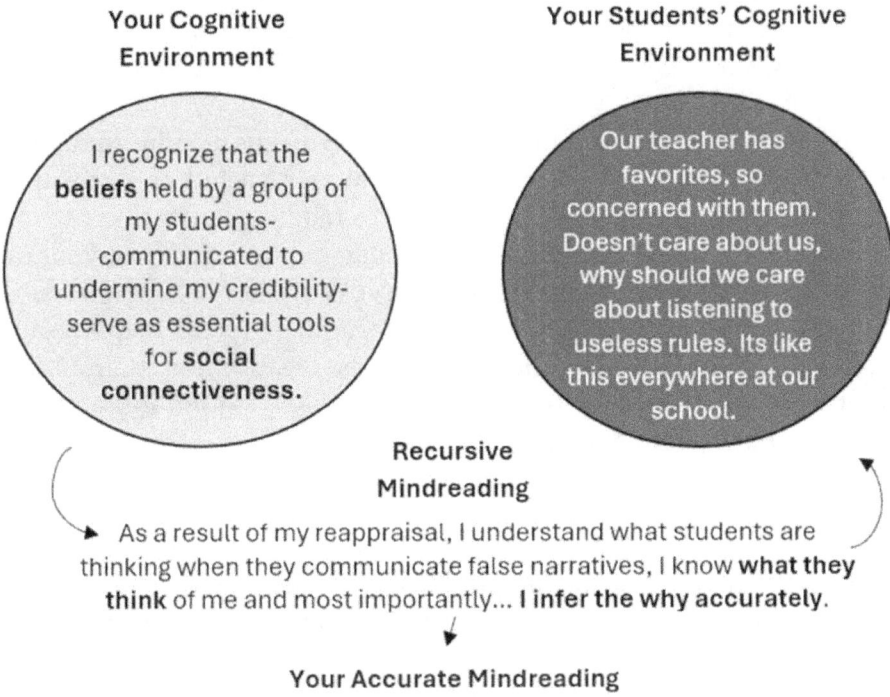

Figure 4.5 Diagram of divergent cognitive environments: the power of cognitive reappraisal.

Although some students respected the deadline, they supported their penalized peers out of social loyalty and peer group hierarchies. Together, they created and spread a false narrative that undermined your credibility. Through **mindreading**—inferring your thoughts, intentions, and values without evidence—these students concluded, or at least endorsed the belief, that your refusal to grant an extension was personal and punitive. However, by engaging in **cognitive reappraisal**, you are able to do your own mindreading—one grounded in evidence and careful inference—to accurately decode your students' motivations and intentions.

Consequence
Even though your students' perceptions (their cognitive environment) are disconnected from reality, your accurate understanding of the situation (through cognitive reappraisal after decoding student inferences) gives you critical insight: their views of your credibility are not based solely on your teaching behaviour, they are also shaped by peer loyalty and social dynamics.

By recognizing this, you can avoid taking the false narrative personally or to heart. Instead of reacting emotionally, like losing your temper or patience, which would only confirm their inaccurate beliefs, you stay calm, protecting both your credibility and your emotional energy (improving your own socio-emotional competence).

This emotional control not only improves your ability to manage student emotions, but also helps you manage your own reactions. It reduces irrational thinking, cuts down on dysfunctional behaviour, and lowers negativity for everyone involved.

However, fully resolving the disconnect also means helping students shift their own thinking and communicative behaviour (including their informative and material cooperation). This involves moving student perception by addressing their recursive mindreading, their assumptions about your intentions and cognitive environment, and improving their ability to accurately reappraise the real classroom climate (through cognitive reappraisal). By decoding their cognitive environment, you can create a less confrontational, calmer atmosphere where students are more likely to rethink and correct their assumptions about you on their own.

Chapter Review

★ Beliefs in your classroom can spread fast—whether they're true or not. This is **social contagion**, and it often affects how students view you and your lessons. Socially motivated students, in particular, tend to adopt the attitudes of their peers to feel accepted.

★ As Burgess and others explain, this isn't just about information—it's about **motivation**. Students want to belong, and that desire can lead them to share or accept distorted beliefs.

★ This pressure to fit in can even override what students personally believe. As James Clear points out, group belonging has deep evolutionary roots. In the classroom, that same instinct drives students to align with peers, sometimes at the cost of truth.

★ Your response matters. By using **cognitive reappraisal**—choosing how to interpret student behaviour—you can avoid reacting emotionally. Staying calm protects your credibility and keeps false narratives from gaining more ground.

Key Takeaway:

In a socially driven classroom, false beliefs about you can spread quickly—not because they're true, but because they help students belong. Your calm measured response is driven by understanding this about your students.

References

Aldrup, K., Klusmann, U., Lüdtke, O., Göllner, R., & Trautwein, U. (2018). Student misbehavior and teacher well-being: Testing the mediating role of the teacher-student relationship. *Learning and Instruction, 58*, 126–136. https://doi.org/10.1016/j.learninstruc.2018.05.006

Burgess, L. G., Riddell, P. M., Fancourt, A., & Murayama, K. (2018). The influence of social contagion within education: A motivational perspective. *Mind, Brain, and Education, 12*(4), 164–174.

Clear, J. (2024). *Why facts don't change our minds.* https://jamesclear.com/why-facts-dont-change-minds

Oberle, E., & Schonert-Reichl, K. A. (2016). Stress contagion in the classroom? The link between classroom teacher burnout and morning cortisol in elementary school students. *Social Science & Medicine, 159*, 30–37. https://doi.org/10.1016/j.socscimed.2016.04.031

Psychology Today. (2023). Cognitive reappraisal. *Psychology Today.* https://www.psychologytoday.com/ca/basics/cognitive-reappraisal

Radel, R., Sarrazin, P., Legrain, P., & Wild, T. C. (2010). Social contagion of motivation between teacher and student: Analysing underlying processes. *Journal of Educational Psychology, 102*(3), 577–587. https://doi.org/10.1037/a0019051

Sacerdote, B. (2011). Peer effects in education: How might they work, how big are they and how much do we know thus far? In E. Hanushek, S. Machin, & L. Woessmann (Eds.), *Handbook of the economics of education* (Vol. 3, pp. 249–277). Elsevier North Holland.

Westman, M., & Etzion, D. (1999). The crossover of strain in the workplace. *Journal of Managerial Psychology, 14*(3/4), 218–230. https://doi.org/10.1108/02683949910263798 Simler K. *Crony beliefs*. Melting Asphalt. https://meltingasphalt.com/crony-beliefs/

5

Echo Chambers and Tribalism in Your Classroom

Overview

This chapter explores the impact of classroom disconnect between teachers' and students' cognitive environments, especially when students spread false narratives about a teacher's credibility. Even if you attempt to reframe students' interpretations of behaviour, their perceptions may remain negative, driven by underlying social motivations. This persistent disconnect causes both teachers and students to misinterpret each other's intentions, creating a cycle of misunderstanding and mistrust.

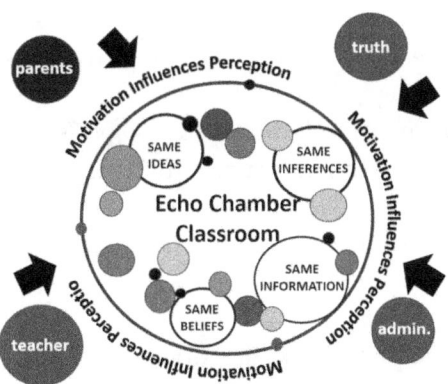

Figure 5.1 Diagram of an echo chamber classroom, showing motivation as the driver of perception.

DOI: 10.4324/9781003644088-7

We examine how "echo chamber" effects and social contagion intensify these dynamics. Within an echo chamber, students reinforce a shared, often inaccurate, narrative about the teacher, fuelled by peer conformity and the need for social belonging. Opposing viewpoints are ignored, and group loyalty begins to take precedence over truth. As students adopt a more tribal mindset, their perceptions of you become increasingly distorted, heightening your stress and risk of burnout.

By understanding these dynamics, we gain deeper insight into how social motivations, group influences, and inaccurate perceptions perpetuate disconnection in the classroom — and why addressing them is critical to restoring a healthy learning environment.

Classroom Disconnect: Divergent Cognitive Environments

What happens if you make the necessary cognitive reappraisal, but your students' cognitive environments remain divergent, and they continue to spread false narratives? Likewise, what if the teacher never incorporates reappraisal and continues to misattribute student behaviour and beliefs? In both cases, the cognitive environments of teacher and students remain misaligned.

Simply put, both the teacher and the students continue operating within different cognitive environments. Students interpret your actions through a lens of negative attributions and may even communicate their inferences deceptively. What makes this disconnect so damaging is that you may often be unaware of, or misunderstand, their motivational perspective. Furthermore, if your inferences about the students are inaccurate—based on different assumptions or prior experiences—this only exacerbates the disconnect, leading to further misinterpretations of intentions and motivations on both sides.

Here's how mindreading often plays out in this scenario:

- **Teacher:** *"I know that you know what I know"*—but this assumption is wrong. The teacher misinterprets the students' behaviour.
- **Students:** *"We know that you know what we know"*—but this assumption is also wrong. The students misunderstand the teacher's intentions.

You'll encounter this dynamic in the upcoming chapter on the "Negative Credibility Ecosystem," where the teacher assumes students are undermining their goals, even though the students have no awareness of those goals at all.

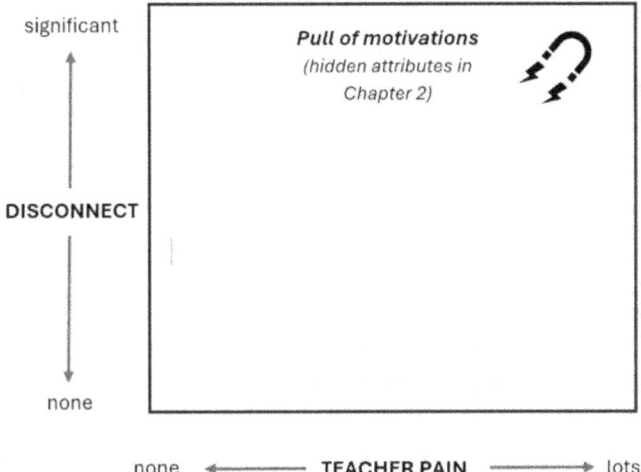

Figure 5.2 Diagram of the pull of hidden student motivations and the pain of disconnect.

Inferential Errors

Both the teacher and the students make inferences based on the available information, but often these inferences are flawed. For example, if a teacher infers that students are following the lesson because they are quiet and nodding along—while in reality, students are lost and not asking questions out of fear or embarrassment—this small disconnect reveals how easily misunderstandings can arise.

These errors highlight the lack of overlap in cognitive environments, leading to serious consequences as both sides interpret actions through incomplete or biased lenses.

The cycle self-perpetuates because the teacher remains unaware of the motivations and social contagion driving students' negative perceptions of credibility. The more unaware the teacher is, the stronger students' beliefs become that the teacher doesn't care, cannot be trusted, and is not competent. As the disconnect deepens, so does the teacher's emotional strain—depicted in the diagram as the increasing pull of motivations fuel disconnect, amplifying the teacher's pain.

The Pain of Classroom Disconnect: Impact on Teachers and Students

A disconnect in the classroom, characterized by a breakdown in communication, can have profound effects on both teachers and students. Here, we explore the emotional, psychological, and behavioural consequences of such disconnects. Research consistently shows that communication breakdowns negatively impact engagement, understanding, behaviour, academic performance, and teacher–student relationships (Goodboy & Myers, 2008; Hamre & Pianta, 2001; McCroskey, 1977).

Misunderstanding of Needs

You may not fully grasp the diverse needs of your students. Social dynamics and social contagion often go unnoticed, misinterpreted, or misattributed. Students' behaviours are frequently driven by their need for social connection—needs that can easily be overlooked. The hidden pull of student motivations (hidden attributes) can derail even your most rational attempts to meet their needs.

Emotional Distance

A lack of emotional connection or trust between you and your students can develop, making it difficult for them to feel safe and supported. Conversely, you may lose trust and connection with students you perceive as undermining your professional credibility. Ouch—that can hurt! Often, students aren't even fully aware of your goals or intentions.

Lack of Engagement

Students may appear disinterested in your lessons because they perceive your intentions as misaligned with their needs, deepening disengagement. For example, if Ms. Smith's students believe she is bored or simply "there for the paycheck," their perceptions of her becomes increasingly negative, leading to decreased effort and participation in her lessons.

Teacher Burnout

When a teacher with strong credibility elsewhere struggles to connect with a specific group of students, the emotional and psychological toll can be severe. Despite your best efforts, not seeing the results you expect or deserve can lead to feelings of helplessness, frustration, and ultimately, burnout.

Impact on Mental Health

A negative classroom climate affects both students and teachers. Students' self-esteem can erode, and their stress and anxiety levels can rise. Similarly, your own sense of self-efficacy can take a significant hit, leaving you emotionally drained. This creates a difficult and challenging classroom—for the next 180 days.

Behavioural Issues

Frustration and disengagement often manifest as behavioural problems, ranging from minor disruptions to full-scale conflicts, as students express their unmet needs and frustrations.

A classroom disconnect can trigger significant emotional, psychological, and behavioural challenges for both teachers and students. For students, it means losing an irreplaceable asset in their education—a teacher like you, who despite earnest efforts, struggles to overcome the distortions caused by divergent cognitive environments and social contagion. For teachers, the consequences include increased stress, emotional exhaustion, and a deep sense of professional disillusionment. Addressing these disconnects is not optional—it's essential for rebuilding trust, fostering engagement, and creating a positive, productive learning environment.

The Insular Echo Chamber Classroom: Motivation as a Driver of Reinforced Narratives and Disconnect

In the echo chamber classroom, motivation plays a crucial role in influencing perception, driving students to reinforce the same ideas, inferences, and beliefs about their teacher. This insularity shapes the cognitive environment, creating a disconnect between students' perceptions and the broader reality. As Sandahl (2020) found in his study of social science classrooms, students' emotional investments in their own beliefs (affective connections) often led them to dismiss alternative viewpoints and reinforce pre-existing narratives rather than engage with differing perspectives. Without intentional efforts to expose students to different perspectives, they tend to stick to their familiar views. Their motivation to defend these views can quickly turn the classroom into an echo chamber, where group beliefs are reinforced even when other viewpoints are available:

1. **Motivation Influences Perception**
   Students' motivation to fit in with their peers or maintain their social status influences how they interpret and reinforce the group's common

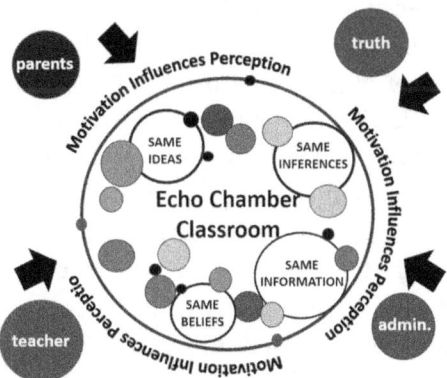

Figure 5.3 Diagram of an echo chamber classroom, showing motivation as the driver of perception.

narrative. This process is amplified by *social contagion*, where beliefs and behaviours spread rapidly through peer influence. The group continuously recycles the same information, filtering out contradictory viewpoints, including those from teachers, parents, or administration. This creates a closed loop of perception, driven by the students' social motivations, and reinforced by the contagious spread of the shared narrative.

2. **Reinforcement of a False Narrative**
Motivated by the need for social connection, students reinforce the same narrative about the teacher's credibility. Even if this narrative is false, the motivation to conform drives its continued spread within the group.

3. **Exclusion of Opposing Views**
Motivated by a desire to maintain their beliefs, students reject or ignore contradictory evidence, whether from parents or administrators, or the teacher's behaviour itself. The exclusion of opposing views maintains the echo chamber.

4. **Social Pressure and Conformity**
The fear of losing social status or being excluded pushes students to conform to the group's narrative, reinforcing their perceptions and blocking out the teacher's reality. This motivation to belong overrides critical thinking.

5. **Positive Reinforcement and Group Identity**
Motivated by a desire for social capital, students who actively support the group's beliefs gain status, while those who challenge it risk rejection. This dynamic ensures the group's shared perceptions remain unchallenged, further entrenching the disconnect (see Peer Attachment, Karpman's Drama Triangle, Anti-School Subcultures and Chronic Hyper and Hypo Arousal).

6. **External Perspectives Blocked**
Despite the presence of external perspectives (from parents, teachers, administration, or objective truth), the insular nature of the classroom prevents these viewpoints from penetrating the echo chamber. The students' motivation to maintain the group's shared beliefs filters out any information that might challenge their established narrative.

In this model, the echo chamber classroom represents a heightened form of classroom disconnect, where the students' insular environment amplifies their misinterpretations of the teacher's credibility. Without an aligned cognitive environment to include the teacher's perspective, the students' inferences remain distorted and divergent, making it difficult to realign their perceptions with reality. (Adapted from Sandahl, 2020)

From Echo Chamber to Tribalism: Loyalty over Truth

In a classroom like *The Ugly*, the echo chamber can evolve into a form of tribalism, where students' loyalty to their peer group takes precedence over objective truth. Scholars such as Farooq et al. (2024) describe behaviours characteristic of tribalism—including in-group loyalty overriding truth and social pressures reinforcing misinformation. In our Ugly scenario, students align themselves with their group and reinforce the false narrative about the teacher, even if it contradicts their own beliefs or observable reality, reflecting a preference for group loyalty over objective truth, as Farooq et al. (2024) emphasize:

Key Characteristics of Tribalism—Group Loyalty in the Classroom

Group Loyalty over Truth
Students may continue promoting the false narrative about the teacher, valuing social cohesion and group loyalty over acknowledging the teacher's credibility.

Us vs. Them Mentality
Students adopt a mindset that positions them as united against the teacher, framing the situation as a conflict between "us" (the group) and "them" (the teacher or school authority).

Social Rewards and Penalties
Conforming to the group's narrative brings social rewards; while challenging it risks social penalties or ostracism. This dynamic pressures students to uphold the shared identity, even at the cost of truth.

In this way, tribalism reflects how students' need for belonging and group identity outweighs the pursuit of truth, sustaining the false narrative about the teacher and deepening the divide between perception and reality. Left unchallenged, both the Echo Chamber and its Tribalism can spread throughout the school environment.

> **Chapter Review**
>
> ★ Classroom disconnect isn't just frustrating—it's damaging. When communication between teachers and students breaks down, it affects engagement, learning, behaviour, and the overall classroom climate. Research shows that these breakdowns can weaken academic performance and strain teacher–student relationships (Goodboy & Myers, 2008; Hamre & Pianta, 2001; McCroskey, 1977).

> ★ One common source of disconnect is a **misunderstanding of student needs**. Teachers may not see the full picture—especially when social dynamics, group pressures, and social contagion influence behaviour. Many student actions are driven by the need for belonging, not by defiance or disengagement. When these deeper needs go unrecognized, communication gaps grow wider, and your credibility can silently erode.

 Key Takeaway:

Classroom disconnect often stems from **divergent cognitive environments** and **unmet social needs**—not simply disobedience. When those needs go unrecognized, communication breaks down, credibility suffers, and students lose the most valuable resource they have: you.

References

Farooq, A., Adlam, A., & Rutland, A. (2024). Rejecting ingroup loyalty for the truth: Children's and adolescents' evaluations of deviant peers within a misinformation intergroup context. *Journal of Experimental Child Psychology, 240*, Article 105654. https://doi.org/10.1016/j.jecp.2024.105923

Goodboy, A. K., & Myers, S. A. (2008). The effect of teacher confirmation on student communication and learning outcomes. *Communication Education, 57*(2), 153–179. https://doi.org/10.1080/03634520701852040

Hamre, B. K., & Pianta, R. C. (2001). Early teacher–child relationships and the trajectory of children's school outcomes through eighth grade. *Child Development, 72*(2), 625–638. https://doi.org/10.1111/1467-8624.00301

McCroskey, J. C. (1977). Classroom consequences of communication apprehension. *Communication Education, 26*(1), 27–33. https://doi.org/10.1080/03634527709378059

Sandahl, J. (2020). Opening up the echo chamber: Perspective taking in social science education. *Acta Didactica Norden, 14*(4), Article 6. https://doi.org/10.5617/adno.8350

6

Why Your Credibility Is So Critical

Overview

Now that we've covered the ABCs of simplifying complex social interaction in your classroom and examined key concepts such as the inferential model of communication, informative and material cooperation, social contagion, and echo chambers, we turn our attention to one of the most critical factors shaping classroom dynamics: **your teacher credibility**.

Your credibility is key to effective teaching—but it can quickly come under pressure. When students misread your actions, spread negative stories, or act out, it creates disconnect. Add stress and burnout, and you get a cycle that's hard to break. These challenges don't just hurt your teaching—they take a real toll on your well-being.

The *Vicious Cycle* infographic illustrates how low perceptions of credibility can lead to increased misbehaviour, emotional exhaustion, and irrational responses from teachers, reinforcing negative outcomes for both students and educators. Similarly, the *Negative Teacher Credibility* Ecosystem infographic highlights the complex and mutually reinforcing nature of these factors.

As students perceive a teacher as lacking credibility, their behaviour often deteriorates. In turn, this elevates teacher stress, contributing to emotional exhaustion and diminishing the ability to manage the classroom effectively. This vicious cycle impacts not only individual teachers, but also broader student outcomes and overall school climate.

DOI: 10.4324/9781003644088-8

Understanding these interrelationships is essential. It reveals that improving your credibility requires more than reactive classroom management—it demands a deeper focus on students' motivations and perceptions **of your credibility: competence, caring, and trustworthiness**. In the following sections, we will explore how even small shifts in student perception can dramatically impact the teacher–student dynamic, either reinforcing or interrupting these destructive cycles.

Negative Teacher Credibility Ecosystem

Losing credibility in the classroom doesn't happen because of one bad moment or mistake. It happens over time, through a mix of factors that work together—like an ecosystem. In this "negative credibility ecosystem," student behaviour, teacher reactions, and school conditions all interact in ways that can quietly erode students' trust in your care, competence, and fairness.

This section breaks down the key causes of credibility loss and shows how they're connected. Use the following diagram to get a quick picture of how these forces build on each other—and how they can be addressed.

Low Teacher Self-Efficacy

Teacher self-efficacy refers to a teacher's belief in their own ability to positively influence student learning and manage the demands of teaching. In a negative credibility ecosystem, low self-efficacy plays a central role.

In their study, Savaş et al. (2014) found that teachers with low self-efficacy experience more burnout. Similarly, Lewis and Riley (2009) explain that when teachers feel their emotional and professional resources aren't enough to handle classroom management challenges, they often feel incompetent and unable to cope. When that happens to you, it becomes easy to shift focus—from what's best for students to protecting your own emotional well-being. As Lewis and Riley point out, under enough stress, you may find yourself reacting aggressively towards students, even when you don't intend to—a kind of fight/flight/freeze response expressed through anger. Over time, this can erode your credibility in ways that are hard to recover. Another internal factor that shapes the negative ecosystem is how teachers interpret student behaviour.

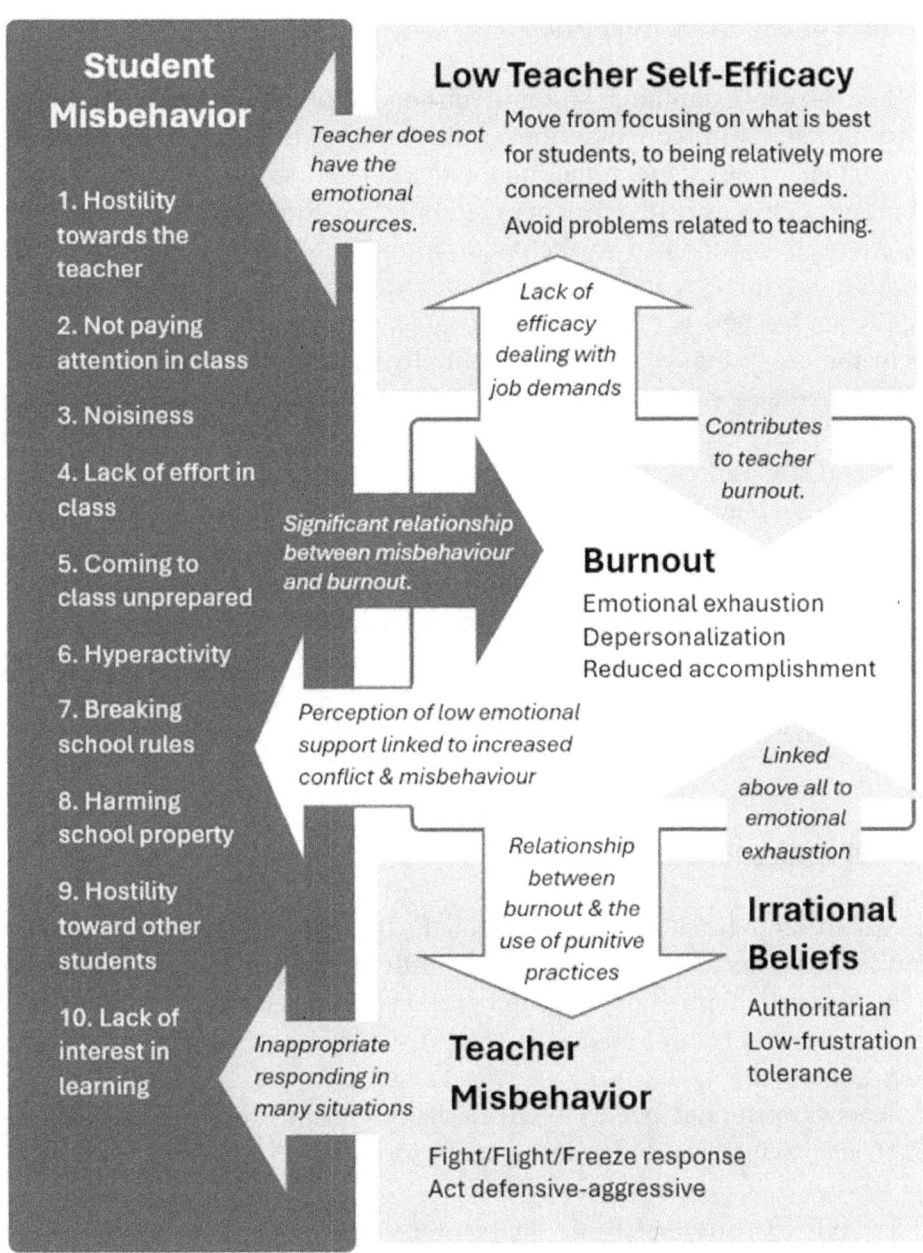

Figure 6.1 Diagram of the negative teacher credibility ecosystem, showing how student behaviour, teacher behaviour, and low self-efficacy interact to erode credibility (Gerving 2007).

Absence of Cognitive Reappraisal

In their article examining student misbehaviour and teacher well-being, Aldrup et al. (2018) conclude that understanding the student's perspective plays a major role in strengthening the teacher–student relationship—a critical foundation for positive teacher credibility. As they explain, "understanding alternative causes of misbehavior from the student perspective could promote cognitive reappraisal and consequently, elicit positive emotions even when teachers are dealing with challenging students."

In the ecosystem of negative credibility, a lack of cognitive reappraisal only exacerbates misunderstandings and attribution errors. Teachers who interpret misbehaviour as intentional are more likely to respond with anger and frustration. As Aldrup et al. point out, teachers' social-emotional competence—their ability to understand and regulate both students' emotions and their own—is key to maintaining a supportive relationship with students, even in the face of behavioural problems.

Without cognitive reappraisal, teachers risk falling into negative patterns of emotional reaction, further weakening their credibility in the eyes of students. Beyond internal challenges, irrational beliefs also play a critical role in undermining teacher resilience and credibility.

Teacher Irrational Beliefs

In their study of teachers' irrational beliefs, Bermejo and Prieto-Ursúa (2006) found that irrational beliefs were significantly associated with higher levels of stress, burnout, depression, psychological symptoms (stress-related physical symptoms, anxiety, and obsessive-compulsive symptoms), and even higher absenteeism.

Teacher irrational beliefs were measured using the Teacher Irrational Belief Scale, which is divided into four factors:

1. Self-Downing Attitude includes the belief in setting unrealistically high personal standards, an excessive need for approval from others, and the belief that making mistakes diminishes personal worth.
2. Low Frustration Tolerance reflects the belief that teaching should be easy and require little effort, along with a low ability to cope with difficulties, frustration, or the inherent challenges of teaching.

3. Attitudes towards School Organization involves the belief that teachers must be heavily involved in all school decision-making, the expectation that all problems should be heard and solved by the organization, and a high emotional dependency on how the school responds to individual concerns.
4. Authoritarian Attitudes towards Pupils includes the belief that any misbehaviour must be severely punished, an inability to tolerate student misbehaviour without an emotional overreaction, and a rigid, inflexible approach to student discipline.

Among these, low frustration tolerance and authoritarian attitudes towards students showed the strongest links to indicators of teacher distress. For example, teachers with irrational beliefs were more likely to experience high stress levels that could hinder the development and use of effective coping skills.

In the ecosystem of negative credibility, two significant impacts emerge: irrational beliefs are closely linked to emotional exhaustion, and authoritarian attitudes towards students are significantly associated with teacher burnout. Both of these patterns directly threaten a teacher's credibility in the classroom. Alongside these internal struggles, external pressures from student behaviour can further accelerate teacher stress and burnout.

Student Misbehaviour and Teacher Burnout

In their meta-analysis, Aloe et al. (2014) highlight the devastating impact of student misbehaviour within the negative credibility ecosystem. They found that student misbehaviour is a major contributor to teacher stress and a significant predictor of burnout. Teachers often spend a considerable amount of time managing problem behaviours, which reduces instructional time, increases job dissatisfaction, lowers self-efficacy, and heightens emotional exhaustion. As Aloe et al. explain, when students perceive low emotional support, this can in turn escalate conflict and misbehaviour in the classroom, creating a damaging cycle.

One of the key risks is emotional exhaustion—the feeling that you no longer have the emotional resources to give of yourself psychologically. This exhaustion can impair your ability to use positive behaviour management strategies, leading instead to punitive practices, which further increase conflict and student misbehaviour.

Consistent with these findings, Aldrup et al. (2018) also note that student misbehaviour undermines teacher–student relationship. Misbehaviour often provokes negative interactions, and teachers may interpret it as a personal rejection or a lack of appreciation. When faced with persistent misbehaviour, you might feel hurt, rejected, and find it difficult to maintain affection towards your students. This emotional strain not only contributes to higher levels of self-reported stress but also to increased emotional exhaustion and reduced enthusiasm for teaching.

Aldrup et al. also point out two important cognitive factors. First, stress increases when your teaching goals are threatened—but students are often unaware of your goals, making their disruptive behaviour feel even more personally discouraging. Second, persistent misbehaviour creates cognitive overload, interfering with your ability to focus on instructional goals and eliciting strong negative emotions. These cognitive and emotional demands can quietly erode your resilience and credibility over time. Even more concerning, students' perceptions of teacher burnout—whether accurate or not—can seriously damage credibility.

Student Perceptions of Teacher Burnout

According to Zhang and Sapp (2009) and Homeo (2020), students' beliefs about a teacher's burnout level—whether accurate or not—significantly influence their perception of the teacher's competence, care, and trustworthiness. Students who perceive their teacher as experiencing high burnout are more likely to view the teacher as uncaring, untrustworthy, and incompetent.

This perception weakens the teacher's credibility across three critical dimensions: the belief that the teacher cannot effectively manage the class, cannot teach content successfully, and cannot maintain appropriate behavioural standards. Even when a teacher's burnout is not extreme, students' assumptions alone can create a damaging credibility gap, reinforcing negative classroom dynamics. Stress and burnout not only affect emotions but can also drive teachers to misbehave in ways that further harm classroom trust.

Teacher Misbehaviour

In their study of teacher misbehaviour, Lewis and Riley (2009) describe research on how students interpret teacher punishments, especially when discipline moves from private to public. They explain that when this shift happens, "the whole class loses focus of the lesson," as students' attention moves away from the content and towards the emotions stirred up by the negative teacher–student interaction. Rather than focusing on learning, students experience heightened stress, anxiety, and fight/flight/freeze reactions.

Elevated stress, they argue, is a major factor that leads to inappropriate teacher responses in many situations. Classroom management difficulties rank among the top three causes of teacher stress, and the pressure can lead teachers to use inappropriate strategies to maintain control. Lewis and Riley highlight two types of teacher misbehaviour: omission and commission. Teachers in distress may fail to act against antisocial behaviour or may fail to recognize prosocial behaviour from "bad" students (omission). Alternatively, they may act out by yelling in anger, using cutting sarcasm, or even name-calling—what the authors describe as misbehaviour by commission.

Within the ecosystem of negative credibility, it is easy to see how this stress-driven cycle of misbehaviour feeds itself. As Lewis and Riley point out, teachers may feel "terrible" about their actions but continue to misbehave, often without full conscious control. This means that teachers can, without realizing it, contribute to the erosion of their own credibility, even as they suffer under the weight of stress and burnout. When these pressures build across many teachers in a school, the effects spread, damaging the entire school's credibility climate.

Schoolwide Teacher Stress: Absence of Collective Efficacy

What happens when stress spreads beyond the individual teacher and their classroom? In the wider school credibility ecosystem, the consequences can be severe. According to *The Epidemic of Teacher Stress* (The Graide Network, 2022), high levels of teacher stress can lead to a downshifting of responsibilities, where roles and tasks that were once held in esteem are handed over to less experienced staff who have not yet earned them through years of work and sacrifice. Teachers may also begin to reframe their professional identities, anchoring their sense of self-worth outside of their teaching roles, and eventually disengaging or quitting altogether. As the article notes, this mental and emotional disengagement results in less effective teaching and a decline in overall school climate.

Savaş et al. (2014) similarly highlight how burnout—specifically emotional exhaustion, feelings of low personal accomplishment, and depersonalization—correlates with negative student outcomes. They found a negative relationship between teachers' emotional exhaustion and average student grades, as well as a strong link between teacher absenteeism and student engagement. As Savaş et al. put it, "Sick and apathetic teachers miss school more often, affecting student engagement and achievement levels."

High teacher turnover, stress, and absenteeism are critical factors that magnify the negative credibility ecosystem across a school. When these pressures build across multiple classrooms, the credibility of the entire teaching staff can be quietly and severely undermined.

A Vicious Cycle

Research has established a strong link between student misbehaviour, teacher burnout, low self-efficacy, and perceived teacher credibility, which can significantly harm both the classroom environment and the well-being of teachers and students. When classroom management strategies prove ineffective, the consequences can persist—or even worsen—over time.

Why does this happen? In many cases, students' perceptions of a teacher's credibility are shaped by forces beyond immediate behaviour or direct control. As a result, classroom management strategies alone are unlikely to significantly improve student behaviour because they do not address the deeper causes shaping credibility. Without enhanced credibility, the cycle of misbehaviour and emotional exhaustion is likely to intensify. Worse, additional management interventions may unintentionally reinforce negative student perceptions if they are seen as punitive or unfair.

To visualize this dynamic, the following illustration highlights the many potential consequences of low teacher credibility:

New teachers are especially vulnerable to this cycle, but even experienced teachers can struggle under its pressures. Teaching is already an emotionally demanding profession, and when students perceive a lack of credibility, maintaining emotional regulation—a key component of effective teaching—becomes even harder. Without effective strategies to address student perceptions, the toll on your well-being, emotional health, and job satisfaction can be severe, particularly when you feel powerless to shift how students view you.

However, recognizing these patterns is the first step toward interrupting the cycle and rebuilding stronger, more resilient classroom relationships.

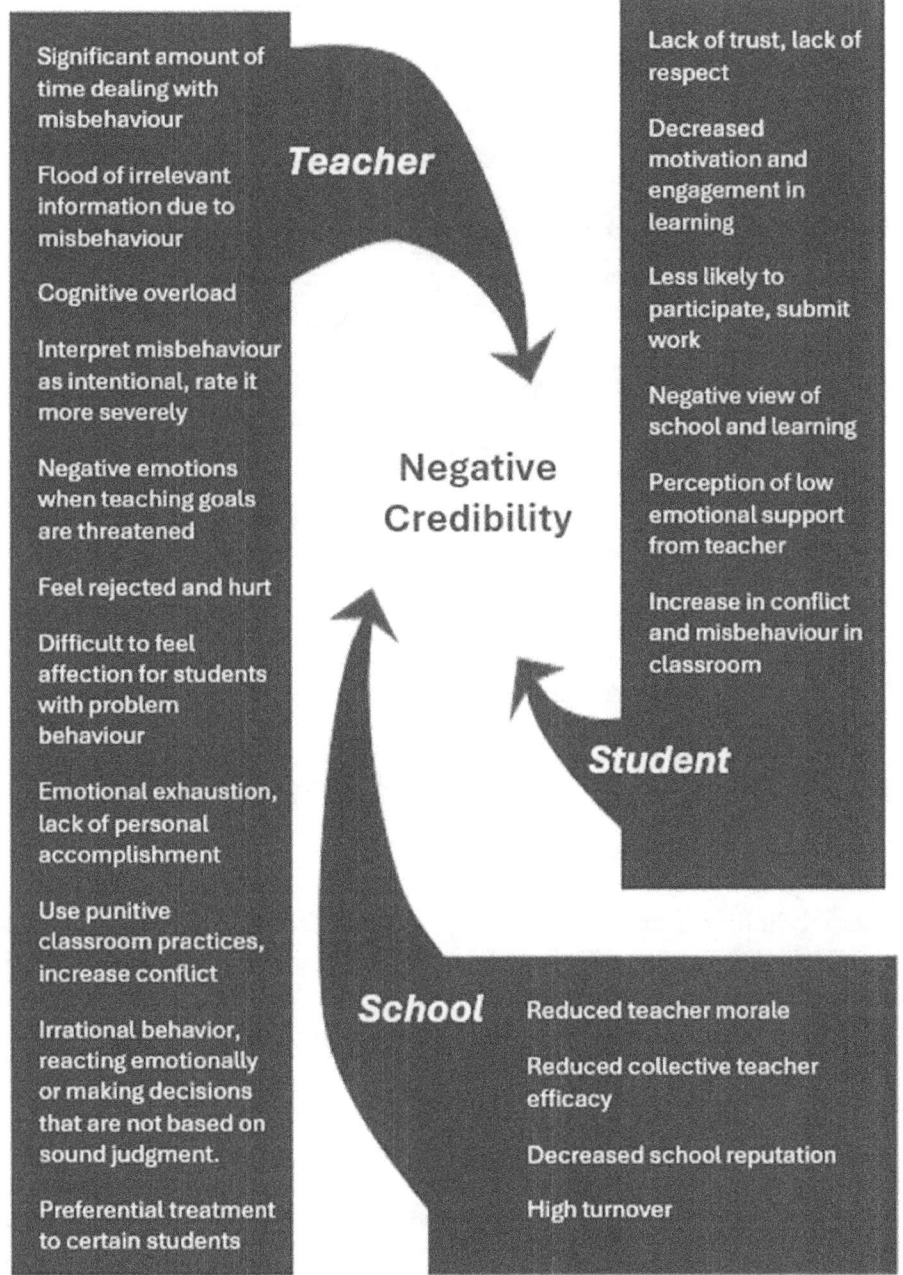

Figure 6.2 Diagram of the vicious cycle, showing how low teacher credibility fuels misbehaviour, burnout, and further credibility loss.

Ecosystem of Negative Teacher Credibility

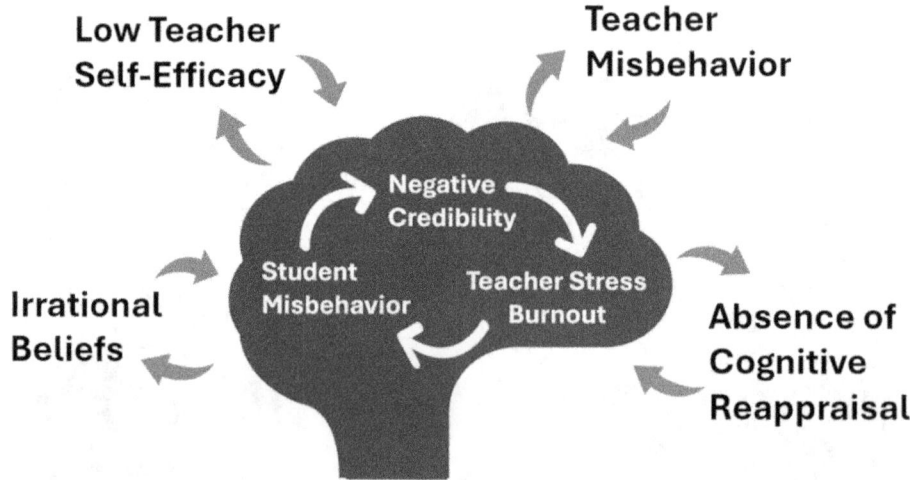

Figure 6.3 Diagram of the ecosystem of negative teacher credibility, showing the interconnections between student misbehaviour, teacher stress, burnout, and low self-efficacy.

To fully appreciate how these pressures converge, the following illustration simplifies the negative teacher credibility ecosystem into its core internal cycle, where stress, misbehaviour, and credibility loss reinforce each other in a self-sustaining negative cycle:

Credibility: What You Need to Know

Teacher credibility is measured through student feedback, using the 18-item *Source Credibility* survey developed by McCroskey and Teven (1999), which evaluates three primary dimensions:

John Hattie's comprehensive meta-analysis on factors influencing student achievement—synthesizing over 800 meta-analyses and covering more than 50,000 studies—highlights the crucial role of teacher credibility. According to Hattie, teacher credibility has a substantial impact on student achievement, with an effect size of 1.09. In the teacher domain, only teacher estimates of achievement (1.29) have a larger effect size. Instructional researchers collectively agree that teacher credibility is a fundamental factor in student learning, with the overriding principle being: "the higher the credibility, the higher the learning" (Hattie, 2024).

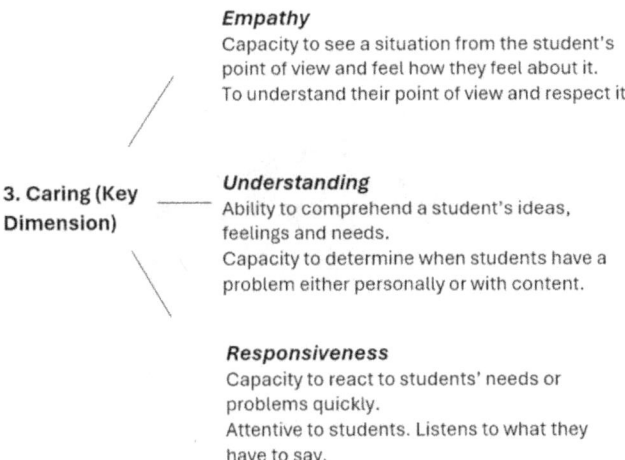

Adapted from: Teven, J. J., & Hanson, T. L. (2004). *The impact of teacher immediacy and perceived caring on teacher competence and trustworthiness. Communication Quarterly,* 52(1), 39–53.

Figure 6.4 Diagram of the three primary dimensions of teacher credibility: caring, trustworthiness, and competence (Hanson & Teven 2004).

Why is Teacher Credibility So Crucial in Education?

A meta-analysis by Amber Finn et al. (2009), encompassing 51 studies and 14,378 participants, reveals that teacher credibility has a substantial positive impact on students' engagement and willingness to participate in learning. Students report greater respect for teachers they perceive as credible, which enhances the overall classroom environment. The three core dimensions of credibility—competence, trustworthiness, and caring—work together to improve student outcomes, with caring having the strongest impact.

The following diagram illustrates the findings of the meta-analysis, highlighting the various ways that increased teacher credibility positively affects students—from greater attention and motivation to enhanced feelings of connection and justice. These findings underscore that teacher credibility is one of the most influential factors in shaping the teacher–student relationship (Myers, 2001). As Myers and Martin (2006) affirm, "teachers who are viewed as being credible exert a tremendous amount of influence on their students."

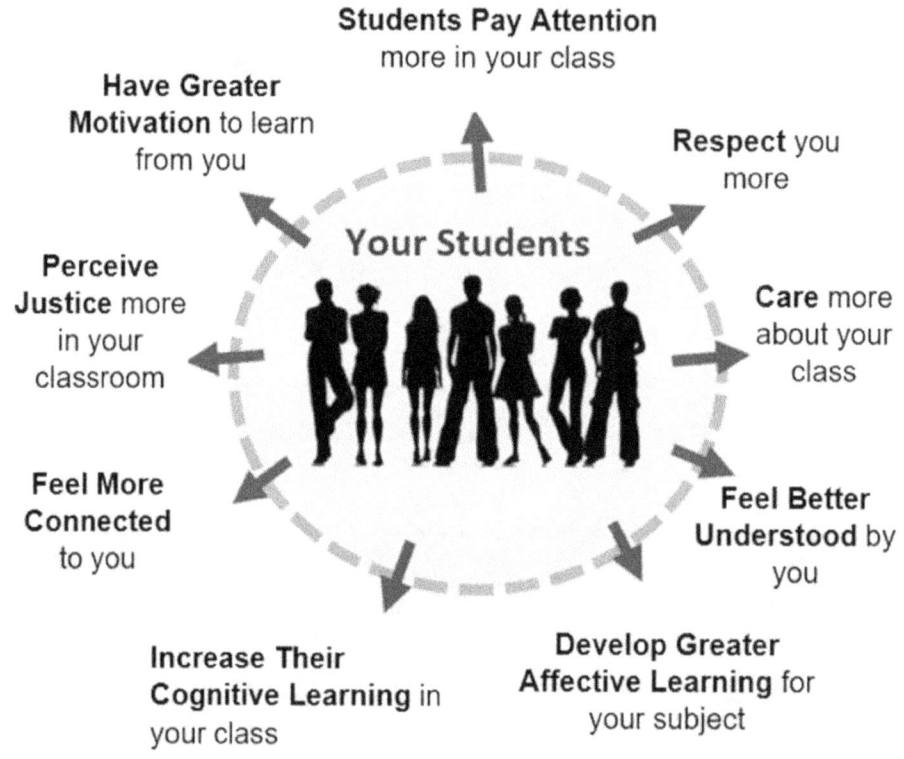

Figure 6.5 Illustration of the substantial impact of positive teacher credibility on student engagement and learning.

Measuring Caring: How Divergent Scores Influence Teacher Credibility

Let's revisit Ms. Smith and the assignment submission scenario. Imagine that her students were asked to provide feedback at the end of class, perhaps through an exit ticket. Recall that Ms. Smith's instructional behaviour has been consistently observed and documented as caring, trustworthy, and competent.

Using the Source Credibility framework, we can measure students' perception of the "caring" dimension in response to the activating event: the teacher enforcing late penalties. The distribution of scores reveals that students' inferences about Ms. Smith's intentions—specifically their perception of her caring—show both divergence from her intent and significant variability across students. While this might seem surprising, such divergence and variability in perception are quite common in classrooms. We will explore the causes and consequences of this divergence and variability in greater depth in a later chapter.

Although this distribution leans towards more positive perceptions overall, it also highlights a significant presence of negative and undecided responses. This raises important questions for every teacher: what are students inferring

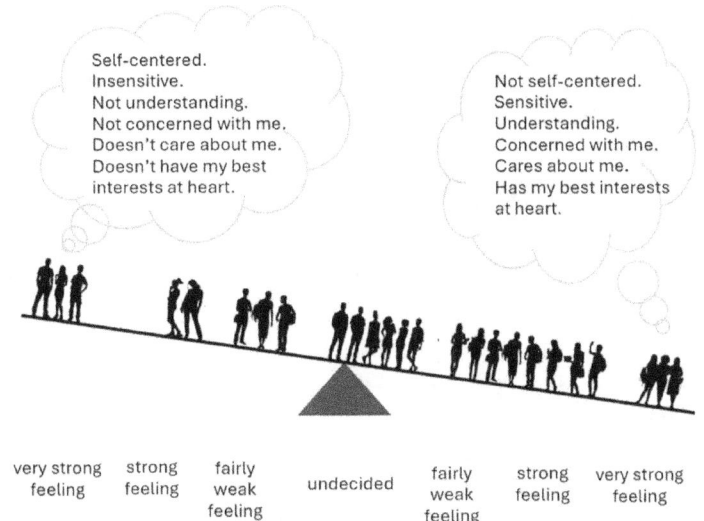

Figure 6.6 Illustration of how divergent caring scores influence perceptions of teacher credibility.

about your intentions and mental states? One clear conclusion is that a considerable number of students may be motivated to perceive you negatively, beyond what your behaviour deserves. This tendency can lead to serious negative outcomes, as false perceptions are often resistant to change due to factors like peer influence, social identity, and emotional commitment to group beliefs.

As we will see in the upcoming section on classroom profiles, challenging student beliefs shaped by identity and group dynamics often triggers a strong defensive response. These reactions are fuelled not by rational evaluation but by an evolutionary drive to defend "social truths" over objective truth. The critical question then becomes: how can you shift these perceptions in your favour?

Be Kind First, Be Right Later: Spectrum of Beliefs

How do you begin to challenge the perceptions and inferences of those who undermine your credibility? First, never tolerate or ignore deceptive and antisocial behaviour—period (remember the two types of teacher misbehaviour: omission and commission). However, as James Clear explains in his essay *Why Facts Don't Change Our Minds*, kindness is essential to reshaping perceptions. Kindness is not a sign of weakness; rather, it's a core component of teacher credibility, alongside competence in classroom management, discipline, instructional strategies, and leadership. Without kindness, credibility suffers. If you're kind but lack strength (competence), you can't protect the vulnerable. So, the question remains: how can you authoritatively correct false narratives while still demonstrating kindness, especially when your credibility is under attack?

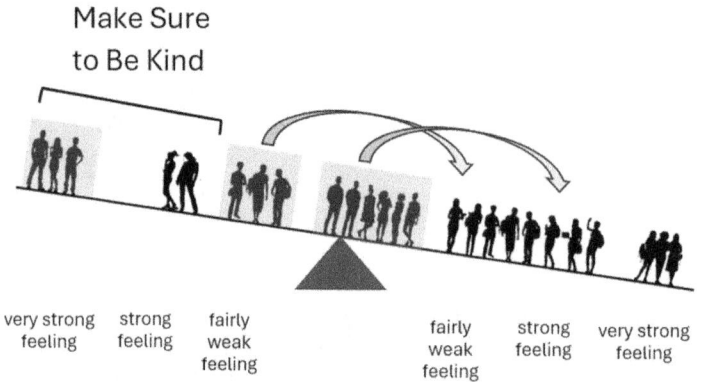

Figure 6.7 Illustration of the spectrum of beliefs: be kind first and be right later.

Spectrum of Beliefs: In the distribution of credibility scores, you may never persuade the outliers. However, how you treat these students profoundly influences the others. Clear explains that arguments often feel like personal attacks, leading to heated debates, especially with those on opposite ends of the spectrum. To influence students effectively, recognize that changing minds is a gradual process—students need to "slide" along the spectrum of beliefs.

Treating outliers with respect is crucial because they are often socially connected to many others in your classroom, touching issues of identity, social hierarchy, and belonging. Many students who disagree are connected to the outliers, but they may be more open—closer in proximity to reconsidering their views. Your treatment of the most resistant students sends a strong signal to everyone watching.

And remember, when discipline moves from private to public, "the whole class loses focus of the lesson." Students' attention shifts from content to the emotions stirred up by negative teacher–student interactions. Those students closer to reconsidering their beliefs are often the ones most vulnerable to heightened stress, anxiety, and fight/flight/freeze reactions. If you respond with losing your temper or sarcasm—what Lewis and Riley describe as misbehaviour by commission—you risk confirming their worst fears. They are watching you carefully: are you kind, trustworthy, and competent with all your students, or only possess some of these qualities?

The best environment for students to reconsider challenging ideas is a non-threatening one. By proactively introducing a "code" or "pre-bunking" common false beliefs (as discussed in Part 3) before conflicts arise, you offer students a safe opportunity to reflect privately, without fear of public judgement. This approach plants the "seed" of a new idea, allowing it to grow on their terms.

When a code is in place, students can openly challenge, debate, and disagree—individually or as a group—without feeling that their identity is under attack. Instead of confronting the teacher or each other directly, they engage with ideas and principles, fostering a reappraisal of their current beliefs. In this way, students feel heard, their perspectives are respected, and they know you have genuinely listened.

By being kind first, you set the stage to be right later.

How to Be Kind and Win the Battle: Confront False Beliefs with a "Scout" Mindset

It's a given that to protect students—whether from a belief that is hurtful or one that undermines your credibility, which, in the short and long term, is harmful to everyone in the class—a teacher must confront false beliefs as they arise. How these situations are handled impacts your credibility with the entire class, including allies, supporters, defenders, or followers of the student(s) holding the false belief.

This is a very tricky business. On the one hand, challenging the belief can risk credibility with students on the opposite side of the spectrum, who might see your handling of the situation as uncaring, incompetent, or unfair to their "tribe". On the other hand, ignoring or tolerating the undermining belief can erode the teacher's competence, caring, and trustworthiness in the eyes of supportive students. To complicate matters further, it's unlikely that a single challenge will change the minds of those students who are farthest from you on the spectrum of credibility perception.

So, you need to adopt a scout mindset well in advance of this situation that you cannot win. What is a scout mindset, and how does it allow you to be kind to those who undermine you and hurt other students? How is it associated with the codebook? In his essay, James Clear's discusses Julia Galef's concept of the "soldier" and "scout" mindsets. Galef explains that a "soldier" mindset focuses on attacking and defeating opposing views, but a "scout" mindset seeks to uncover the truth and to understand reality as accurately as possible. As Galef explains in her TED Talk, the scout's job is not to attack or defend but to understand. The scout goes out to identify potential obstacles. The scout may learn that there's a bridge, but really, they want to learn what is really there, as accurately as possible. Making good judgements, accurate predictions, and good decisions. Importantly, these mindsets are emotionally rooted: your feelings determine whether you react defensively or seek understanding.

By exposing students to codes in a safe environment in advance, based on your scout mindset that goes out to find bridges and identify obstacles, you can prevent bad outcomes and mitigate risks before the soldier is needed. It allows the soldier to win battles without all the unnecessary casualties because students have the tools to perceive the challenging of false beliefs more rationally. So, when dealing with students who spread false beliefs, possibly through deception or antisocial behaviour, the scout mindset not only aids in uncovering truth but also helps regulate your emotions and those of your students. This way, you have the necessary tools to be perceived as kind and caring as you fight and win the battle against those beliefs and behaviours that diminish and undermine your credibility as you move students toward you on the spectrum.

The Paradox of Kindness and Authority in Teacher Credibility

There is a seemingly paradoxical relationship between the authoritative classroom management necessary to uphold teacher credibility (as supported by research on compulsive communicators and perceptions of classroom justice, e.g., McPherson & Liang, 2007; Chory, 2007) and the essential demonstration of kindness towards students who may challenge this authority. In both the application of justice and in dealing with uncooperative students, the research is clear: students need to feel that they have been listened to and understood. Research on prosocial communication behaviours further supports this view, showing that teachers who consistently use confirming messages, clarity, and nonverbal immediacy significantly enhance students' perceptions of their credibility (Schrodt et al., 2009). Research on classroom justice (Chory, 2007) and the management of compulsive communicators (McPherson & Liang, 2007) shows that failing to respond fairly and consistently to disruptive behaviour—errors of omission—undermines teacher credibility more seriously than the discomfort caused by addressing the issue. In this sense, omission—not confrontation—is the greater threat to maintaining credibility.

As referenced in James Clear's essay, the writer Haruki Murakami aptly reminds us, "Always remember that to argue, and win, is to break down the reality of the person you are arguing against. It is painful to lose your reality, so be kind, even if you are right." Using codes, as you will see in Part 3, allows teachers to maintain effective authority and classroom management while also demonstrating kindness and care to even their most ardent critics—elements vital to establishing and sustaining teacher credibility.

Chapter Review

- ★ Credibility breaks down over time—not because of one mistake, but through a mix of student misbehaviour, unmet expectations, and classroom disconnect. Rebuilding it takes more than management strategies. It requires consistent behaviour that students interpret as **competent, caring, and trustworthy**.
- ★ But perception alone isn't enough. As James Clear notes, reshaping beliefs requires **kindness**, not just logic. Kindness is not weakness—it's a critical part of credibility. When paired with **competence**, kindness protects vulnerable students and strengthens your authority.
- ★ Students don't always change their minds through facts. Beliefs shift gradually, across a **spectrum of perception**—influenced by how they feel they're treated. That's why the **scout mindset**, as described by Julia Galef, is so valuable: it helps teachers stay calm, seek understanding, and prepare students to interpret challenging situations with clarity, not defensiveness.
- ★ Proactively teaching students how to interpret your behaviour—through clear, prosocial codes—reduces the spread of false beliefs and softens future conflicts. And research is clear: students are more likely to trust teachers who are **consistent, fair, and emotionally available**. Ignoring harmful behaviour to avoid discomfort does more damage than addressing it with empathy and authority.
- ★ Ultimately, credibility is preserved not just through what you do, but **how you help students interpret what you do**—and how you respond when that interpretation is distorted.

Key Takeaway:

Teacher credibility is sustained not just by what you do, but by how students interpret your actions—and how you respond when those interpretations go wrong. Balancing competence (protecting vulnerable students, discipline) with kindness, protects your credibility in even the most challenging moments.

References

Aldrup, K., Klusmann, U., Lüdtke, O., Göllner, R., & Trautwein, U. (2018). Student misbehavior and teacher well-being: Testing the mediating role of the teacher-student relationship. *Learning and Instruction, 58*, 126–136. https://doi.org/10.1016/j.learninstruc.2018.05.006

Aloe, A. M., Shisler, S. M., Norris, B. D., Nickerson, A. B., & Rinker, T. W. (2014). A multivariate meta-analysis of student misbehavior and teacher burnout. *Educational Research Review, 12*, 30–44. https://doi.org/10.1016/j.edurev.2014.05.003

Bermejo, L., & Prieto-Ursúa, M. (2006). Teachers' irrational beliefs and their relationship to distress in the profession. *Psychology in Spain, 10*, 88–96.

Chory, R. M. (2007). Enhancing student perceptions of fairness: The relationship between instructor credibility and classroom justice. *Communication Education, 56*(1), 89–105. https://doi.org/10.1080/03634520600994300

Finn, A. N., Schrodt, P., Witt, P. L., Elledge, N., Jernberg, K. A., & Larson, L. M. (2009). A meta-analytical review of teacher credibility and its associations with teacher behaviors and student outcomes. *Communication Education, 58*(4), 516–537. https://doi.org/10.1080/03634520903131154.

Galef, J. (2016, February). *Why you think you're right — even if you're wrong* [Video]. TED Conferences. https://www.ted.com/talks/julia_galef_why_you_think_you_re_right_even_if_you_re_wrong

Gerving, A. M. (2007). Identifying the types of student and teacher behaviors associated with teacher stress. *Teaching and Teacher Education: An International Journal of Research and Studies, 23*(5), 624–640.

Hanson, T. L., & Teven, J. J. (2004). The impact of teacher immediacy and perceived caring on teacher competence and trustworthiness. *Communication Quarterly, 52*(1), 39–53. https://doi.org/10.1080/01463370409370177

Hattie, J. (2024). *Visible Learning MetaX* (Version 1.3). Retrieved from https://www.visiblelearningmetax.com/

Homeo, R. C. (2023). Effects of teacher burnout on their credibility. *International Journal of Research Publication and Reviews, 4*(3), 709–719. https://doi.org/10.55248/gengpi.2023.32015

Lewis, R., & Riley, P. (2009). Teacher misbehaviour. In L. J. Saha & A. G. Dworkin (Eds.), *International handbook of research on teachers and teaching* (pp. 401–412). Springer. https://doi.org/10.1007/978-0-387-73317-3_27

McCroskey, J. C., & Teven, J. J. (1999). Goodwill: A reexamination of the construct and its measurement. *Communication Monographs, 66*(1), 90–103. https://doi.org/10.1080/03637759909376464

McPherson, M. B., & Liang, Y. (2007). Students' reactions to teachers' management of compulsive communicators. *Communication Education, 56*(1), 18–33. https://doi.org/10.1080/03634520601016178

Myers, S. A. (2001). Perceived instructor credibility and verbal aggressiveness in the college classroom. *Communication Research Reports, 18*, 354364.

Myers, S. A., & Martin, M. M. (2006). Understanding the source: Teacher credibility and aggressive communication traits. In T. P. Mottet, V. P. Richmond, & J. C. McCroskey (Eds.), *Handbook of instructional communication: Rhetorical and relational perspectives* (p. 67–88). Pearson.

Savas, A. C., Bozgeyik, Y., & Eser, i. (2014). A study on the relationship between teacher self-efficacy and burnout. *European Journal of Educational Research, 3*(4), 159–166. https://doi.org/10.12973/eu-jer.3.4.159

Schrodt, P., Witt, P. L., & Turman, P. D. (2007). Instructor credibility as a mediator of instructors' prosocial communication behaviors and students' learning outcomes. *Communication Education, 56*(1), 1–17. https://doi.org/10.1080/03634520601080332

The Graide Network. (2022). *The epidemic of teacher stress*. https://www.thegraidenetwork.com

Zhang, Q., & Sapp, D. A. (2009). The effect of perceived teacher burnout on credibility. *Communication Research Reports, 26*(1), 87–90. https://doi.org/10.1080/08824090802637122

Part 2

Beyond Contagion
Making Sense of Group Perceptions in Your Classroom

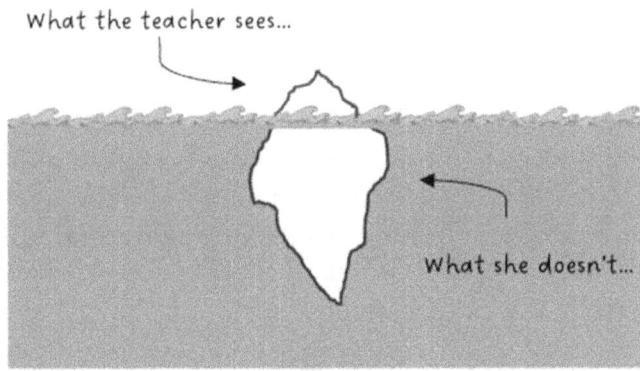

Figure P.2 Illustration of hidden motivations that can hurt your credibility.

Overview

So far, we've looked at how your students form perceptions of your credibility—sometimes accurately, sometimes not. These perceptions are shaped by the inferences they make about your intentions, and whether they choose to communicate those inferences honestly (informative cooperation) or deceptively. We've also considered how students' behaviour, whether prosocial or antisocial, reflects material cooperation. Up to this point, our focus has been on how peer influence and social contagion shape these classroom dynamics.

DOI: 10.4324/9781003644088-9

In Part 2, we'll go deeper. You'll see how distorted perceptions of your credibility aren't always the result of peer dynamics. Sometimes, they come from your students' internal motivations and histories—past negative experiences, underlying psychological influences, or difficulty with self-regulation. These "hidden attributes" can shape how your class collectively interprets your behaviour, forming classroom profiles that may differ greatly from how you or an outside observer would understand the same actions.

These classroom profiles can be aligned or divergent, depending on how your students' internal filters guide their interpretations of you.

Chapter 7: What Most of Your Students Have in Common
Classrooms are socially complex, with students responding to your behaviour in different, and sometimes unpredictable, ways. But you can reduce this complexity by identifying one common characteristic shared by the majority of your students.

Chapter 8: When Your Class Doesn't See You the Same Way
This chapter explores why students in the same classroom can interpret the exact same teacher behaviour in completely different ways. Drawing on Schenke's et al. (2018) research, we examine how prior experiences, personal traits, and perception shape student beliefs, often more than the teacher's actual behaviour itself.

Chapter 9: The Two Classroom Profiles and What They Mean for You
This chapter introduces two classroom profiles—Aligned and Divergent—based on shared student characteristics that influence how your behaviour is perceived. Using a real example of two classes taught identically, we explore how hidden motivations shape student beliefs and explain why credibility can break down in one group but not the other.

Chapter 10: What You Can't See Can Still Hurt You
This chapter explores how students in divergent versus aligned classrooms interpret the same teacher behaviour in very different ways, shaped by the positive or negative form of a hidden attribute. You'll use simulated student narratives to practice identifying internal motivations and distorted beliefs, helping you build insight, empathy, and credibility through reflective teaching.

Reference

Schenke, K., Ruzek, E., Lam, A. C., Karabenick, S., & Eccles, J. S. (2018). To the means and beyond: Understanding variation in students' perceptions of teacher emotional support. *Learning and Individual Differences*, *67*, 87–99. https://doi.org/10.1016/j.lindif.2018.06.004.

7

What Most of Your Students Have in Common

Overview

Classrooms can be very complicated and complex social environments. In this chapter, we'll take a quick look at how you can reduce that complexity by identifying common characteristics shared by your students. Specifically, we'll explore how to identify a **common attribute**, a variable or trait shared by the majority of students in your class, that can be used to define the **profile** of a group of students, known as a *classroom profile*.

Recognizing a common attribute helps set the stage for understanding broader patterns in student behaviour and perception, especially when divergence and variance arise from sources beyond social contagion.

Common Attribute: A variable or characteristic that is shared by the majority of students in your class.

Figure 7.1 Illustration of the balance between positive and negative perceptions of teacher credibility.

DOI: 10.4324/9781003644088-10

Common Attribute

Classroom A

Do you see the black desks? They represent students who share a common attribute. All the "black desk" students take the bus to school.

Do you see the white desks? They represent students who also share a common attribute, but they're different. They walk to school.

So, one way of looking at classrooms is based on student composition. Here, we have a class where the majority of students take the bus. You could call Classroom A the "bus class" for example.

Classroom B

In Classroom B, you'll notice that the proportion of students who take the bus is significantly smaller compared to Classroom A. You could call Classroom B the "walking class".

Consider that both classes are:

1. Taught by the same teacher.
2. At the same grade level and subject.

 Take the bus    Walk to school

Figure 7.2 Illustration of a common attribute in your classroom: taking the bus.

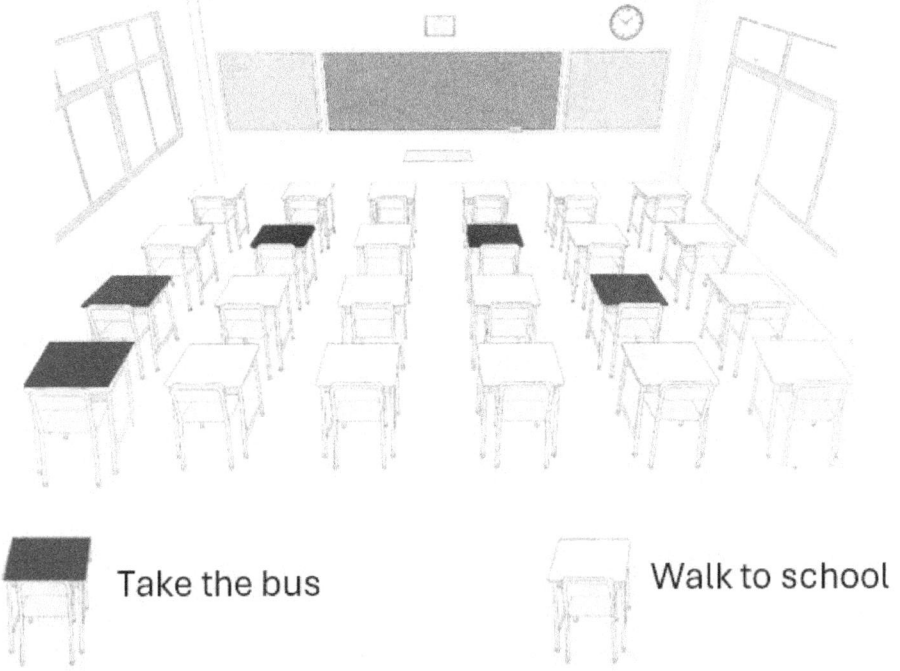

Figure 7.3 Illustration of a common attribute in your classroom: walk to school.

This example illustrates the simplification of a complex system filled with interacting variables. By isolating and focusing on a single variable at a time, such as a common attribute, we facilitate a direct comparison between how two distinct student groups interpret their teacher's behaviour.

Simplifying a Complex System

Moving forward, each classroom's unique identity will be defined by a dominant student attribute. This approach involves categorizing classrooms based on a key characteristic shared by the majority of its students.

In this comparative analysis, Classroom A is characterized by having a predominant number of students with one specific attribute (ex. bus), while Classroom B is distinguished by a significant majority of students who possess a different attribute (ex. walkers).

Algebra 1 vs Remedial Math*

As we take a closer look at Classrooms A and B, it's essential to consider that both are taught history 201 by the same teacher. However, there's a distinct difference in their academic compositions: Classroom A consists of grade 10 students who are in remedial math, whereas Classroom B is composed of grade 10 students in algebra 1.

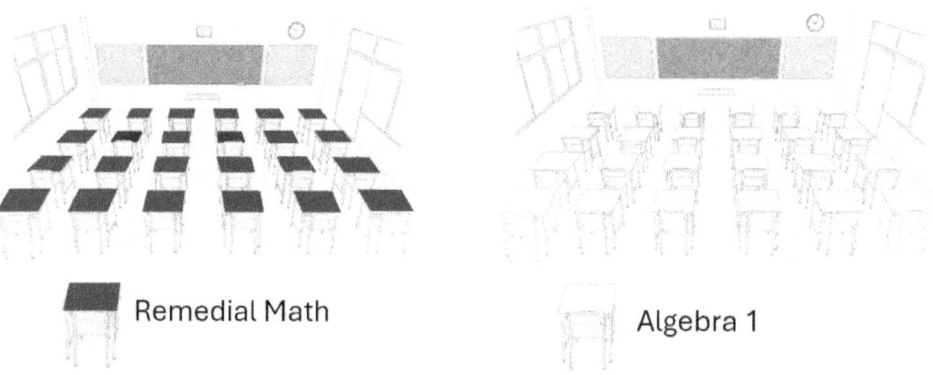

Figure 7.4 Illustration comparing common attributes in two history classrooms.

We will therefore focus on defining the dominant student attribute in Classroom A as remedial math and that of Classroom B as algebra 1. This distinction moves us beyond superficial differences, such as transportation to school.

It's important to emphasize that these distinctions in classroom attributes—remedial math vs. algebra 1—represent just a few of the many attributes that can be applied for comparative analysis.

Teacher Behaviour

To keep things simple as we explore classroom dynamics, let's control for the variable of teacher behaviour. Imagine you're teaching the same history 201 lesson in both Class A and Class B. A trained observer or instructional coach has confirmed that in both cases, your teaching reflects positive teacher credibility—you're consistent, clear, caring, and competent in both settings.

In other words, just like we outlined in Part 1, your behaviour is not the variable that's changing—**the difference lies in how your students are perceiving you.**

Chapter Summary

★ Classrooms can feel complex and unpredictable—but some of that complexity can be reduced by identifying a common attribute shared by most students. This might be a trait, orientation, or past experience that shapes how they perceive your behaviour.

- ★ By defining a classroom profile based on this shared attribute, you can better understand patterns in student behaviour and perception—especially when divergence isn't just caused by peer influence or social contagion.
- ★ The key idea: you're staying consistent in your teaching. What's changing is how your students are interpreting you.

 Key Takeaway:

To understand classroom dynamics, don't just focus on your actions—look at what most students in the room bring with them. Their shared traits shape how they see you.

Note

* *"Remedial Math" can be replaced with "Foundational Math" or "Standard Math," etc. The primary characteristic of students in this class is that they did not qualify for Algebra 1.*

8

When Your Class Doesn't See You the Same Way

Figure 8.1 Illustration representing students' divergence in perception from trained observers, as a result of motivations such as past classroom experiences.

Overview

In the next few chapters, we'll draw heavily from Katerina Schenke's (2018) work *To the Means and Beyond: Understanding Variation in Students' Perceptions of Teacher Emotional Support*. Her research sheds light on how and why students within the same classroom can hold very different views of the exact same teacher behaviour.

Schenke's synthesis of multiple studies offers a powerful lens to help us better understand this variation in perception. We'll explore key ideas such as alpha and beta press—two different ways students evaluate teacher behaviour—and what happens when student perceptions align with or diverge from observed reality.

Even in a single class, your students may interpret praise, feedback, or goal-setting messages in completely different ways. Often, that's because they bring different classroom histories and expectations with them. As researchers like Ames and Brophy have shown, these prior experiences can strongly influence how students make sense of your behaviour (Ames, 1992; Brophy, 1981).

And sometimes, what matters most isn't what's actually happening—but how your students interpret it. The meaning they assign to your actions can carry more weight than even the evaluations of trained observers—what Ryan and Grolnick (1986, as cited in Schenke, 2018) referred to as the *functional significance* of the environment. Schenke captures this clearly:

"Student perceptions of teacher quality may be more indicative of student-level factors than their experiences with that teacher" (Schenke, 2018).

In short, how your students *perceive* you may say more about **them** than it does about **you**.

Evaluating Teacher Behaviour: Two Lenses

As you begin to examine Classroom A (remedial math) and Classroom B (algebra) for variance (differences) in student perception, it helps to consider

Alpha Press : This lens involves evaluating the objective, measurable characteristics of your teaching—what a trained observer or instructional coach might see.

Beta Press : This lens shifts the focus from what you're doing to how your students interpret it. It captures their subjective perceptions of your behavior—how they personally experience your tone, support, or feedback. This includes both the individual perspective (*private press*) and the shared group perspective (*consensual press*) held by most students in the same classroom.

Figure 8.2 Illustration of two lenses of assessing teacher behaviour: alpha and beta press.

your own behaviour through two distinct lenses or frameworks. These perspectives can offer insight into why students may interpret the same teacher actions in very different ways—even when you're teaching consistently across both groups.

When Everyone Sees It the Same Way: Alignment in the Algebra Group

In Classroom B—algebra—you, your students, and a trained observer all see your teaching the same way. Both the Alpha Press (objective evaluations by you and the coach) and Beta Press (student perceptions) are in alignment. Everyone shares a common understanding of your behaviour—your intentions are being received as you meant them, and the classroom climate reflects that mutual understanding:

In Katerina Schenke's study, students' perceptions of a teacher's emotional support are measured using three key indicators: care, friendliness, and fairness. When we apply these criteria to students in Classroom B, we find strong agreement between their perceptions and the assessment of a

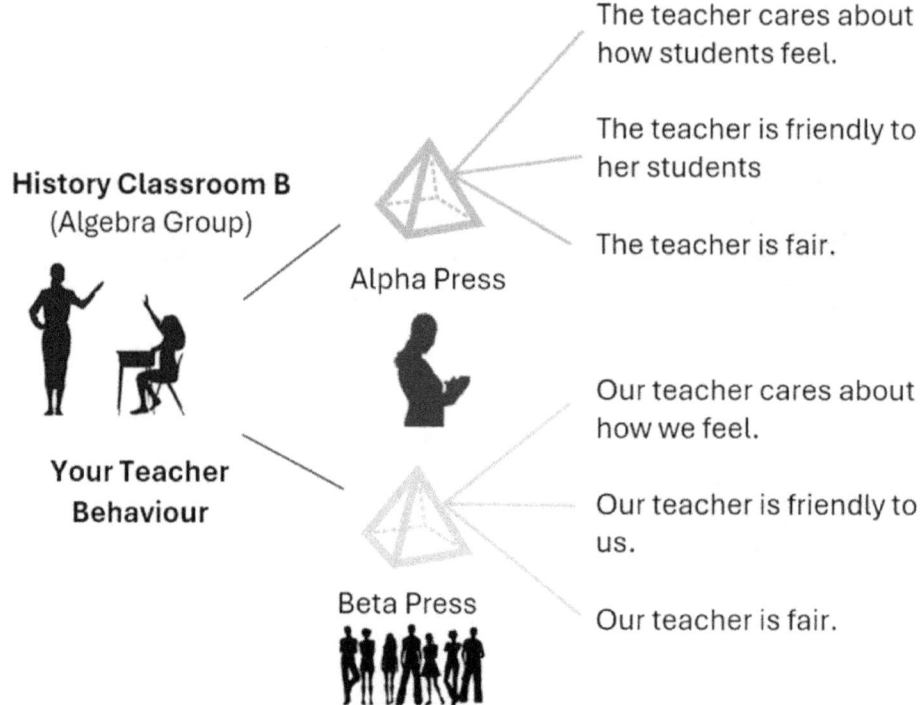

Figure 8.3 Illustration showing alignment in perception between alpha press (trained observer) and beta press (student perception).

trained observer. This suggests that your behaviour is being interpreted as intended, a sign that your credibility and emotional support are landing with your students the way you mean them to.

When Students See It Differently: Divergence in the Remedial Math Group

Perception variability shows that it's not unusual for students in the same classroom to hold very different interpretations of their teacher's behaviour, even when a trained observer (Alpha Press) rates that behaviour as clear, supportive, and effective.

In fact, student perception divergence isn't the exception, it's the norm. Research shows that students often interpret the same teaching in different ways, shaped more by their own histories, beliefs, and values than by the teacher's actual behaviour (Ames, 1992; Gencoglu et al., 2021).

Studies also reveal that teachers and students frequently disagree about what's happening in the classroom—teachers may believe they're being clear or caring, while students perceive confusion or distance (den Brok et al., 2006; Karamane et al., 2023).

So, even in a history class like your remedial math group Class A, where a trained observer rates your instruction and emotional support as high-quality, that doesn't guarantee your students will perceive it the same way. This is where divergence comes in: students' perceptions (Beta Press) may significantly differ from the observable reality.

And it's not just individual. When students share similar past experiences or talk among themselves, their interpretations can begin to align, not with you, but with each other. That's how a collective perception forms: a shared classroom narrative that may depart dramatically from your intent or from what an observer would report.

This is known as **consensual divergence**—when students arrive at a common, yet inaccurate, interpretation of your behaviour:

Students Seeing You Differently

Consensual divergence illustrates how students' personal experiences and inner psychological environments can lead to shared misinterpretations of teacher behaviour. When these individual perceptions align socially, they form a collective viewpoint that may not only differ from, but even challenge, the evaluations made by trained observers—despite consistent, high-quality teaching.

98 ◆ The Teacher Credibility Codebook

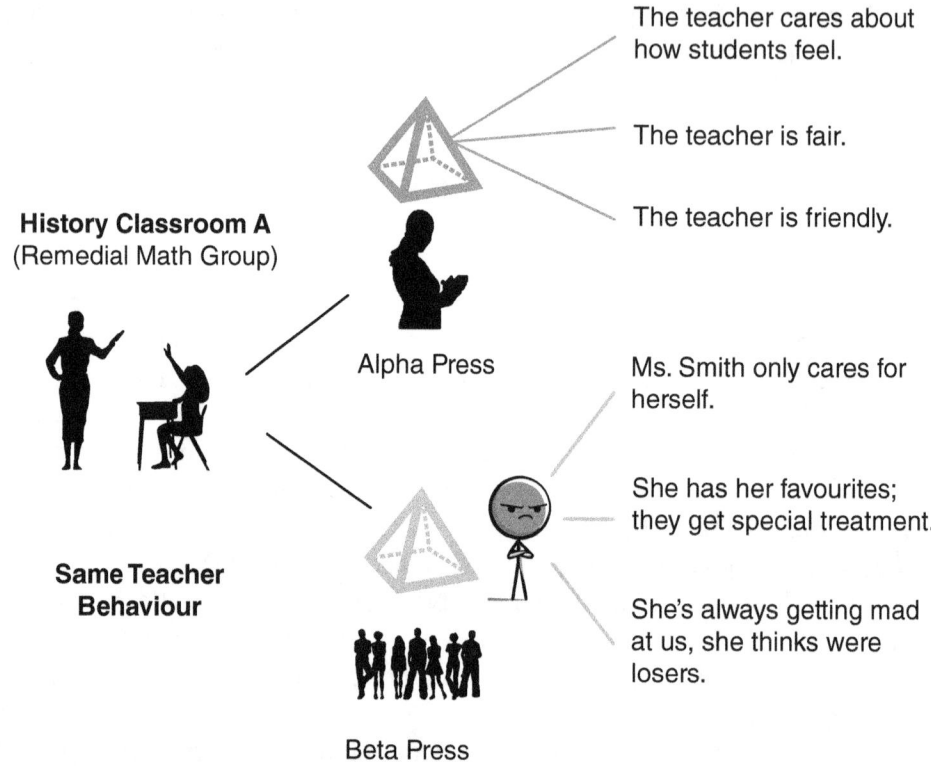

Figure 8.4 Illustration of divergence in perception: alpha vs. beta press.

> **Chapter Summary**
> ★ Even when your teaching is consistent, students may interpret it in very different ways. That's because they bring unique past experiences and expectations into the classroom, which shape how they understand your feedback, tone, and support.
> ★ Schenke's research introduces two helpful lenses: Alpha Press: What an outside observer sees—objective teaching behaviours. Beta Press: What students experience—their personal or group interpretation of your behaviour.
> ★ Research shows that perception variability is normal. Students often disagree not only with each other, but also with their teacher. What matters most isn't always what you're doing—it's what students believe you're doing.

Key Takeaway:

Your credibility isn't determined by what you do alone—it's shaped by how students *interpret* what you do. That interpretation is influenced more by their past than your present.

References

Ames, C. (1992). Classrooms: Goals, structures, and student motivation. *Journal of Educational Psychology, 84*(3), 261–271. https://doi.org/10.1037/0022-0663.84.3.261

Brophy, J. (1981). Teacher praise: A functional analysis. *Review of Educational Research, 51*(1), 5–32. https://doi.org/10.3102/00346543051001005

den Brok, P., Bergen, T., & Brekelmans, M. (2006). Convergence and divergence between students' and teachers' perceptions of instructional behaviour in Dutch secondary education. *Educational Research and Evaluation, 12*(1), 3–25. https://doi.org/10.1080/13803610500392193

Gencoglu, B., Helms-Lorenz, M., Maulana, R., & Jansen, E. P. W. A. (2021). A conceptual framework for understanding variability in student perceptions. *Frontiers in Psychology, 12*, 725407. https://doi.org/10.3389/fpsyg.2021.725407

Karamane, A., Zaragas, H., & Kounenou, K. (2023). Divergence between teachers' self-perceptions and students' perceptions of interpersonal teacher behaviour in Greek secondary education. *European Journal of Psychology and Educational Research, 6*(1), 1–10. https://doi.org/10.12973/ejper.6.1.1

Schenke, K., Ruzek, E., Lam, A. C., Karabenick, S., & Eccles, J. S. (2018). To the means and beyond: Understanding variation in students' perceptions of teacher emotional support. *Learning and Individual Differences, 67*, 87–99. https://doi.org/10.1016/j.lindif.2018.06.004

9

The Two Classroom Profiles and What They Mean for You

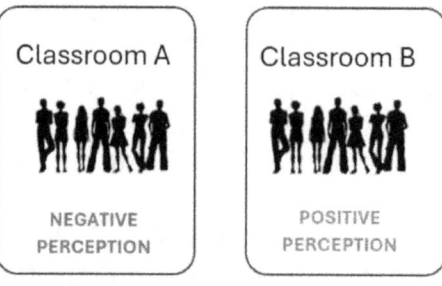

Figure 9.1 Illustration of Classroom A (negative perception) and Classroom B (positive perception), showing divergent and aligned profiles.

Overview

In this chapter, we create classroom profiles based on shared student characteristics, what we call common attributes. Both Classrooms A and B are history classes taught by the same teacher, using consistent, high-credibility teaching behaviours. The key difference lies in the students themselves:

- ♦ Classroom A is made up of students in remedial math. These students share a common tendency towards perceptual divergence, forming what we'll call the Divergent Profile.
- ♦ Classroom B includes students enrolled in algebra, whose perceptions of the teacher closely align with those of a trained observer. This becomes the Aligned Profile.

DOI: 10.4324/9781003644088-12

To explain the divergence seen in Classroom A, we apply the Motivation Influences Perception Model. In this case, students' hidden motivations—**beyond math level**—act as perceptual filters, shaping how they interpret the teacher's intentions and behaviour.

The hidden attribute, often unknown to the teacher, becomes the focus of the analysis that follows. Within the Divergent Profile, this attribute drives students' inference-making (beliefs) about teacher behaviour (activating event), often leading to significant negative impacts on teacher credibility (consequence).

This chapter explores how divergence can emerge even in classrooms with high-credibility instruction, and why understanding perception variability is essential for recognizing and responding to hidden dynamics that influence learning.

Quick Review: How Do Students Form Perceptions of Their Teacher?

1. Student Perception Influences Motivation

In this model, students form judgements about their teacher's effectiveness based on *their* classroom interactions and experiences.

- ★ When those interactions are viewed positively, students are more likely to feel motivated, ask questions, take academic risks, and engage.
- ★ When interactions are perceived negatively, motivation tends to drop.

This model highlights the crucial role of students' perception of their interactions with the teacher in shaping motivation in the classroom, including how willing they are to participate, take risks, and persist with learning.

2. Student Motivation Influences Perception

This model flips the lens. It suggests that students enter the classroom with pre-existing motivations, shaped by past experiences, beliefs, and individual differences.

- ★ A student who is already motivated may see a tough task as a challenge.
- ★ Another student, less motivated, might see the same task as unfair or discouraging.

In this view, it's not the interaction that shapes perception, it's the student's internal motivation that colours how they interpret the classroom environment, especially the teacher's intentions and behaviour.

> **Quick Note**
> Both history 201 classes were taught with the same high-credibility teaching behaviours. The key difference? Classroom A, composed of students in remedial math, holds a predominantly negative perception of you. In contrast, Classroom B, made up of algebra students, perceives the same teaching more positively. One class's perception diverges from observable reality—while the other aligns. This contrast sets the stage for understanding how hidden attributes shape classroom narratives.

The Essential Question

Why do students in Classroom A perceive you so differently from how the trained observer does? And what actions can you take in response? To work towards an answer, we will apply our two models of student perception to Classroom A.

Classroom Profiles: Aligned and Divergent

To better understand what's driving the divergence in Classroom A, we'll create two classroom profiles using the lens of **Alpha and Beta Press**. This approach helps isolate the key attributes that shape student perception.

Classroom A, which includes students in remedial math and shows a clear divergence in perception, becomes the **Divergent Profile**.

Classroom B, where students' perceptions align with those of a trained observer, becomes the **Aligned Profile**.

By comparing these profiles, we can begin to identify the **hidden motivations** or **common attributes** that may be shaping the disconnect in Classroom A.

The alpha–beta dynamics of student perception are defined in the illustration as divergent and aligned profiles. These profiles categorize perceptions of quality teaching based on students' collective interpretation of teacher credibility characterized as either positive or negative. Teacher credibility is defined by students' attitudes towards their teacher, influenced by perceived caring, competence, and trustworthiness. As discussed in Part 1, credibility significantly influences student motivation, engagement, behaviour, and academic achievement, shaping students' overall learning experience and outcomes.

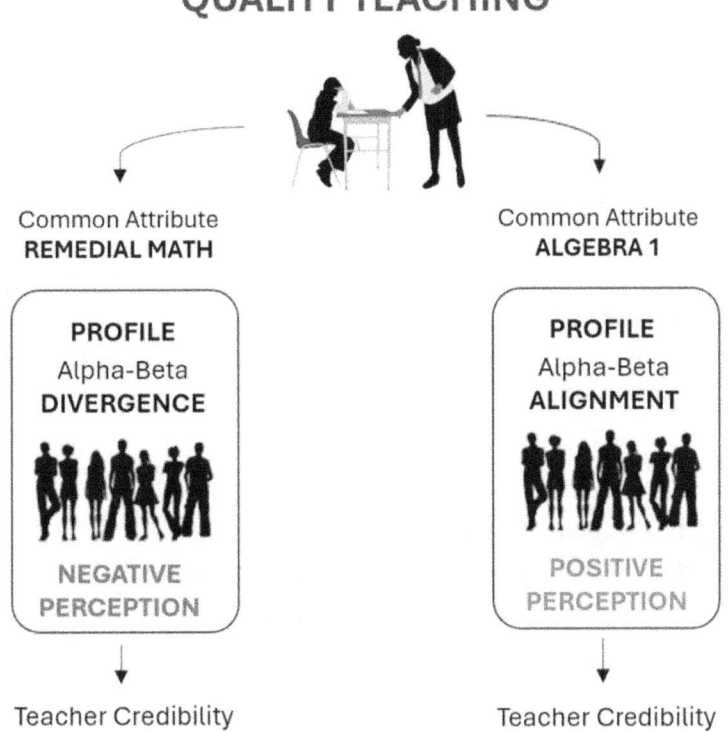

Figure 9.2 Illustration of profiles showing alpha–beta divergence in remedial math and alpha–beta alignment in algebra.

Apply Perception Influences Motivation Model

Using this model, we look at the obvious common attribute—remedial math—to answer the question:

Why do the students in Classroom A perceive your teaching behaviour so negatively? And what actions can you take in response?

Target the Common Attribute—Remedial Math

Recognizing that the collective perception of your behaviour significantly impacts the classroom's overall motivation and attitude, you might re-evaluate your instructional strategies, especially in light of the unique needs of your remedial math students enrolled in your history class. Negative perceptions of your behaviour and credibility can deeply affect students' motivation and engagement, making a targeted response not only helpful, but necessary.

Independently or with the support of an instructional coach, you could identify high-impact teaching strategies—often referred to as The Big Four:

- Content planning
- Formative assessment
- Instruction
- Community building (classroom management)

These strategies, drawn from Jim Knight's work on instructional coaching (*The Impact Cycle*, 2018), are designed to help you increase your effectiveness and credibility with students, and shift their perceptions towards a more engaged and motivated learning experience.

<u>OR</u>

Apply Perception Influences Motivation Model
Using this model, we focus on the hidden common attribute—Motivation—to answer the question: *Why do the students in Classroom A perceive your teaching behaviour so negatively? And what actions can you take in response?*

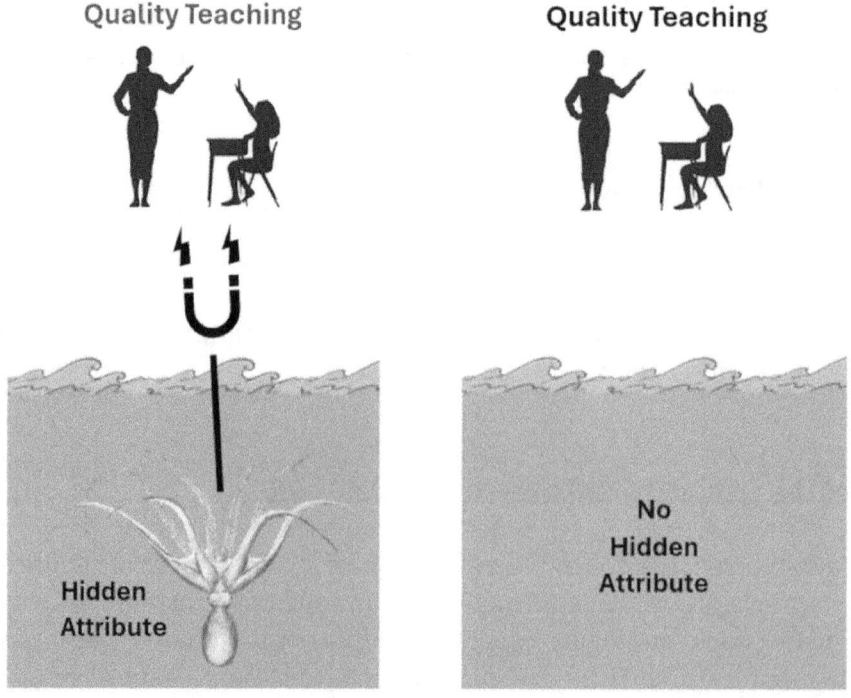

Figure 9.3 Illustration of the influence of hidden attributes on teacher credibility perception.

In the first model, students' judgements are based primarily on direct interactions. So, in response, you might adapt your instruction to better meet the needs of remedial math learners in your history class. However, this second model suggests that student perceptions are shaped by many other factors, beyond what happens in direct interactions with you.

Divergence in Classroom A can be better understood by examining **the meaning students assign** not only to your behaviour, but also to the classroom itself. This meaning, rooted in their psychological environment, may carry more weight than any observable measure of teaching, including your instructional strategies. In short, your practices alone may not fully explain the disconnect. The perception gap arises not just from what you do, but from how students interpret it—and what they believe their classroom represents: **The Hidden Attribute.**

Meet the Common Attribute: Motivation, Not Remedial Math

If the negative perceptions in Classroom A stem from internal student factors—such as orientation or past experience—you might consider strategies aimed at changing students' negative inferences about your behaviour. This could involve addressing social contagion, attributions, or helping students reinterpret your intentions more accurately. With or without the support of an instructional coach, you can begin to uncover the deeper "motivations" behind these perceptions—what we call **hidden attributes**. These often lie beneath the surface and can be masked by other classroom behaviours, making the classroom dynamic harder to interpret.

What You Can't See Might Be Driving Everything

Hidden attributes, like past experiences, orientation, or self-regulated learning, often lie beneath the surface, masked by student behaviour and misattributed by you.

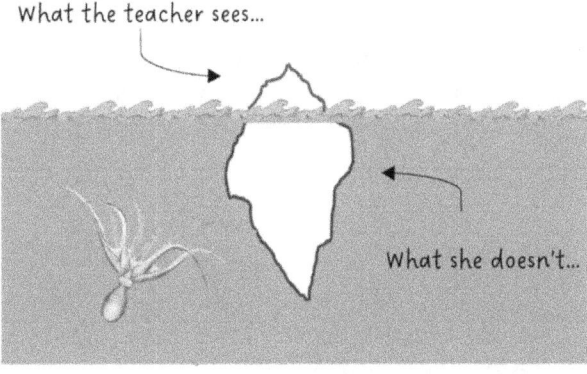

Figure 9.4 Illustration showing that hidden attributes, although unseen, can undermine teacher credibility.

These internal motivations may be the real reason students in Classroom A perceive your credibility differently, even when your teaching is strong and consistent.

> **Chapter Summary**
>
> ★ Classrooms A and B are both taught by the same teacher using consistent, high-credibility strategies. But the outcomes are very different, not because of what the teacher is doing, but because of who the students are.
>
> ★ In Classroom A (remedial math), students tend to interpret the teacher's actions more negatively. This group forms what we call the Divergent Profile, a classroom shaped by internal factors like past negative experiences or motivational traits that distort perception. In contrast, Classroom B (algebra) forms an Aligned Profile, where student perceptions closely match those of a trained observer.
>
> ★ This chapter explored how hidden student characteristics, called hidden attributes, can influence how your teaching is received. Using the Alpha and Beta Press framework, we looked at how students assign meaning not just to your actions, but to the classroom itself. These interpretations are often stronger than any objective measure of instructional quality.
>
> ★ Even strong teaching can fall short if students interpret it through a distorted lens. That's why understanding divergence is critical: it helps you uncover the real reasons for disconnect—and respond more effectively by addressing student perceptions, not just surface behaviours.

 Key Takeaway:

Great teaching doesn't guarantee credibility, what matters is how students interpret it. In divergent classrooms, hidden attributes like past experience and low motivation shape meaning more than your methods.

Reference

Knight, J. (2018). *The impact cycle: What instructional coaches should do to foster powerful improvements in teaching.* Corwin.

10

What You Can't See Can Still Hurt You

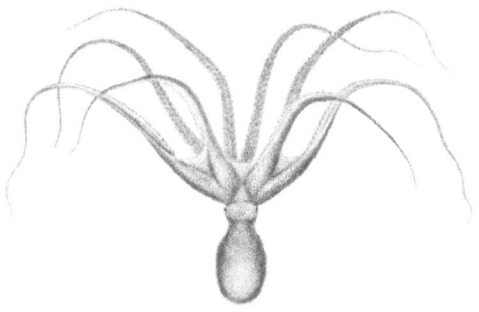

Hidden Attribute

Figure 10.1 Visual metaphor, an unseen attribute lurking beneath the surface of teacher awareness.

Overview

In this chapter, we explore key research findings on student motivations that shape how they perceive your credibility—including trait orientation, past classroom experiences, perceptions of teacher burnout, and self-regulated learning.

DOI: 10.4324/9781003644088-13

Classroom A vs. Classroom B

As we continue comparing our two history classes, you'll notice that Classroom A, marked by collective divergence, includes a majority of students influenced by the negative form of a hidden attribute. This often leads to inaccurate inferences about your behaviour (the activating event).

By contrast, Classroom B has an aligned profile, where most students are shaped by the positive form of the same attribute—resulting in higher perceptions of your credibility, even though your teaching remains consistent across both groups.

Simulating Student Narratives

To help you apply these insights, we'll simulate how students with different orientations interpret key classroom moments. This involves mapping how student beliefs (B) are triggered by activating events (A)—like a major assignment—and how their internal narratives drive behaviour.
Example:
An ambivalent student who believes "life starts after school" might interpret a term assignment as pointless. Their internal narrative might sound like:

- Why do I need to do this? It doesn't really matter in real life."
- "I'll do the bare minimum to get it over with, it's just a waste of time."

A Reflective Tool for Teacher Insight

This simulation exercise is designed to help you recognize and better understand student disengagement, resistance, or misinterpretation, especially when it's driven more by internal motivations than by your actual behaviour.

Why is this important? Because this is how you experience them in the classroom. These aren't abstract concepts. They're real, and they often hurt.

By generating and exploring these student narratives, you'll strengthen your scout mindset: the ability to recognize when students are interpreting your actions through a distorted lens.

This activity also supports recursive mind reading, the awareness that you and your students may be operating in divergent cognitive environments without even realizing it. If left unaddressed, this disconnect can slowly erode your credibility, with real consequences for learning.

Research Findings—Looking at Hidden Attributes

Exploring why students in Classroom A perceive high-credibility teaching negatively requires applying the Motivation Influences Perception model. This approach allows us to examine research findings that reveal how student orientations, past experiences, and other pre-existing factors shape perceptions of teacher credibility.

The following hidden attributes will be explored:

- **Trait Orientations**: Your students' pre-existing trait orientations significantly influence how they perceive your credibility.
- **Influence of Previous Perceptions**: Your students' past experiences with teachers create a perceptual lens that shapes how they interpret and respond to you today.
- **Perceptions of Teacher Burnout**: When students perceive you as burned out, they tend to see you as less credible—regardless of your actual teaching quality.
- **Self-Regulated Learning (SRL)**: Students' capacity to manage their own learning significantly impacts how credible they perceive you to be.

These research findings help explain why students with the same teacher can arrive at such different conclusions about their credibility. But to make sense of these patterns in your own classroom, we need to go one layer deeper, into the hidden attributes your students carry with them. These are the unseen filters that shape how your behaviour is interpreted, and they often determine whether your efforts are perceived as credible or dismissed altogether.

Hidden Attributes: How Students Misread Your Intentions

1. **Understanding Hidden Attributes:**
   Hidden attributes act as perceptual filters through which your students interpret classroom interactions (activating events), including your behaviour, instructional strategies, interactions among themselves, and the overall classroom climate.
2. **Impact on Classroom Narratives:**
   These inferences of intention can quickly become accepted classroom norms or false beliefs, creating a shared narrative that strongly shapes how your students collectively perceive your credibility (see Chapter 1).

3. **Challenges in Addressing Hidden Attributes:**
   Uncovering and addressing hidden attributes is challenging because they are deeply rooted in your students' internal motivations, individual differences, and past experiences—factors that may not be directly observable to you or even fully understood by the students themselves. These attributes can also be masked by other visible behaviours, leading you to make inaccurate assumptions. And often, these perceptions are influenced by elements entirely beyond your control.

Quick Recap: Power of the Collective Hidden Attribute

To understand hidden attributes, it's important to recognize that their power doesn't come from the factual accuracy of students' perceptions—it comes from their collective acceptance by the group (*see Chapter 1*). Even when these perceptions are inaccurate, they can become "factually false, socially true"—and what your students agree upon often matters more than what is objectively correct.

You may be entirely disconnected from the assumptions your students are making about you. Yet if those assumptions are shared and reinforced by the group, they gain validity—not because they are true, but because they are believed.

This creates a powerful collective narrative in Classroom A—one that's difficult for you to detect or challenge, especially when students' conclusions feel irrational or are formed without concrete evidence. Their inaccuracy and seemingly irrationality are often what allow them to go unrecognized or unchecked. You are operating in one cognitive environment; your students are sharing and reinforcing another.

As we look further into the research, it becomes clear that the decoding and interpretation of your everyday communication behaviours (activating events) in Classroom A can be deeply shaped by students' hidden motivations and the negative intentions they attribute to you.
Even routine statements like:

Distribution of Justice

★ "Let's address this fairly and hear both sides before making a decision."

Task Completion

★ "Complete your weekly lab assignment by tomorrow—late submissions won't be accepted."

…can be misread through the lens of a hidden attribute. What you intend as clarity, fairness, or structure may be interpreted as unfair, cold, or uncaring. Because of this, even small moments can dramatically affect how students perceive your caring, trustworthiness, and competence—and over time, these distorted inferences can seriously erode your teacher credibility.

Quick Note

Hidden attributes shape how students interpret even routine classroom interactions.

Perceptions don't need to be true to be powerful—they just need to be *shared* and *reinforced* by the group.

Teachers may be unaware of the gap between their intended meaning and students' interpreted meaning.

Everyday teacher behaviours can be misread when students operate from a different cognitive environment.

Over time, these distorted inferences can quietly undermine your credibility, even when your teaching is strong.

"You and your students may be seeing the same classroom events but processing them through entirely different cognitive environments. When beliefs become shared, they become powerful—whether they're true or not."

Figure 10.2 Illustration of the spectrum of teacher credibility scores, demonstrating how hidden attributes can tip perception in either direction.

Hidden Attribute: Trait Orientations

In his 2006 study, *Communication Organizational Orientations in an Instructional Setting*, David Tibbles explored how students' attitudes toward school shape how they see their teachers. He found that students fall into three types: Upward Mobile (driven and motivated), Indifferent (disengaged), and Ambivalent (critical and resistant). These underlying mindsets—what I refer to as *hidden attributes*—affect how students judge your credibility, care, and trustworthiness.

This means two students can see the exact same behaviour from you and interpret it in completely different ways. As Tibbles suggests, even when you're consistent, students' internal attitudes towards school, authority, and *you* will shape how they respond.

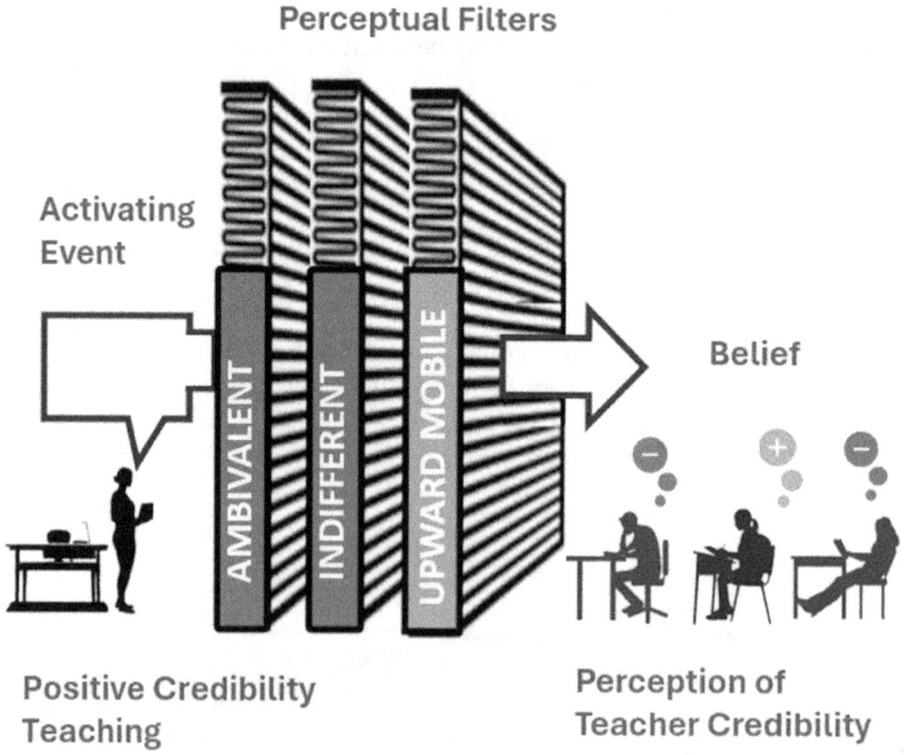

Figure 10.3 Illustration of perceptual filters for hidden attribute: trait orientations, during an activating event. How student orientations filter the same teaching behaviour into divergent perceptions of credibility.

According to Tibbles' study, the more strongly a student holds an ambivalent or indifferent orientation, the more likely they are to see their teacher as noncredible—even if the teacher is doing a good job. As these negative orientations increase, students are more likely to:

These students are often intelligent and capable, but their internal stance toward school and authority leads them to resist—even sabotage—classroom relationships.

The more upward mobile a student is, the more likely they are to see you as credible—competent, trustworthy, and caring. When students hold this positive orientation, they're more likely to:

Ambivalent

Watch you closely for anything that confirms their negative view of you.

Dislike being told what to do or how to think.

Believe you have ill will toward them.

Complain often or openly reject your authority in class.

Believe they're smarter or more capable than you.

Look for and assume the worst in your behavior.

Challenge your authority and initiate confrontations.

Dislike both your subject and your presence.

Put in the bare minimum effort and show little interest in learning.

See school—and your class in particular—as a waste of time.

Indifferent

See your class as something to get through—not something to care about.

Assume you're just doing your job, not personally invested in them or their success.

Dislike both the content and your teaching, but instead of pushing back, they quietly check out.

Show emotional detachment and apathy, making it clear they just don't care.

Avoid challenge, and when things get hard, disengage even more.

Put in the bare minimum, showing little effort or interest in learning.

Believe life "starts after school," making them more likely to skip, coast, or eventually drop out. Treat your class like a transaction, time and effort in exchange for grades.

Feel no connection to your goals, the subject, or the school's values—just going through the motions.

Figure 10.4 Table showing student tendencies based on Ambivalent and Indifferent orientations.

Upward Mobile

See you as smart, supportive, and invested in their success.

Work hard and stay driven, even when circumstances aren't ideal—they're resilient and goal-oriented.

Perceive you as warm and engaging, responding positively to your immediacy and presence.

View school as a meaningful challenge, something that prepares them for future goals.

Feel good about both the subject and your teaching, creating a strong foundation for engagement.

Believe they've learned all they could from your class, seeing it as a valuable experience.

Trust in their own ability to succeed, showing persistence and a willingness to take on challenges.

Gravitate toward peers with similar goals, forming a motivational peer group.

See challenges as chances to grow, not setbacks to avoid.

Figure 10.5 Table showing student tendencies based on upward-mobile orientation.

Simulating What Students Might Be Telling Themselves: How Motivation Shapes Inference

This simulation uses three trait orientations—Indifferent, Ambivalent, and Upward Mobile—to model how students might interpret classroom events. These narratives are emotionally charged, socially reinforced, and often inaccurate—but they form the beliefs that shape how your credibility is perceived. Many of these negative statements may sound familiar—and that's the point. They're not about you personally; they're about how perception works:

When your class is mostly composed of ambivalent students, even neutral or supportive actions can be misinterpreted. These students can share and reinforce false inferences—turning "what happened" into a collective narrative that questions your caring, competence, or trustworthiness. Over time,

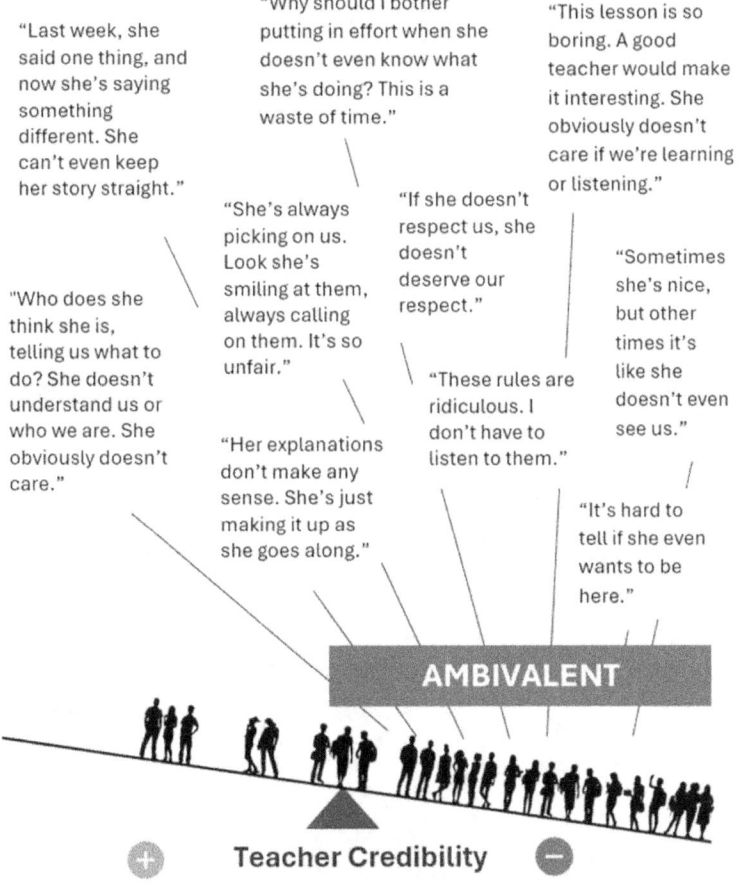

Figure 10.6 Illustration showing simulated student narratives for the Ambivalent orientation, demonstrating how this hidden attribute influences perceptions of teacher credibility.

this can quietly reduce engagement and motivation, not because you're doing something wrong, but because of how your behaviour is being decoded.

Indifferent

In a class dominated by indifferent orientations, you may encounter pervasive apathy. You may struggle to foster motivation or a sense of purpose, as indifferent students tend not to identify with the goals or values of the school. This orientation often manifests as minimal effort, poor engagement, and a view that life "begins after school," reinforcing a detachment from the class and the learning process. Consequently, your efforts to build credibility may be undermined, as indifferent students remain largely unmotivated, disconnected, and uninvested your class and in school.

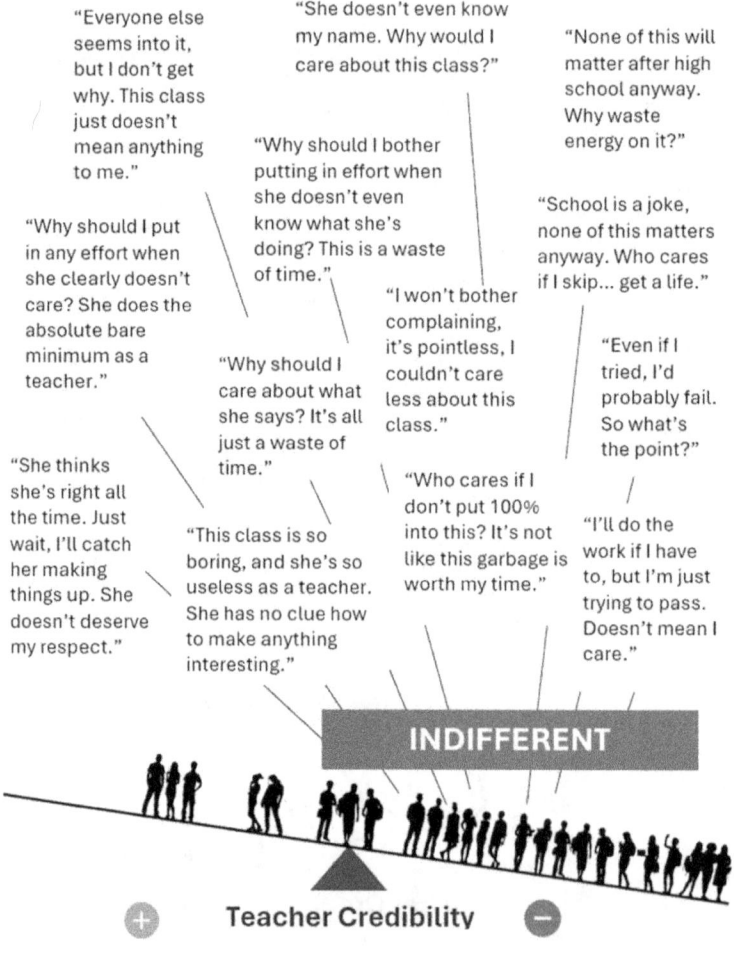

Figure 10.7 Illustration showing simulated student narratives for the Indifferent orientation, demonstrating how this hidden attribute influences perceptions of teacher credibility.

Upward Mobile

In a class dominated by upward-mobile students, you're likely to experience a motivated, growth-focused environment. These students see challenges as opportunities, view you as knowledgeable and supportive, and often surround themselves with peers who share similar goals. Your credibility—rooted in caring, competence, and fairness—is more likely to be recognized, respected, and reinforced.

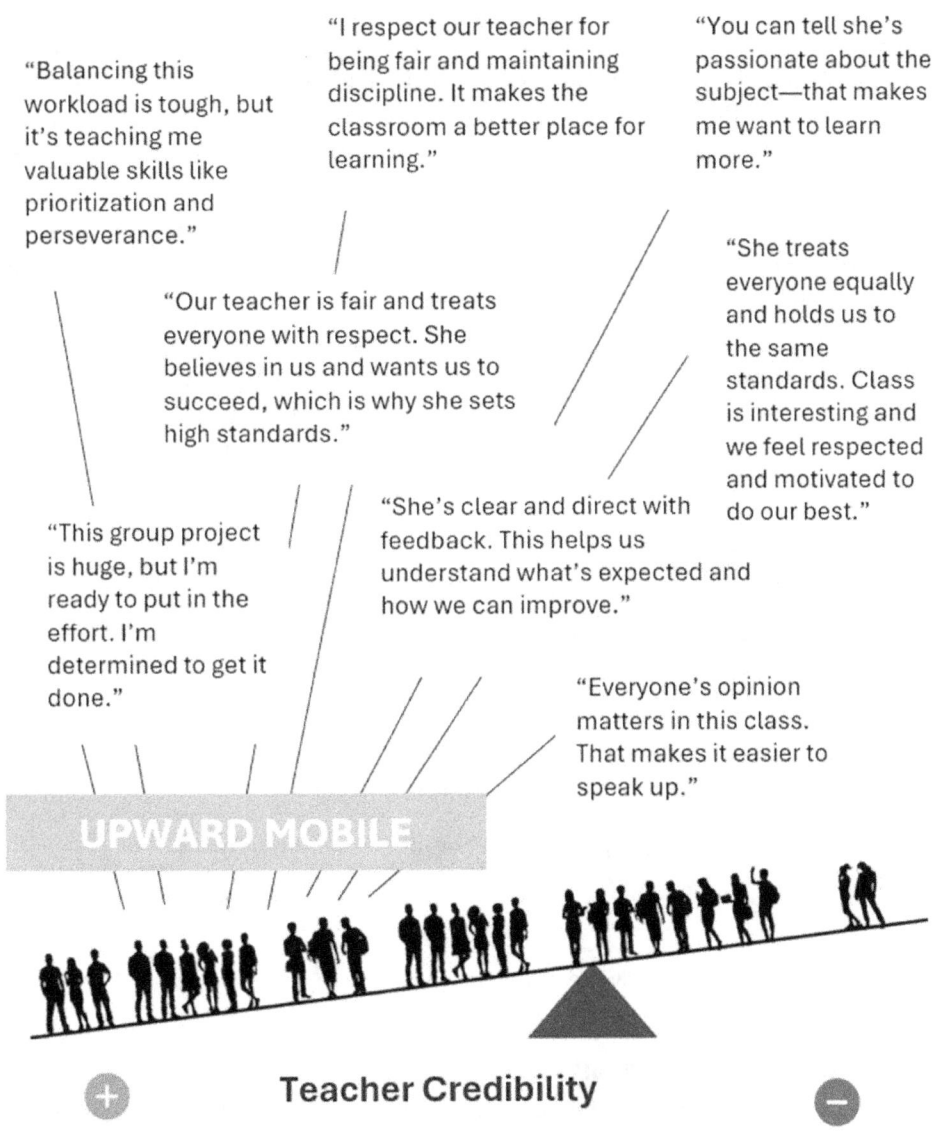

Figure 10.8 Illustration showing simulated student narratives for the upward-mobile orientation, demonstrating how this hidden attribute influences perceptions of teacher credibility.

Hidden Attributes—Ambivalent and Indifferent Orientations: What You Can't See Can Hurt You

In this scenario, Classroom A is dominated by hidden student attributes—ambivalent and indifferent orientations—that drive alpha–beta divergence. These students are more likely to interpret your actions negatively, skewing perceptions of your credibility. In contrast, Classroom B shows alignment, where upward-mobile students are more likely to see your behaviour in a positive light.

If you're unaware of the hidden dynamics in Class A, you risk misreading student intentions (recursive mindreading), leading to misunderstandings about how your behaviour is perceived. This can create a harmful cycle—your credibility erodes further as students continue to misinterpret your efforts.

Importantly, this isn't necessarily a reflection of your teaching ability—it's the result of how these hidden student orientations filter your behaviour through a lens of scepticism and/or disengagement.

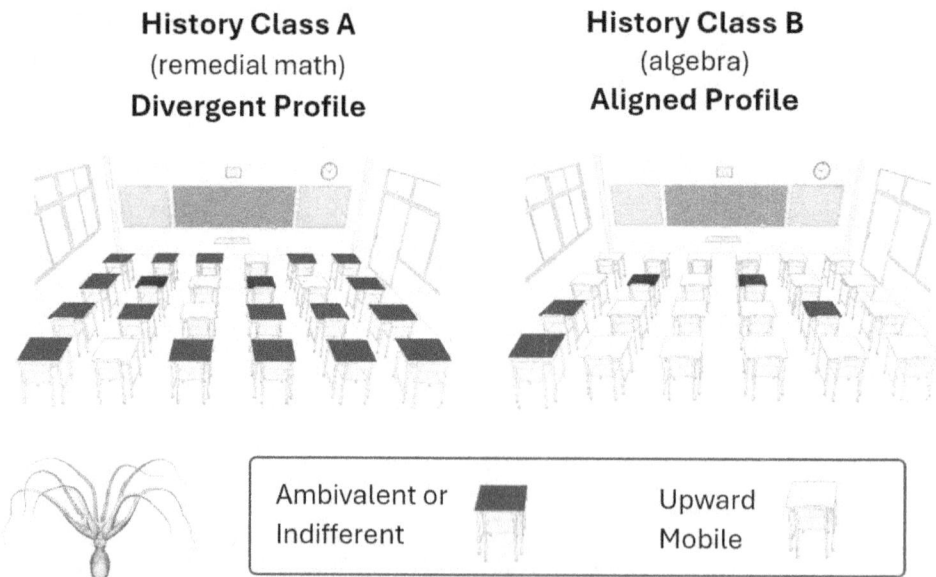

Figure 10.9 Illustration comparing divergent and aligned classroom profiles by trait orientations.

Hidden Attribute: Past Classroom Experience

In her study *To the Means and Beyond: Understanding Variation in Students' Perceptions of Teacher Emotional Support*, Katerina Schenke found that students' **past classroom experiences** significantly shape how they perceive their current teacher's emotional support. This "experiential baggage" means students often carry forward consistent perceptions—about caring, fairness, and friendliness—that influence how they interpret your behaviour now.

Importantly, Schenke's research suggests that these emotional support perceptions—and possibly perceptions of other classroom constructs such as classroom management, feedback, assessment, peer relationships, and academic expectations—tend to remain consistent within students over time.

While the study focused specifically on emotional support, its indicators closely align with the core dimensions of **teacher credibility**: care, trustworthiness, and fairness. In other words, students may not be reacting to you alone—they may be responding to the climate and teaching of their past classrooms:

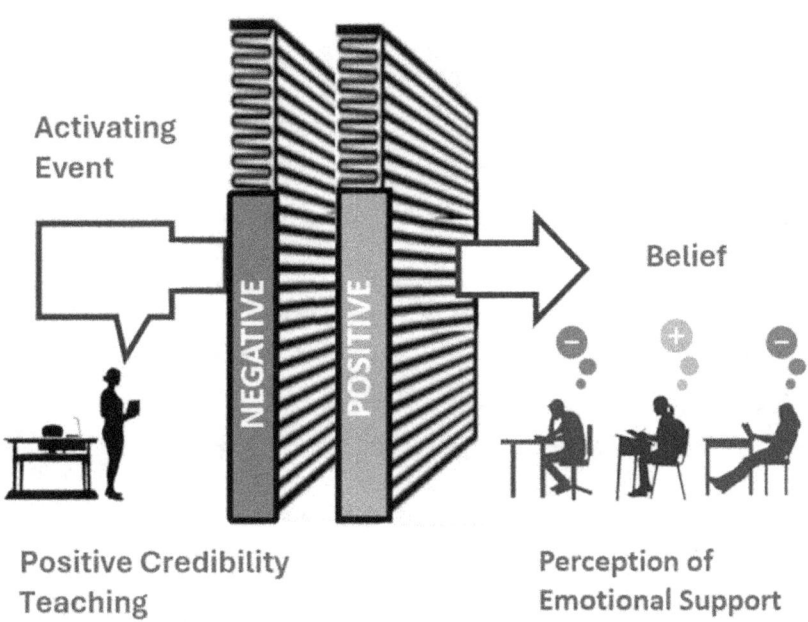

Figure 10.10 Illustration of perceptual filters for hidden attribute: past classroom experiencess, during an activating event.

In Katerina Schenke's study, students who previously viewed their teacher as uncaring, unfriendly, or unfair were significantly more likely to perceive their current classroom climate negatively. Given this tendency, students with such negative perceptions are likely to see you, their current teacher as:	Just as negative experiences tend to predict negative perceptions, positive ones often lead students to view their current teacher more favorably. Students who previously saw their teacher as caring, friendly, or fair are more likely to carry those expectations forward. As a result, they tend to see you, their current teacher as:

Past Negative Experience	Past Positive Experience
Unable to control the class or administer justice.	**Able to control** the class and ensure a safe, respectful environment.
Blaming them for things that aren't their fault.	**Fair** in enforcing rules and handling issues.
Enforcing rules that are unfair.	
Only pointing out what students do wrong.	**Appreciative** of their efforts and providing helpful feedback.
Giving unfair tests and assignments.	**Fair** in tests and assignments, rewarding hard work.
Never treating them fairly, showing biased grading.	**Creating a positive environment** for group work and encouraging cooperation.
Setting unrealistic expectations.	**Setting high** but achievable expectations, motivating students to try their best.
Misunderstanding them and not being supportive.	
Ignoring their individual needs and learning styles.	**Trustworthy**, understanding, and supportive, providing help and guidance.
Failing to foster a positive classroom community.	**Contributing** to a positive and supportive school environment, making students feel optimistic about their future
Believing that nothing will ever change in the school.	

Figure 10.11 Table showing student tendencies based on passed negative and positive past experiences.

Simulating What Students Might Be Telling Themselves: How Past Classroom Experience Shapes Inference

In Classroom A, many of your students bring negative past experiences with them. This means they're more likely to interpret your neutral or even supportive actions as controlling, unfair, or insincere. Before you've

Figure 10.12 Illustration showing simulated student narratives for past negative experiences, demonstrating how this hidden attribute influences perceptions of teacher credibility.

had a real chance to build trust, a negative narrative can take hold. As students reinforce each other's negative perceptions, a shared belief of your credibility may form—one that persists even when you're doing everything right.

In Classroom B, your students bring positive expectations shaped by past supportive experiences. They're more likely to see your behaviour as

Figure 10.13 Illustration showing simulated student narratives for positive past experiences, demonstrating how this hidden attribute influences perceptions of teacher credibility.

fair, caring, and competent—even during moments of stress or uncertainty. These students tend to give you the benefit of the doubt and reinforce each other's positive perceptions, building a shared narrative of trust and emotional safety. This positive outlook strengthens your perceived credibility and makes classroom cooperation easier to build and maintain.

Hidden Attributes—Past Classroom Experiences: What You Can't See Can Hurt You

In a classroom dominated by students with past negative experiences, the implications for teacher credibility are profound. These students are likely to begin the year with strong biases that lead them to assume the worst about their current teacher's intentions and actions. When students interpret your behaviour as a continuation of past grievances, it reinforces a collective belief that your teaching is uncaring or unfair, creating a "false truth" within the classroom that sustains a negative perception of teacher credibility.

Even genuine efforts by you to foster a positive environment may be misinterpreted or dismissed, as students view these actions with suspicion or perceive as attempts at control rather than support. Additionally, you may misinterpret student behaviour as defiance rather than as a reaction to past negative experiences, deepening misunderstandings. Over time, these entrenched negative perceptions can have a lasting impact on your teacher credibility.

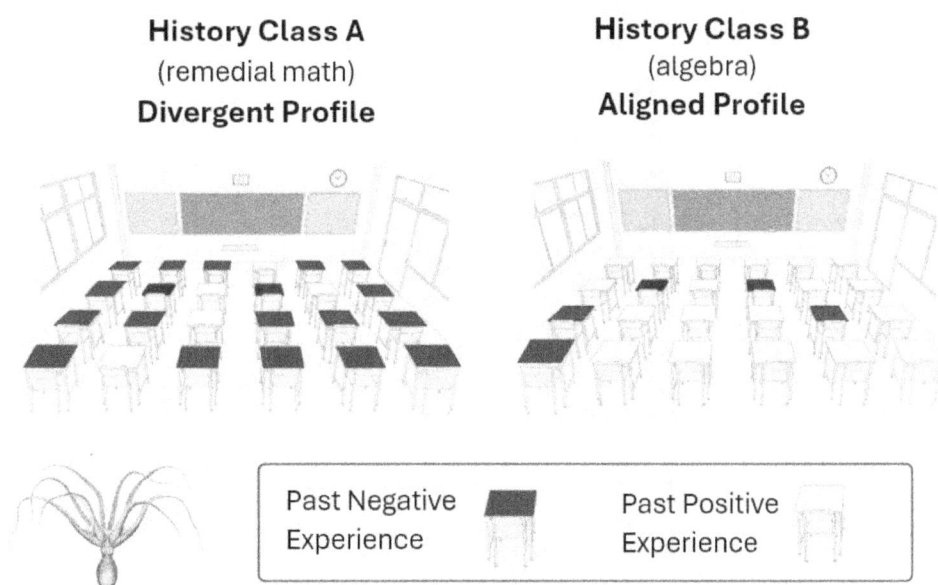

Figure 10.14 Illustration comparing divergent and aligned classroom profiles by past classroom experiences.

Hidden Attribute: Perceived Teacher Burnout

According to Zhang's article *"The Effect of Perceived Burnout on Credibility"* and Homeo's article *"Effects of Teacher Burnout on Their Credibility,"* students' beliefs about a teacher's burnout level, whether accurate or not, can significantly influence their perception of the teacher's competence, caring, and trustworthiness.

Students who perceive you as experiencing high burnout are significantly more likely to view you as uncaring, untrustworthy, and incompetent. They are also more likely to believe you can't manage the class, teach effectively, or maintain control.

This perception creates a significant divergence between your actual behaviour (Alpha Press) and the students' interpretation of it (Beta Press). That divergence can produce a collective classroom narrative of burnout—one that can further erode your credibility and authority, even if your actual performance hasn't changed.

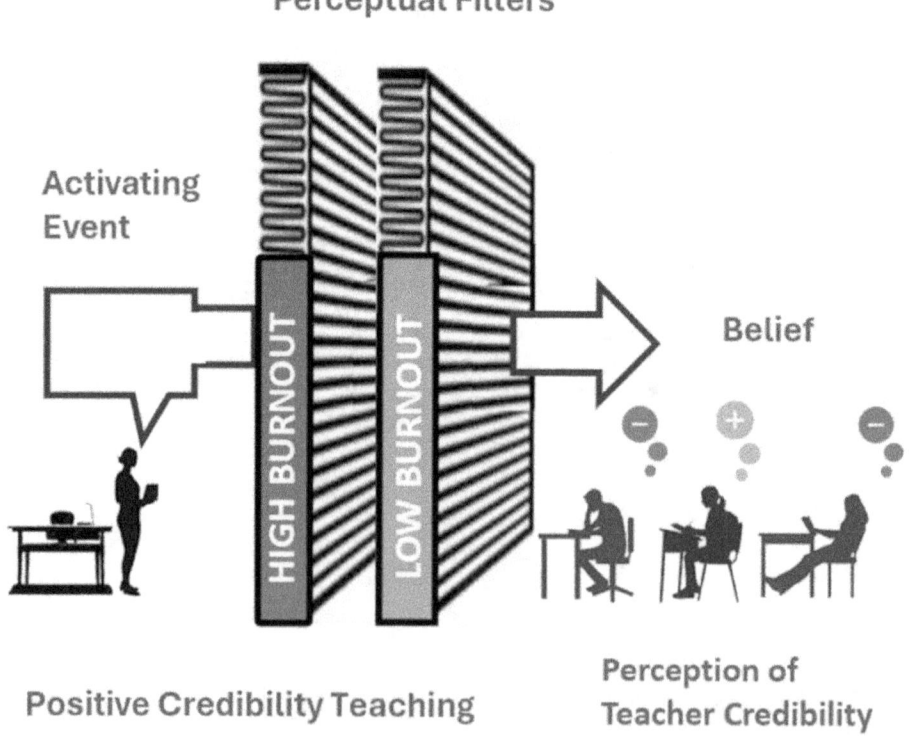

Figure 10.15 Illustration of perceptual filters for hidden attribute: perceived teacher burnout, during an activating event.

Several studies describe teaching as one of the most demanding and emotionally exhausting professions. According to Zhang and Homeo, it's not surprising that perceptions of burnout, especially when compounded by a classroom where interpretations diverge, contribute to a collective belief that undermines the teacher's credibility. In such environments, students are more likely to:

High Burnout Perception

Spread the burnout story, telling others you're overwhelmed and not in control.

Projecting bad past experiences with teachers onto you. which may justify their disengagement or disruptive behavior.

See your rules as weakness, mistaking firmness for frustration or emotional struggle.

Dismiss your support, thinking you're just pretending to care.

Lower their expectations, assuming you're checked out and not able to teach well.

Doubt your fairness, blaming your burnout for grades or discipline they don't like.

Stop asking for help, thinking you're too drained to be supportive.

Act out more, assuming you won't follow through or hold them accountable.

Tell others you're not capable, using classroom chaos as evidence.

Add to your stress, not always on purpose, but making burnout worse.

Create a self-fulfilling loop, where their low trust and effort make your job even harder.

Figure 10.16 Table showing student tendencies based on high burnout perception.

When students don't perceive you as burned out, they're more likely to see you in a positive light—enhancing your credibility and contributing to a more productive classroom climate. In these classrooms, students are more likely to:

Low Burnout Perception

Respect your authority and credibility, reinforcing a positive view of your role in the classroom.

Bring positive past experiences into your class, making them more open, trusting, and receptive to your teaching.

See your structure and discipline as care, recognizing your commitment to a productive, well-managed environment.

Appreciate your efforts to support them, viewing your actions as genuine rather than performative.

Stay cooperative and engaged, helping you maintain a calm and focused classroom climate.

Reinforce your reputation for fairness and competence, encouraging their peers to adopt a similar respectful attitude.

Contribute to a supportive environment, helping you stay motivated and reinforcing a shared commitment to learning.

Feel comfortable asking for help, trusting that you're available, invested, and capable of guiding their success.

Trust your decisions, seeing them as fair, balanced, and consistent—fostering a greater sense of emotional safety.

Figure 10.17 Table showing student tendencies based on low burnout perception.

Simulating What Students Might Be Telling Themselves: How Burnout Perception Shapes Inference

In Classroom A, when students perceive high teacher burnout, they often create and reinforce negative narratives—regardless of the teacher's actual behaviour or competence. These inferences spread quickly, erode

Figure 10.18 Illustration showing simulated student narratives for high burnout perception, demonstrating how this hidden attribute influences perceptions of teacher credibility.

credibility, and make it harder for you to re-establish trust. What you're seeing may not reflect what you're doing—it reflects what students *believe* they're seeing.

When students perceive low burnout, they're more likely to interpret your behaviour as caring, competent, and fair. These students assume good intentions, respond positively to structure, and reinforce a classroom culture built on trust and shared purpose. Their inferences support—not erode—your credibility.

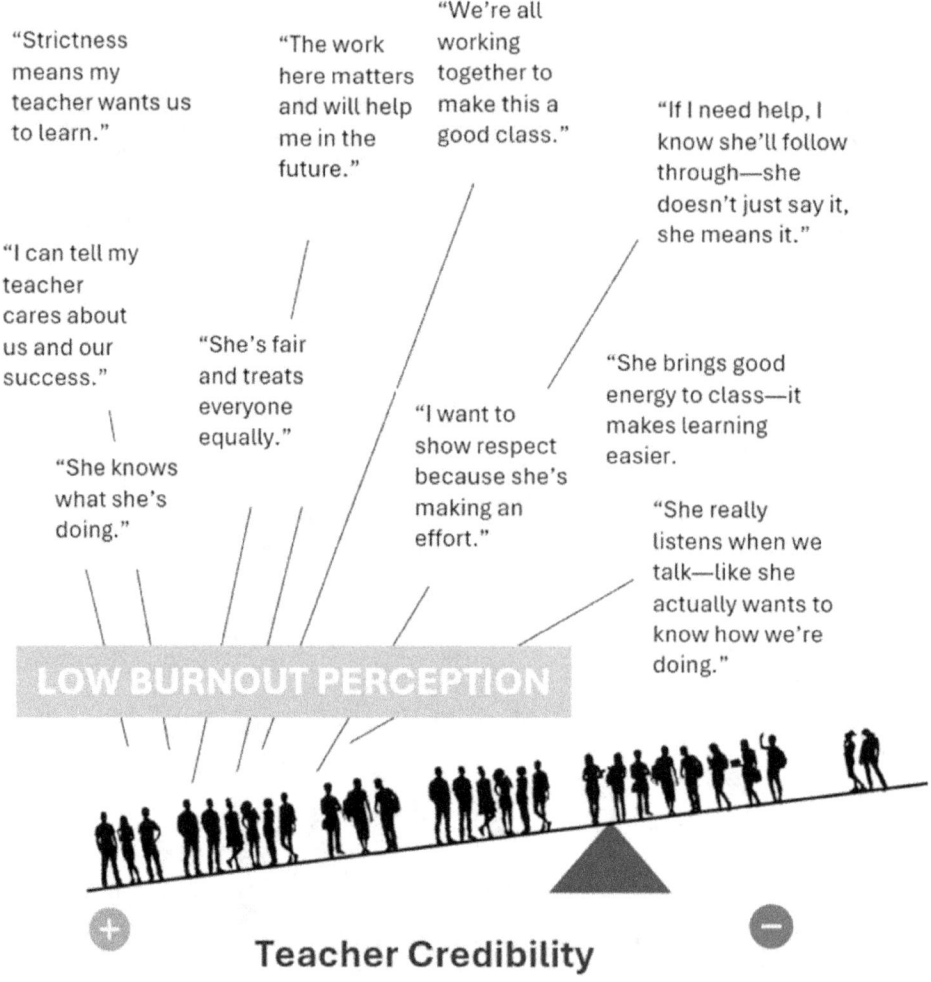

Figure 10.19 Illustration showing simulated student narratives for low burnout perception, demonstrating how this hidden attribute influences perceptions of teacher credibility.

Hidden Attributes—Burnout Perception: What You Can't See Can Hurt You

In a classroom where the majority of your students **perceive** you as burned out; your credibility is at high risk. Even if you're doing your best, students may interpret your actions as signs of weakness, incompetence, or a lack of care. This perception is often shaped by past negative experiences and reinforced by peers.

Efforts to support students can be dismissed—or worse, seen as covering up your inability to manage the class. When students believe you're emotionally checked out, they're more likely to test boundaries, withdraw effort, or question your authority.

Over time, this narrative of burnout can become a self-fulfilling prophecy: engagement drops, classroom conflict rises, and your reputation suffers. Without intervention, both student learning and teacher well-being are likely to decline—sometimes to the point where teachers consider leaving the profession.

What students perceive matters—even when it's not true.

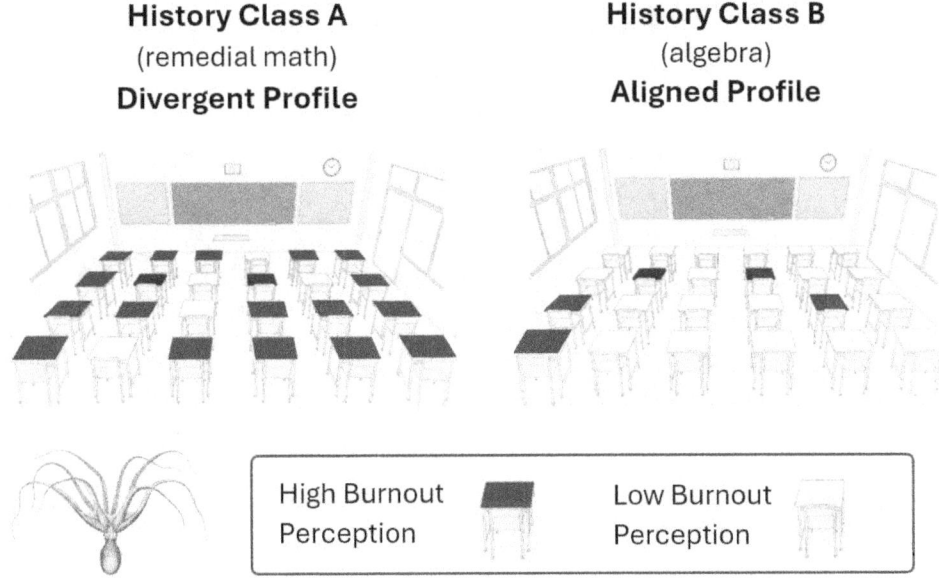

Figure 10.20 Illustration comparing divergent and aligned classroom profiles by perceived teacher burnout.

Hidden Attribute: Self-Regulated Learning

According to Yu et al. (2021), students with strong SRL skills are much more likely to see their teachers as credible—especially in terms of **care** and **trustworthiness**. In their study, SRL had both a direct impact on academic performance and an indirect one by shaping how students viewed their teachers.

While the study doesn't directly test students with low SRL, the message is clear: when students struggle to manage their learning, they may become frustrated and disengaged. That frustration can quickly shift how they interpret your behaviour. Even supportive actions might be dismissed or misread, eroding perceptions of your credibility. In classrooms where SRL is low, caring and trustworthiness may be harder for students to see—even when you're showing both.

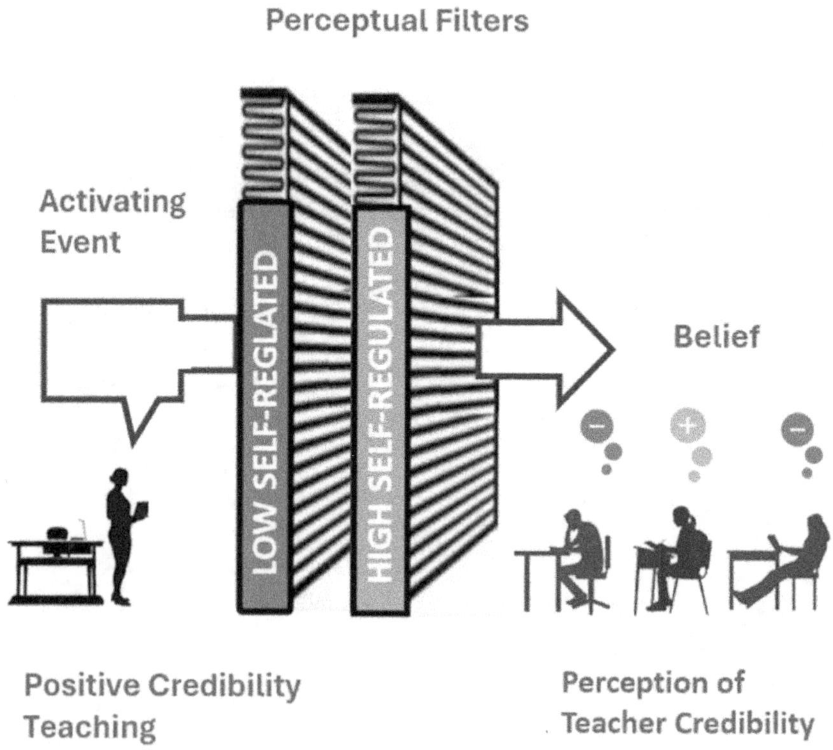

Perceptual Filters

Activating Event

Belief

Positive Credibility Teaching

Perception of Teacher Credibility

Figure 10.21 Illustration of perceptual filters for hidden attribute: self-regulated learning, during an activating event.

Students who lack SRL skills—like goal setting, time management, or self-monitoring—often struggle academically. This can leave them frustrated, disengaged, and unsure of how to succeed. In that state, it's easy to see why they might:	Since your high-SRL students have strategies like goal setting, time management, and self-monitoring, they tend to feel confident, successful, and in control of their learning. Given those strengths, it's easy to see why they might:

Low Self-Regulated	High Self-Regulated
See you as unsupportive, especially when they're overwhelmed by tasks.	**See you as caring,** believing you genuinely value their well-being and academic success.
Feel like you don't understand their academic or personal challenges, creating distance.	**Trust your guidance,** seeing you as honest, reliable, and invested in their progress.
Misinterpret your help as proof that you think they're incapable.	**Take constructive feedback** as encouragement, not criticism—they know it's meant to help them grow.
Believe you're biased, giving more attention to higher-performing students.	**Respect your authority,** recognizing your role in helping them learn and succeed.
Dismiss your methods as ineffective and assume you don't really care about their success.	**Appreciate your course structure** and organization, interpreting it as a sign you care about their learning.
Feel misunderstood and treated unfairly—even when you're trying to help.	**See your teaching methods** as supportive of their goals, which increases their motivation and engagement.
Take constructive feedback as criticism, believing you see them as failures.	**Value your support** when it's given purposefully, because they know how to manage most tasks on their own.
Blame you for their struggles instead of recognizing their own habits or lack of effort.	**See your caring behavior** as a reason to trust and follow your lead—they connect emotional support to academic success.
Expect constant guidance, and if you don't provide it, assume you're disengaged or don't know how to help.	

Figure 10.22 Table showing student tendencies based on low and high self-regulated learning.

Simulating What Students Might Be Telling Themselves: How Self-Regulated Learning Shapes Inference

Even when you show care, offer support, and act with integrity, students with low SRL may still see you as less credible. They often struggle to engage and, because of their frustration, misread your efforts as unhelpful—or even unfair.

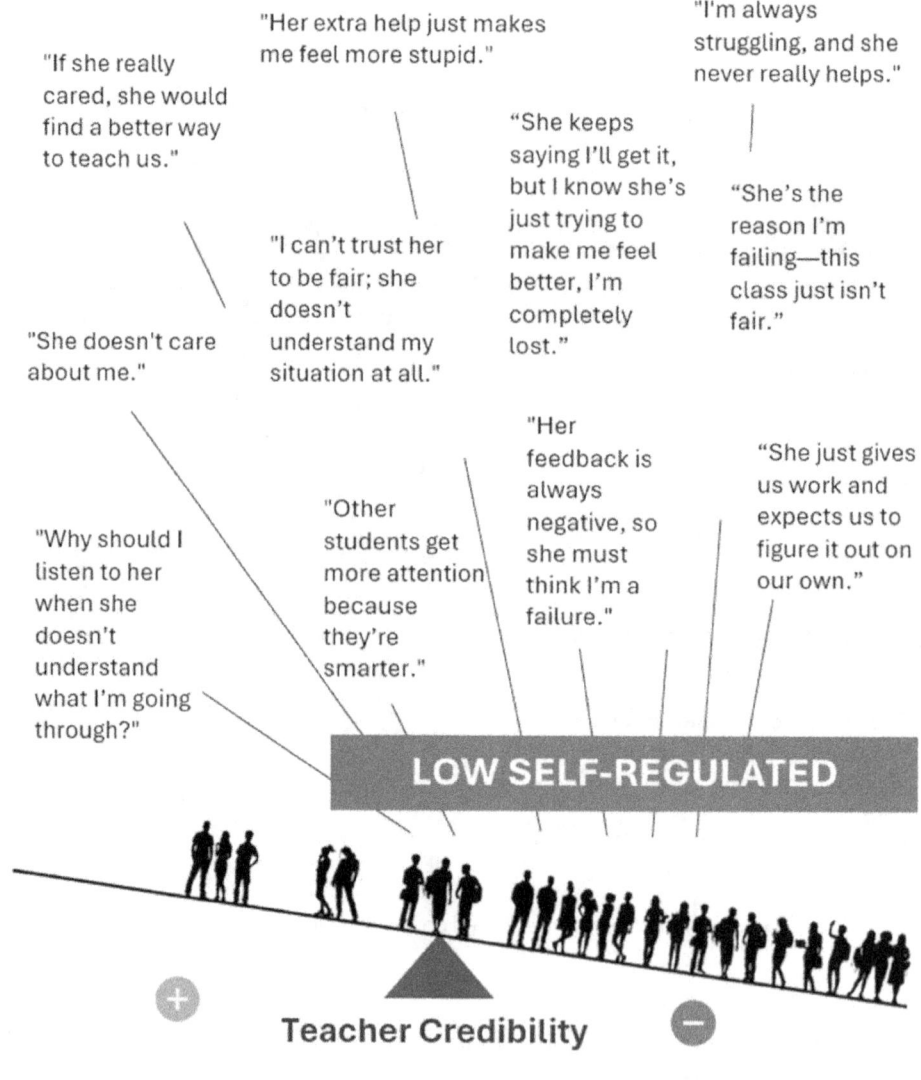

Figure 10.23 Illustration showing simulated student narratives for low self-regulated learning, demonstrating how this hidden attribute influences perceptions of teacher credibility.

When your students have strong self-regulation skills, they're more likely to see your actions in the best possible light. They interpret your feedback as support, your expectations as a sign that you care, and your guidance as trustworthy. Even when challenges arise, these students tend to give you the benefit of the doubt—because they feel capable, connected, and respected in your classroom. Their belief in their own effort helps reinforce their belief in you.

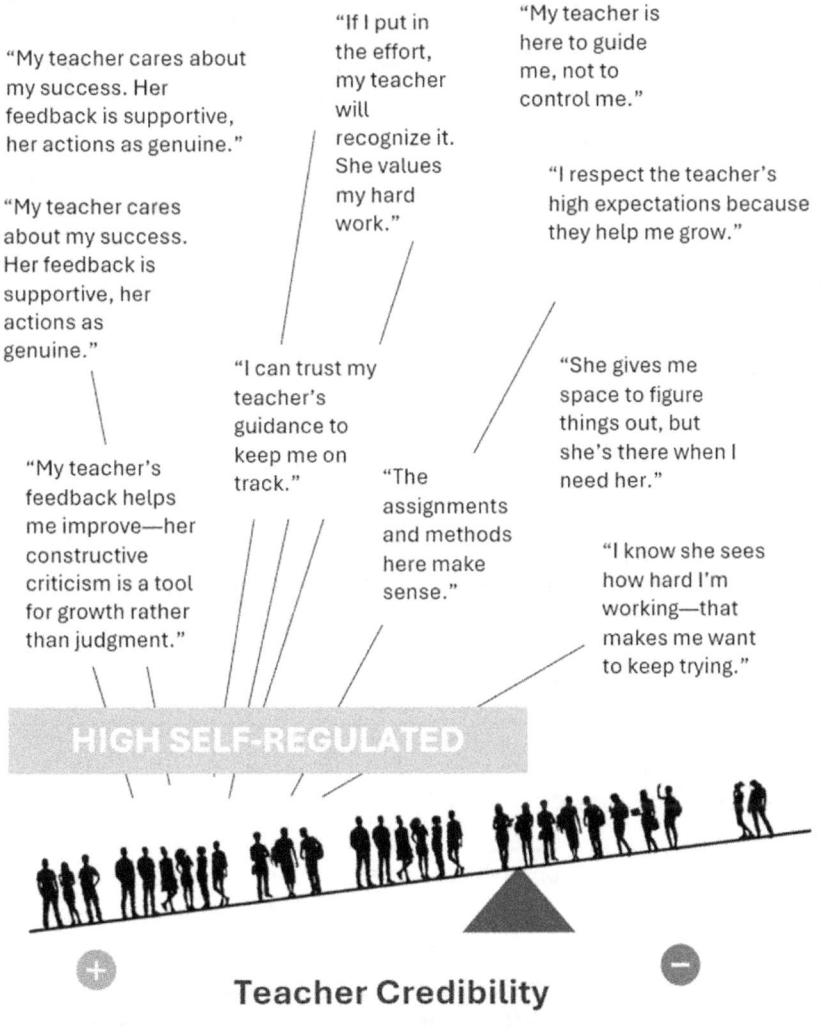

Figure 10.24 Illustration showing simulated student narratives for high self-regulated learning, demonstrating how this hidden attribute influences perceptions of teacher credibility.

Hidden Attributes—Self-Regulated Learning: What You Can't See Can Hurt You

In a classroom dominated by students with low SRL, your credibility is at risk—even when you're doing the right things. These students often interpret constructive feedback as personal criticism, making them feel judged rather than supported. They may see your support for other students as favouritism, especially if they perceive those peers as more capable. This can erode their trust in your fairness.

Structured tasks and organized routines—meant to support learning—can feel overwhelming, irrelevant to them or not aligning with their needs. As a result, your efforts may be dismissed as controlling or impersonal, rather than recognized as help. This disconnect lowers their perception of your care and support, often leading to disengagement, resistance, or outright defiance.

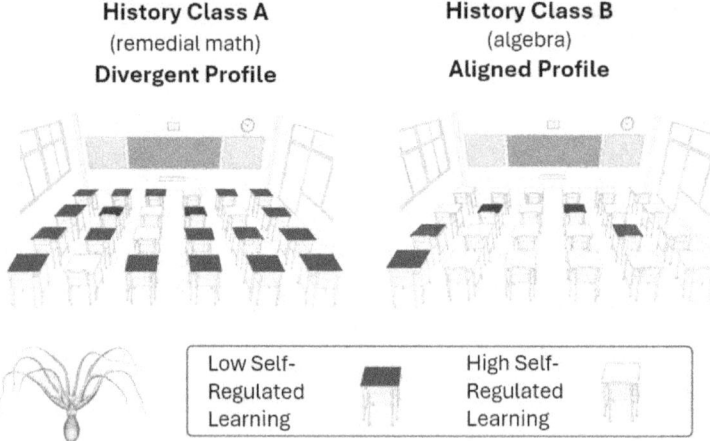

Figure 10.25 Illustration comparing divergent and aligned classroom profiles by self-regulated learning.

 Key Takeaway:

The simulated student narratives you've seen so far—based on research into teacher credibility—highlight something important: students' internal motivations or hidden attributes (like low SRL) can shape how they see you, even when your behaviour is fair, caring, and competent. These distorted perceptions aren't about what you're doing wrong—they're about how students are interpreting it.

Before we dive into Part 3: The Codebook, here's a quick checklist to help you reflect on the biggest takeaways from Parts **1** and **2**—so you're ready to apply them in practice.

Checklist for Understanding Hidden Attributes

How do I know if hidden motivations and social contagion are at work in my classroom—and what do I do about it?

You Likely Need the Codebook If
1. ☑ You're consistently demonstrating credible, supportive teaching.
2. ☑ Yet a significant number of students still interpret your behaviour negatively, even when your actions clearly demonstrate caring, trustworthiness and competence.

This Suggests
3. ☑ Student interpretations are being shaped by hidden attributes, irrational thinking and peer influence, not by your actual behaviour.
4. ☑ That's why perception varies across students, and why some develop persistently inaccurate inferences, a pattern I call the *Divergent Profile*.
5. ☑ These inaccurate inferences aren't just misunderstandings. They're emotionally charged, rigid beliefs, central to the ABC model, that distort how students interpret your actions (A) and lead to negative emotional or behavioural responses (C).
6. ☑ Hidden attributes and social contagion explain how distorted beliefs can take root, and how they can erode your credibility, even when your teaching is strong.

So What Do You about It?
7. ☑ At the root of informatively and materially uncooperative behaviour are distorted beliefs, shaped by internal student motivations like social contagion and other hidden attributes. These beliefs distort how students interpret your behaviour (A) and lead to the negative consequences you see (C).

Change the Belief to Change the Perception
8. ☑ To shift student perception, you must target not just the belief—but the motivation behind it. These motivations shape how students interpret everything you do.

So How Do You Do That?
9. ☑ Use the **Credibility Codebook** to target *B*—students' beliefs—through practical, research-informed strategies. These are organized into *codes*: tools designed to help students form more accurate inferences, resist peer-driven distortions, and adopt healthier, more rational beliefs about your behaviour.

Figure 10.26 Illustration showing focus on targeting students' beliefs (B) using the Credibility Codebook.

Chapter Summary

★ In Classroom A, many students are shaped by **hidden attributes**—like negative past experiences, low self-regulation, or a belief that their teacher is burned out. These factors distort how they interpret your behaviour, even when you're doing everything right.

★ This chapter explores how those distorted perceptions form, using **student narrative simulations** to show how activating events (like assignments or corrections) can trigger irrational beliefs and negative responses. These aren't abstract ideas—you experience them every day in the form of misbehaviour, resistance, or disengagement.

★ The problem isn't just that these perceptions exist—it's that they're often **shared and reinforced by the group**. Even when inaccurate, they become "factually false but socially true"—and that social truth can quietly erode your credibility.

★ By understanding these hidden attributes, you'll improve your ability to recognize when student reactions are driven by internal beliefs, not your actual teaching. That awareness—your **scout mindset**—is the first step in bridging the gap between your intention and their interpretation.

 Key Takeaway:

Student beliefs don't need to be accurate to impact your credibility—they just need to be shared. In Classroom A, it's not the facts that shape perception, but the group's story about you.

References

Homeo, R. C. (2023). Effects of teacher burnout on their credibility. *International Journal of Research Publication and Reviews, 4*(3), 709–719. https://doi.org/10.55248/gengpi.2023.32015

Schenke, K., Ruzek, E. A., Lam, A. C., Karabenick, S. A., & Eccles, J. S. (2018). To the means and beyond: Understanding variation in students' perceptions of teacher emotional support. *Learning and Instruction, 55*, 13–21. https://doi.org/10.1016/j.learninstruc.2017.09.009

Tibbles, D. (2006). *Communication organizational orientations in an instructional setting* (Master's thesis, West Virginia University). West Virginia University Research Repository. https://researchrepository.wvu.edu/etd/792

Yu, L., Chen, S., & Recker, M. (2021). Structural relationships between self-regulated learning, teachers' credibility, information and communications technology literacy and academic performance in blended learning. *Australasian Journal of Educational Technology, 37*(4), 33–47. https://doi.org/10.14742/ajet.6575

Zhang, Q., & Sapp, D. A. (2009). The effect of perceived teacher burnout on credibility. *Communication Research Reports, 26*(1), 87–90. https://doi.org/10.1080/08824090802637122

Part 3

Activating the Codebook
Replacing Irrational Thinking and Inoculating Against Coercion and False Beliefs

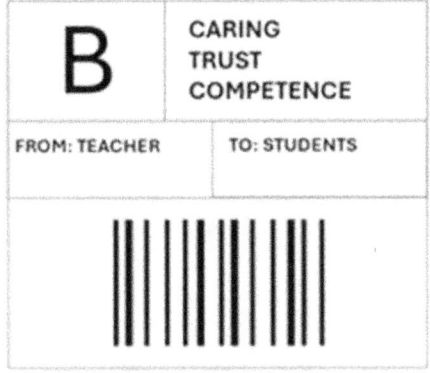

Figure P.3a Illustration using a barcode as a metaphor for decoding teacher behavior accurately and rationally.

Overview

In Parts 1 and 2, you explored why students perceive the same teacher so differently, and how internal filters like trait orientations, past experiences, and peer dynamics shape their beliefs. Now it's time to shift from insight to action.

Part 3 activates the Codebook, a practical framework for reshaping distorted student beliefs, protecting your credibility, and creating a classroom environment more resilient to manipulation, misinformation, and irrational thinking.

DOI: 10.4324/9781003644088-14

You'll start by identifying the irrational beliefs that quietly drive disengagement, defiance, and disrespect (Chapter 11). From there, you'll explore the one belief that, if left unchallenged, most reliably destroys student trust and credibility (Chapter 12). With that groundwork, you'll explore rational alternatives that promote ownership, fairness, and emotional self-regulation (Chapter 13).

Then, you'll apply two powerful classroom codes:

- **Code 1** shows you how to replace irrational student beliefs using strategies from Rational Emotive Education (Chapter 14).
- **Code 2** equips you with prebunking techniques to counter peer coercion, misinformation, and false narratives—before they take hold (Chapter 15).

Together, these five chapters give you a tested set of tools to **rebuild the beliefs that shape behaviour**, reinforce your credibility, and inoculate your classroom against the forces that so often work against both teachers and students.

To guide your work in this section, here's a visual of the two core strategies, Code 1 and Code 2, that you'll use to reshape student beliefs and stabilize your classroom climate.

Two Classroom Codes to Reshape Student Beliefs and Protect Credibility

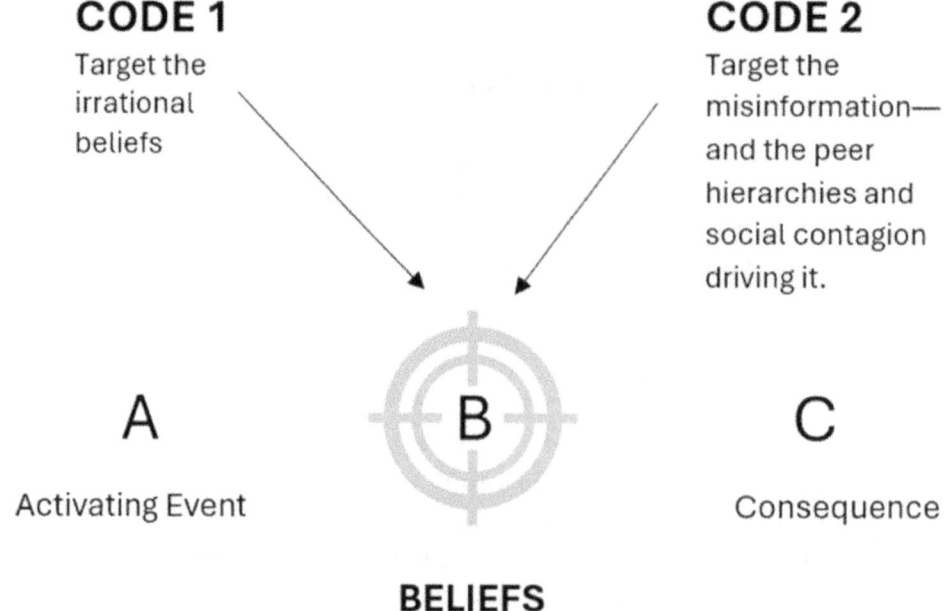

Figure P.3b Illustration showing how Code 1 and Code 2 target irrational beliefs and peer-driven misinformation to reshape student perceptions.

Code 1: Rational Emotive Education (REE) teaches students how to identify and challenge irrational beliefs by guiding them to uncover the belief that caused their emotional reaction—then helping them replace it with a more rational, constructive one.

Code 2: Social Inoculation teaches students to recognize misinformation and understand how it's spread.

In classrooms with strong peer influence, social contagion can mimic misinformation, spreading beliefs based on shared emotion and group loyalty rather than facts. This peer-driven dynamic works much like media-driven misinformation but moves student-to-student instead of media-to-student.

11

The Irrational Beliefs That Derail Student Thinking

Figure 11.1 Illustration representing demandingness, a core irrational belief that can distort student perceptions.

Overview

Much of the work in this chapter, and throughout Part III, draws from two key sources: Rational Emotive Education (REE) developed by Dr. William Knaus, and the clinical framework laid out in Dr. Ray DiGiuseppe's Rational Emotive Behaviour Therapy (REBT): Distinctive Features. These foundational models guide how irrational beliefs can be identified and addressed in educational settings.

Many of the most frustrating student behaviours, disrespect, hostility, defiance, ridicule and disengagement are not random. They're driven by

irrational beliefs students carry with them into the classroom. In this chapter, you'll learn how to identify the four most common types of irrational beliefs—**Demandingness, Catastrophizing, Low Frustration Tolerance, and Self/Other Rating**—and how they silently shape students' perceptions, emotions, and behaviours.

When these beliefs go unchallenged, they distort how students interpret your instructions, feedback, and classroom norms. A simple request becomes a humiliation. Enforcing a deadline becomes an attack. A grade becomes a judgement of self-worth.

But once you recognize the beliefs underneath these reactions, you can respond more effectively, not just with discipline or reassurance, but by helping students question the thinking that fuels their behaviour.

This chapter sets the foundation for **Code 1**, where you'll learn how to help students replace irrational beliefs with rational, constructive alternatives that support classroom learning and support your credibility.

I Learned about Irrational Beliefs on the Ice—Not in a Classroom

Before I ever connected irrational beliefs to the classroom, I ran into them coaching football and hockey for over 20 years. In that time, I was introduced to cognitive-behavioural strategies designed to improve player performance. One of the most effective is REBT, developed by psychologist Albert Ellis in 1962.

REBT is built on a simple but powerful idea: it's not the event itself that causes distress, it's what you believe about the event. For example, if a quarterback throws an interception and tells himself, "I'm never going to be good," or "It's all my fault we lost," those thoughts reflect irrational beliefs. They're emotionally charged, unrealistic, and disconnected from the facts. Left unchecked, these beliefs can quietly erode confidence, derail performance, and damage mental health.

Research shows that irrational beliefs are strongly linked to anxiety, burnout, poor focus, and low motivation in athletes (Turner, 2016). That's why REBT is now widely used in sports psychology, from Olympic programmes to the NFL, NHL, and Major League Baseball (MLB), to help athletes stay mentally strong under pressure and reframe their thinking when it matters most.

Later, I discovered this same framework applied to education. It's called REE, a classroom-ready version of REBT, grounded in decades of research and supported by meta-analyses (Trip et al., 2007). REE helps students reduce disruptive behaviour, build healthier beliefs about themselves, their school experience, and the inevitable setbacks that come with learning. And it's designed specifically for people like you and me—teachers, not therapists.

You Don't Need a Psychology Degree—It's Practical, Proven, and Easy to Use

Before we dive deeper into REBT and its classroom adaptation, REE, here's something important to know… you don't need to be a trained therapist to use it effectively. In fact, as Dr. William Knaus notes, REE can be "self-taught without formal training or exposure" (Knaus, 1974).

In fact, a meta-analysis on Rational Emotive Therapy with children and adolescents found that educational professionals—like teachers and coaches—often achieved better outcomes than mental health professionals (Gonzalez et al., 2004). That's a powerful finding.

It means you can apply these strategies directly in your classroom—with confidence and impact. REE is designed to be simple, flexible, and easy to weave into your existing routines. And most importantly, it works.

It Starts with Demands

How does this actually work in a classroom? And how does it help you build, protect, and maintain your credibility? You're a busy teacher with a lot going on, so let's keep it simple and practical.

We'll start with sports. I'll use examples from coaching to break it down, then connect it directly to what you face in the classroom. This way, you get the essentials of REBT and REE quickly, and you'll be able to use them right away to understand your students (cognitive reappraisal-mindreading) and even teach these ideas to them.

Meet the King of Irrational Beliefs: Demandingness

At the heart of nearly all irrational thinking, emotional distress, and disruptive behaviour is one key belief: Demandingness (Dr. DiGiuseppe). Demandingness, it's the belief that things *must* go a certain way:

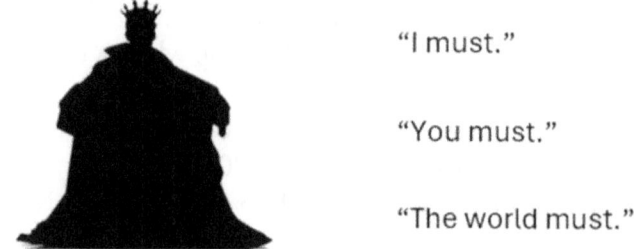

Figure 11.2 Illustration of demandingness: the belief that self, others, and the world must conform to one's expectations.

Let's say you have a rough morning: speeding ticket on the way to school, you miss most of an important Professional Development (PD) staff meeting and forget your lunch. Then your principal seems to wave off your morning like it's an excuse, and Human Resources (HR) isn't flexible, you lose a half-day. It's frustrating, sure. But what really drives the potential emotional spiral is what you might start telling yourself:

"I must have everything under control every morning."
"My principal must understand how hard my morning was."
"The school must care more about people than policies."

If those irrational demands aren't met, the reaction kicks in: guilt, anger, anxiety, and self-doubt. The beliefs, not the events, cause the emotional storm. **Thank you, King**!

This is how Demandingness works. And yes, it shows up in your students too. Let's take a look at a simple coaching and classroom scenario.

Demandingness: In Sports and in the Classroom

Demandingness is the core irrational belief behind most emotional distress—whether you're coaching athletes or teaching students (Dr. DiGiuseppe). It shows up as rigid expectations like "I must always perform well," "The coach must play me more," or "The league should always be fair." In the classroom, it might sound like "I must always get good grades," "The teacher must always listen to my side," or "School should always feel fair."

Understanding **Demandingness** is key, because it fuels all the other irrational beliefs. Recognizing signs of Demandingness, on a sports team or in your classroom, is essential to protecting your credibility. These inflexible "must" or "should" beliefs are often what drive emotional reactions, resistance, and disruptive behaviour—**not your actual coaching or teaching**.

What follows are two graphic organizers showing how Demandingness plays out in both scenarios:

- One shows the irrational demands an athlete might place on themselves, their teammates, their coach, the league, and the referees.
- The other shows the irrational demands a student might place on themselves, their classmates, their teacher, and the school system.

Who Must What? Demandingness on the Team

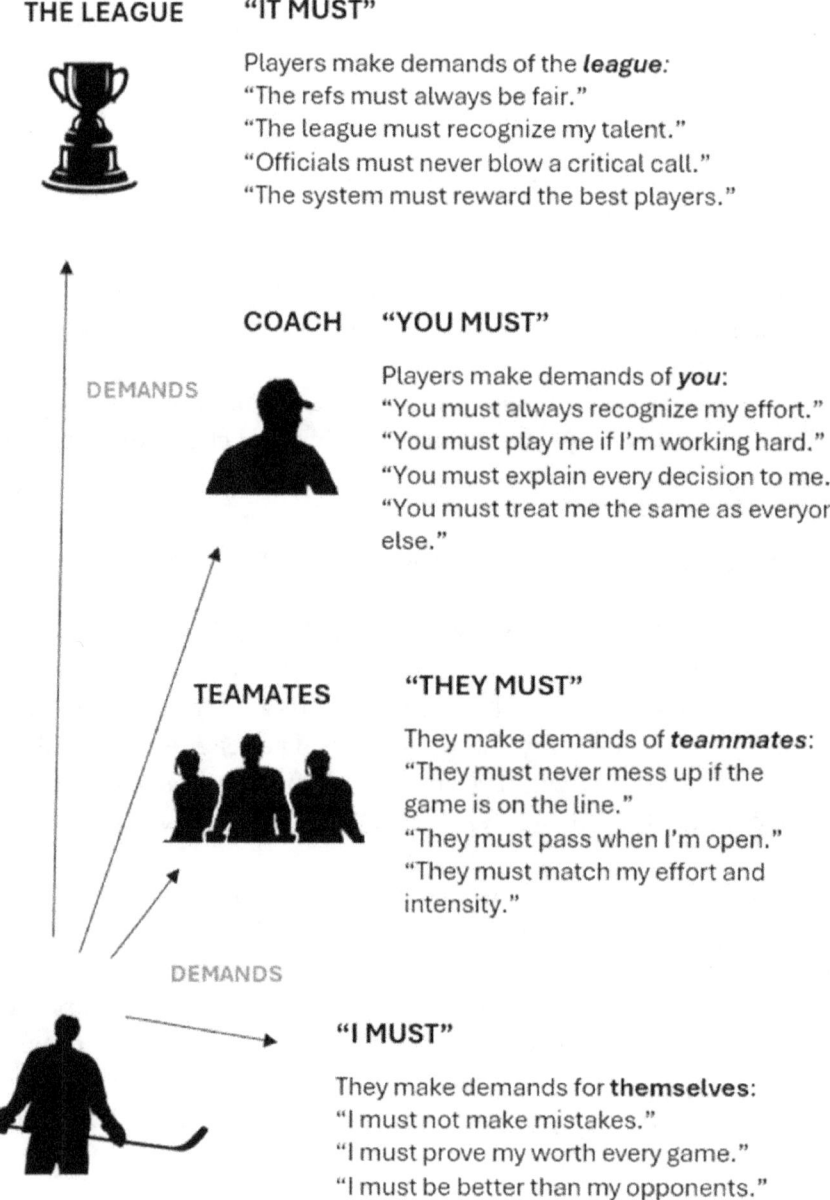

THE LEAGUE — **"IT MUST"**

Players make demands of the *league*:
"The refs must always be fair."
"The league must recognize my talent."
"Officials must never blow a critical call."
"The system must reward the best players."

DEMANDS

COACH — **"YOU MUST"**

Players make demands of *you*:
"You must always recognize my effort."
"You must play me if I'm working hard."
"You must explain every decision to me."
"You must treat me the same as everyone else."

TEAMATES — **"THEY MUST"**

They make demands of *teammates*:
"They must never mess up if the game is on the line."
"They must pass when I'm open."
"They must match my effort and intensity."

DEMANDS

"I MUST"

They make demands for *themselves*:
"I must not make mistakes."
"I must prove my worth every game."
"I must be better than my opponents."

All Infographics Adapted from Dr. DiGiuseppe's Distinctive Features of REBT

Figure 11.3 Infographic: Demandingness on the Team.

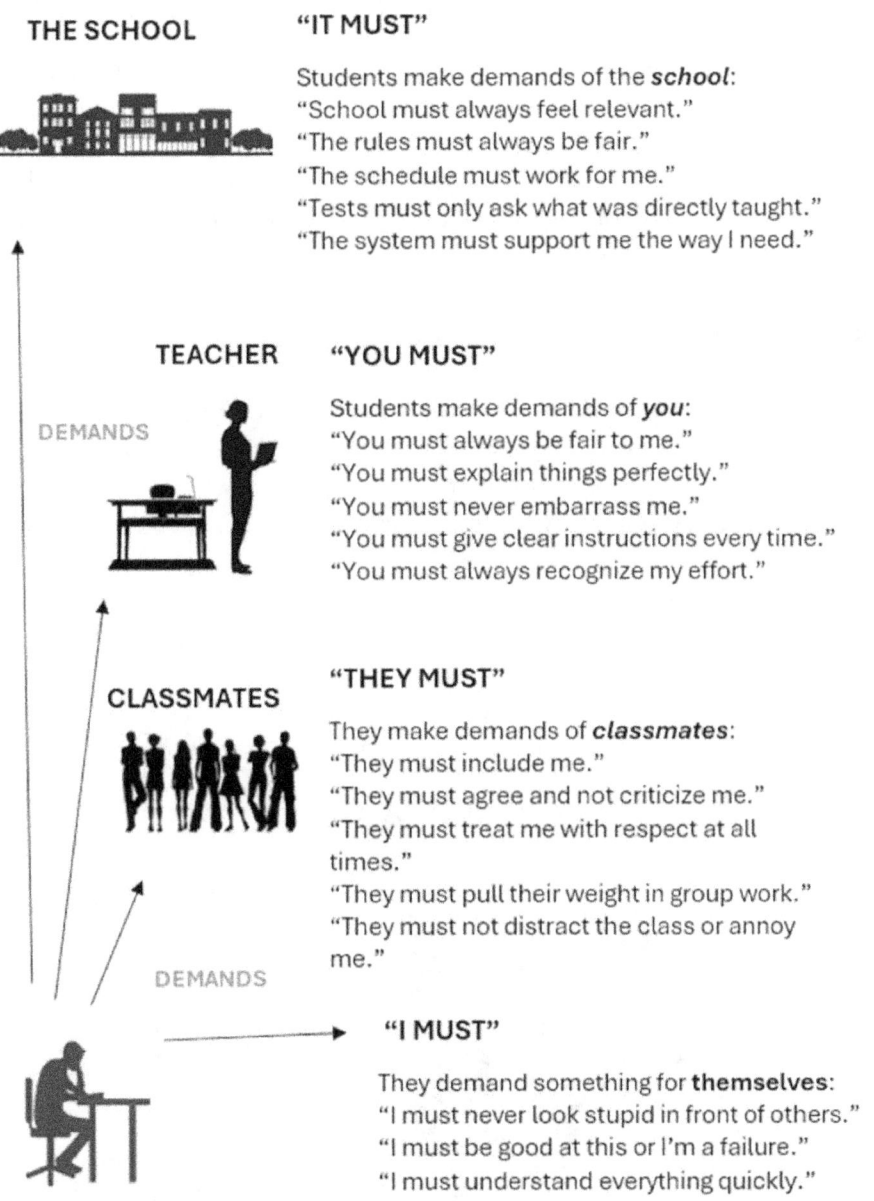

Figure 11.4 Infographic: Demandingness in the Classroom.

That Doesn't Sound So Bad

Let's be honest, some of these demands don't sound all that bad at first. A hockey player says, "I must be better than my opponent." A student insists, "My group members must pull their weight." A teacher promises to "get her morning routine organized." It almost sounds like goal setting, maybe even high standards or motivation in action.

But here's the trap: these aren't goals or preferences. They're rigid, absolute expectations. In REBT, that's why they're called **irrational beliefs**, non-negotiable demands we place on ourselves, others, or the world.

The Real Problem Starts When the Demand Isn't Met

The moment a demand isn't met, the **Factory of Troubles** kicks into gear. That's when emotional distress hits, irrational thinking flares up, and the King of Demandingness takes over.

Here's what the **Factory** typically produces:

- **Catastrophizing:** "If the demand isn't met, it will be awful."
- **Low Frustration Tolerance (LFT):** "If the demand isn't met, I can't handle it."
- **Self/Other Rating:** "If the demand isn't met, I'm a failure—or the person responsible is a bad person."

Figure 11.5 Illustration of the 'Factory of Troubles', a metaphor for how unmet demands trigger irrational thinking and its derivatives.

That's how a seemingly harmless "must" can spiral into emotional outbursts, conflict, disruptive behaviour, disengagement or worse. **These are all very harmful to your credibility.**

Your Rough Morning—Through a Distorted Lens

Remember that tough morning? You're running late. You get a speeding ticket. You miss most of the PD staff meeting. You forgot your lunch. And you still have a full day of meetings ahead. Stress is high, but the day isn't ruined. Not yet.

Here's where things start to shift:

When we hold rigid demands: on ourselves, our principal, or the school, and those demands aren't met, the **Factory of Troubles** can kick into full production.

If we start to believe these demands won't be met, not now, not ever, then irrational beliefs can start to take over. In the next few pages, you'll see how this can happen.

I'll break it down into three common sources of demand:

- **Yourself**
- **Your Principal** (others)
- **The School System** (the world)

And for each, you'll see what happens when those demands are perceived to go unmet, and how they trigger the three major distorted beliefs from the Factory of Troubles:

- **Catastrophizing:** "This is horrible!"
- **Low Frustration Tolerance:** "I can't stand this!"
- **Self/Other Rating:** "I'm no good. You're no good."

> **Quick Note**
> The examples that follow are intentionally exaggerated. They're designed to illustrate how irrational beliefs can distort thinking in moments of stress, just like they do for our students. While your own experience may look very different, these examples help us recognize the thought patterns that often drive emotional reactions in the classroom.

 **Demand on the Self:** "I must have everything under control every morning."

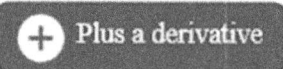

 **Catastrophizing** — And if I do not, the belief becomes: **"It's horrible."**

- "I'll never recover my credibility."
- "Admin will think I'm incompetent."
- "Parents and colleagues will all judge me."
- "Maybe I shouldn't even be teaching."

 **Low Frustration Tolerance** — And if I do not, the belief becomes: **"I can't stand it."**

- "I can't take messing up again—it's too much."
- "This pressure is unbearable."
- "Trying to be perfect will drain me—I can't keep this up."

 **Self Rating** — And if I do not, the belief becomes: **"I am no good!"**

- "I'm clearly not cut out to be a teacher."
- "I'm a disorganized mess—no one should trust me."
- "This one slip proves I'm a failure."

Figure 11.6 Infographic showing self-directed demandingness in teachers and its three derivatives: Catastrophizing, Low Frustration Tolerance, and Self-Rating.

The Irrational Beliefs That Derail Student Thinking ◆ 151

 **Demand on Others:** "My principal must understand how hard my morning was."

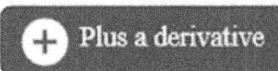 Plus a derivative

 Catastrophizing — And if she does not, the belief becomes: **"She's awful."**

- "She doesn't care about me at all."
- "I'll never get support in this school."
- "This proves I'm on my own."

 Low Frustration Tolerance — And if I do not, the belief becomes: **"I can't cope."**

- "I can't work for someone so cold."
- "Having to explain myself is exhausting."
- "It's draining to hold it together when leadership doesn't get it."

 Other Rating — And if she does not, the belief becomes: **"Then she's the problem. She needs to be reprimanded."**

- "She's just the kind of leader who shouldn't be in charge."*
- "People like her make this job impossible. She should be replaced"*

Figure 11.7 Infographic showing others-directed demandingness in teachers and its three derivatives: Catastrophizing, Low Frustration Tolerance, and Other-Rating.

 **Demand on the World:** "The school must care more about people than policies."

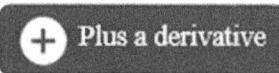

 **Catastrophizing** — And if it does not, the belief becomes: **"This school is awful."**

- "This proves the school doesn't value people—just compliance."
- "I can't keep working in a place like this."
- "This confirms the system is toxic."

 **Low Frustration Tolerance** — And if it does not, the belief becomes: **"I can't take it."**

- "I'm worn down by this inflexibility."
- "This kind of response just breaks me."
- "Justifying myself every time is exhausting."

 **Other Rating** — And if it does not, the belief becomes: **"They're no good, they need to be investigated."**

- "This system doesn't care about teachers—only appearances. There needs to be an audit on how they treat staff."
- "This district is broken. Someone needs to step-in, and tear out the incompetence"*

Figure 11.8 Infographic showing world-directed demandingness in teachers and its three derivatives: Catastrophizing, Low Frustration Tolerance, and Other-Rating.

Why This Exercise Works

These exaggerated thoughts reflect the same irrational patterns your students often fall into, just flipped. In a classroom where your credibility is under constant attack, students' distorted perceptions aren't really about you. It's about a belief that something must happen, and when it doesn't, their thinking become irrational. The result isn't logical—**it's emotional**. Their reaction isn't based on what you did; it's fuelled by a rigid belief that wasn't met.

That's why it matters: the pushback you face isn't personal, it's often predictable. And once you can spot the pattern, you can respond by working with your students to challenge those beliefs together.

It's Actually Pretty Simple

There's a lot of new language here, and the "derivatives" might seem like a lot to take in. But don't worry, all of these irrational beliefs come from one basic pattern. And once you see it, things really start to click.

Because you're right there in the moment with your students, you're in the best position to help shift their thinking and change the beliefs behind their behaviour. More effective, actually, than a mental health professional.

Here's the basic pattern behind irrational beliefs, and the simple switch that can change everything. **Just replace the irrational belief with a rational one:**

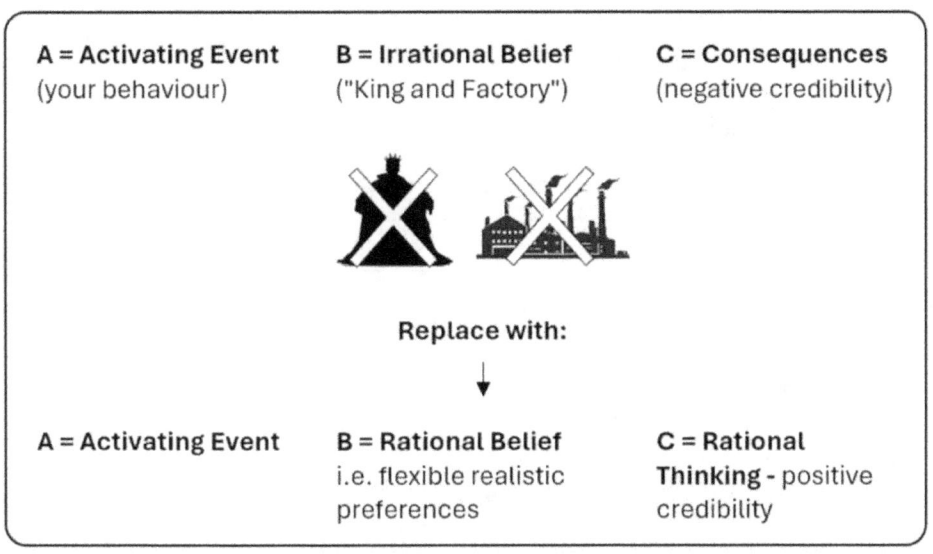

Figure 11.9 Infographic showing how to replace irrational beliefs with rational ones to improve teacher credibility.

Irrational Beliefs in the Locker Room: Demandingness and Its Derivatives at Play

Before we move on to how to replace irrational beliefs with rational ones, let's pause and look at the whole picture. Based on what you know about the King and the Factory, take a moment to observe this team. What do you think is

Derivatives & Drama: Inside the Irrational Locker Room

ACTIVATING EVENT Close game, we lose again. The coach has us learning skating drills every practice. We should be working on systems and tactics more. No one is working hard in practice today and coach keeps on with his drills.

 DEMANDS    **DERIVATIVES**

I MUST

I work hard so I **must** have a winning team and a good coach.

CAT- I'll never get scouted and this whole season will be a waste.

LFT- I'm done—what's the point of pushing myself if no one else cares and the coach isn't changing anything?

SOR- Then my coach clearly isn't good enough to lead us.

MY TEAMMATES MUST

My teammates **must** work as hard as me and care as much as I do.

CAT- With teammates like this, we're never going to win, I might as well give up now.

LFT- I can't deal with this anymore, no one's taking it seriously, it's a waste of time.

Other Rating- Some of these guys are just useless, they don't care, they don't work, dragging us down. They need to get cut.

YOU MUST

You **must** recognize my hard work and listen to what I say about practice and do it.

CAT- It means nothing's ever going to change, this team is going nowhere, there's no point even trying.

LFT- I can't take this anymore; there's no point showing up if you're just going to ignore us.

Other Rating- You're clearly clueless and don't deserve to coach this team.*

Figure 11.10 Infographic showing demandingness within a sports teams with derivatives: catastrophizing, low frustration tolerance, and other-rating.

driving their distorted perceptions? Which core irrational belief would you target and replace?

Don't worry, we haven't covered the tools and strategies that replace distorted thinking yet. Just focus on noticing the pattern.

And keep this in mind: this team has a credible coach, caring, trustworthy, and competent. Just like the "Rough Morning" scenario, if you can spot how irrational beliefs show up in your own thinking when you're upset, you'll be better equipped to help your students do the same.

Here's how Demandingness—and its emotional derivatives—play out on a sports team, like in hockey. And if you can recognize how the King and the Factory show up on the soccer field, basketball court, or baseball diamond, you'll start to see exactly how they operate in your classroom too.

One Conclusion about This Locker Room: False Beliefs Target Leadership

Let's be clear: the Factory isn't producing accurate versions of reality. These players aren't drawing conclusions based on what their coach or teammates actually do. The issue isn't behaviour; it's interpretation. The inferences being made are distorted and not backed by facts or evidence.

But here's the thing: a person's cognitive environment doesn't have to reflect reality for it to feel true. And once that "truth" takes hold, it spreads. When it does, your credibility as a coach, or teacher, is at risk. A false belief becomes a shared story. A story becomes the team's social truth.

The more leadership you carry, the more likely you are to become the target of irrational demands. Why? Because you represent the standards, the systems, the success, or the lack of it. And when things feel unfair, uncomfortable, or unsuccessful, it's easier to pin those feelings on you.

And when that narrative spreads? It wreaks havoc.

Thanks, King. Thanks, Factory

> **Chapter Summary**
>
> ★ Disrespect, defiance, and disengagement often seem random—but they're not. These behaviours are usually driven by irrational beliefs students bring with them into the classroom.
>
> ★ This same problem shows up in sports. Athletes who hold rigid, unrealistic expectations struggle with anxiety, burnout, and low motivation. That's why professional and Olympic teams use REBT to help athletes reframe their thinking under pressure.

- ★ In education, REBT has been adapted into REE—a research-backed, classroom-ready version of the same framework. REE gives teachers tools to help students replace irrational thinking with healthier beliefs about themselves, their school experience, and how to handle setbacks.
- ★ At the heart of REE is one core irrational belief: Demandingness—the idea that "things must go my way," or "others must treat me how I expect." This belief doesn't just cause emotional distress. It distorts how students interpret your behaviour and how they respond to your leadership. And once distorted beliefs spread, they become shared stories—what the group sees as "truth," even when it isn't grounded in fact.
- ★ As a teacher or coach, the more responsibility you carry, the more likely you are to become the target of these irrational expectations. That's why recognizing and addressing Demandingness is essential—not just for behaviour management, but for protecting your credibility.

Key Takeaway:

The problem isn't always what you're doing—it's how students are interpreting it through irrational beliefs like Demandingness. Unless those beliefs are addressed, your credibility will suffer, no matter how well you teach.

References

DiGiuseppe, R. *Distinctive features of cognitive behavioral therapy and REBT* [PowerPoint slides]. Albert Ellis Institute & St. John's University. https://www.numc.edu/wp-content/uploads/old/our-services/primary-care/Distinctive%20Features%20of%20cognitive%20behavioral%20therpay%20and%20REBT.pdf

Gonzalez, J. E., Nelson, R. J., Gutkin, T. B., Saunders, A., Galloway, A., & Shwery, C. S. (2004). Rational emotive therapy with children and adolescents: A meta-analysis. *Journal of Emotional and Behavioral Disorders, 12*(4), 222–235. https://doi.org/10.1177/10634266040120040301

Knaus, W. J. (1974). *Rational emotive education: A manual for elementary school teachers* [PDF]. Institute for Rational Living. Retrieved from REBT Network https://albertellis.org/rebt-cbt-therapies/rational-emotive-education-ree/

Trip, S., Vernon, A., & McMahon, J. (2007). Effectiveness of rational-emotive education: A quantitative meta-analytical study. *Journal of Cognitive and Behavioral Psychotherapies, 7*(1), 81–93.

Turner, M. J. (2016). Rational Emotive Behavior Therapy (REBT), irrational and rational beliefs, and the mental health of athletes. *Frontiers in Psychology, 7*, Article 502. https://doi.org/10.3389/fpsyg.2016.00502

12

The One Core Irrational Belief That Destroys Your Credibility

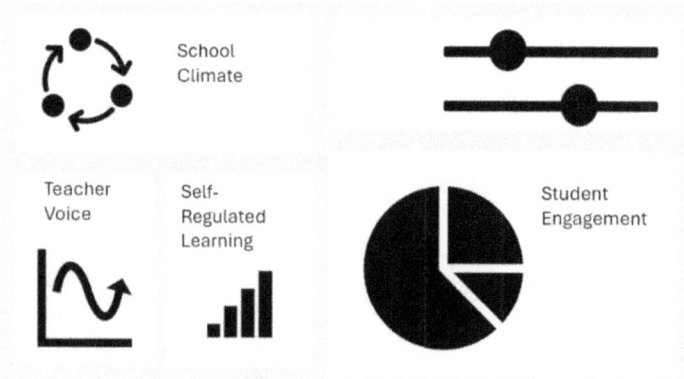

Figure 12.1 Data visualization highlighting the importance of assessing irrational thinking in schools.

Overview

In every classroom, there's one irrational belief that does more damage to your credibility than any other:

"If you don't meet my expectations perfectly, you're a bad teacher—and I don't need to respect you."

This belief falls under what Rational Emotive Education identifies as **Other's Rating**—the tendency to assign absolute, all-or-nothing judgements to

DOI: 10.4324/9781003644088-16

others based on isolated events or unmet demands. When students adopt this mindset, a late assignment, a misunderstood consequence, or even a neutral tone of voice can be interpreted not just as a mistake, but as proof that you're unfair, uncaring, and/or unworthy of respect. Your credibility isn't just questioned, it's attacked.

By addressing this core irrational belief directly, you don't just protect your credibility—you help students move beyond blame, defensiveness, and justification for defiance toward more rational, respectful interpretations of your behaviour.

Divergent Profile, Hidden Attributes… Meet the King and His Factory

You've already seen irrational beliefs in action back in Chapter 11. But what do they have to do with Classroom A, our history class made up of remedial math students?

Here's what we know:

Classroom A isn't just marked by divergent student perceptions, where their view of your credibility doesn't match your own or a trained observer's. It's also shaped by Hidden Attributes—but this time, in their negative form:

- Indifferent Orientation
- Ambivalent Orientation
- Past Negative Experiences
- Low Self-Regulated Learning
- High Perceived Teacher Burnout

Each of these factors negatively influences how students interpret your behaviour. But there's something else they all have in common: the simulated student narratives tied to these motivations all map directly onto Rational Emotive Behaviour Therapy's (REBT) core irrational belief, Demandingness, and its derivatives:

- Catastrophizing
- Low Frustration Tolerance
- Self/Other Rating

That's not a coincidence.

The King and his Factory of Troubles are alive and well in Classroom A. Let's take a closer look at how that plays out.

Classroom A: Where Irrational Thinking and Credibility Collide

	Demanding	Catastrophizing	Low Frustration Tolerance	Self/Others Rating
Ambivalent	"These rules are ridiculous. I don't have to listen to them." "Who does she think she is, telling us what to do?"	"This lesson is so boring. A good teacher would make it interesting."	"Why should I bother putting in effort when she doesn't even know what she's doing?"	"Sometimes she's nice, but other times it's like she doesn't even see us".
Indifferent	"Why should I put in any effort when she clearly doesn't care?"	"This class is so boring, and she's so useless as a teacher."	"Even if I tried, I'd probably fail."	"School is a joke. None of this matters anyway."
Negative Past Experience	"Rules are so unfair as usual."	"I'm going to fail again, no matter what she does."	"Nothing ever changes. She sets unrealistic expectations."	"No matter who the teacher is, I can't trust any of them."
High Burnout Perception	"She is so 'unfair.' Everyone should complain."	"Once she loses control again, it'll be clear she's incompetent."	"She always looks tired and annoyed. Just being in her class stresses me out.	"She never smiles-she hates this job." "She's useless actually." –
Low Self-Regulated Learning	"I can't trust her to be fair."	"She keeps saying I'll get it, but I'm completely lost." -	"Her extra help just makes me feel more stupid."	"She doesn't care about me."

Figure 12.2 Table categorizing simulated student narratives within demandingness and its derivatives.

> **Quick Note**
> Multiple demands can stack, intensifying resistance and undermining instruction. When these demands are shared and reinforced by peers, teacher credibility can erode fast.

Sound Familiar? How Hidden Motivations Fuel Irrational Beliefs

Notice how the four irrational beliefs seem almost to perfectly echo the student narratives we explored earlier? Both reflect the same core issue: students' negative perceptions of your credible teaching or coaching aren't based on what's actually happening in the classroom, on the ice or on the field,—they're shaped by internal psychological motivations like trait orientation, past experience, perceived burnout, low self-regulated learning, and social contagion. It's as if the King and the Factory work hand-in-hand with student motivation.

This is exactly why Rational Emotive Education (REE)—along with Social Inoculation strategies in the Credibility Codebook—provides a powerful way to name, understand, and respond to distorted student inferences, perceptions, and interpretations.

Let's take a closer look at a classroom scenario where Irrational Beliefs play out, almost to the exact tune of hidden attributes:

One Core Irrational Belief That Destroys Your Teacher Credibility

Have you noticed the second pattern yet? (If not, go back and take a look—I bolded key statements in the earlier irrational scenarios. There's a reason they stand out.)

This core irrational belief appears in various scenarios, such as the "Rough Morning" and "Irrational Locker Room." It hides in the Self/Other Ratings derivative, specifically the **Others Rating**. Unlike catastrophizing and low frustration tolerance, this belief actively fuels retaliation:

- "People like her make this job impossible. She should be replaced."
- "This district is broken. Tear out the incompetence."
- "You're clearly clueless and don't deserve to coach this team."
- "If you won't listen, you don't deserve my respect."

The Core Irrational Belief

Other people (like my teacher) must treat me fairly, kindly, and competently at all times—or else they are bad and deserve to be punished.

Derivatives & Drama: Inside the Irrational Classroom

ACTIVATING EVENT Before class starts, a student leaves their assigned seat to sit with friends. When asked to return, they refuse, calling it unfair and undeserved. Several classmates support the defiance.

 **DEMANDS**　　 **DERIVATIVES**

I MUST

 **AND IF I DON'T**

I **must** never be treated unfairly, and I must be respected at all times.

CAT- If I can't even sit with my friends, what's the point of coming?

LFT- This is too much; I'm done with this teacher.

Self Rating- Only bad students get treated this way, I must be a bad student."

MY CLASSMATES MUST

 **AND IF THEY DON'T**

My friends **must** support me and see how unfair this is.

CAT- We're all standing up and it still doesn't matter; this class is useless!

LFT- This is so unfair, I'm over it. Other people sit wherever they want, and I can't take it anymore.

Others Rating- "My classmates are awful if they don't see how unfair this is. If so, they don't deserve my friendship."

YOU MUST

 **AND IF YOU DON'T**

You **must** treat me like I matter and let me make my own choices. The school has got to stop controlling everything.

CAT- This teacher is just here to control me; I can't learn in a place like this. The school doesn't care about us, it's all about power.

LFT- I can't keep putting up with this kind of treatment. It's humiliating in front of my friends over and over again.

Others Rating-. If you won't even listen, you don't deserve my respect. She's just another puppet of the school.*

Figure 12.3 Infographic showing classroom demandingness and derivatives—catastrophizing, low frustration tolerance, and other rating.

Impact on Teacher Credibility

The sub-beliefs help us see just how deeply this core irrational belief can damage teacher credibility. Adapted from Will Ross's summary of the Three Major Musts (REBT Network, n.d.), I've applied these distortions directly to how students may view a teacher:

"If the teacher acts unfairly, incompetently, or unwisely, they're a worthless idiot. They should be ashamed. They shouldn't expect anything good. If they criticize me unjustly, they're no good—and don't deserve respect, success, or even basic cooperation."

When students hold this belief, any perceived failure by the teacher to meet expectations justifies defiant behaviour. This defiance can manifest as:

- Refusal to comply: "I don't have to listen to you."
- Lack of respect: "You don't deserve my respect."
- Negative judgements: "You don't care. You're untrustworthy. You're incompetent."
- Openly challenging the teacher
- Undermine them
- Withdraw cooperation
- Rally peers
- Retaliation or sabotage

Students' Internal Logic Based on Core Irrational Belief II

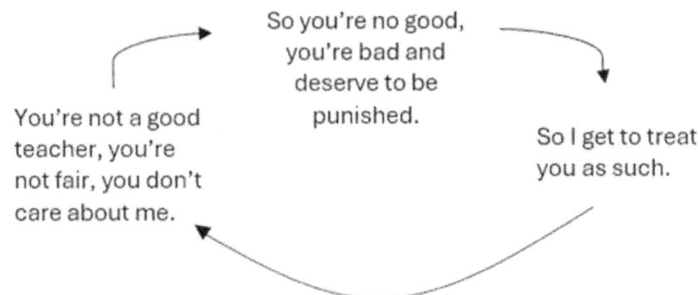

Figure 12.4 Illustration showing the internal logic chain of Core Irrational Belief II in students.

REBT Perspective

- Irrational Belief: Drives emotional fallout (anger, disgust, contempt).
- Justification: "Because you didn't meet my demand, you're not worthy of your role, my respect, or good treatment."
- Behaviour: Condemnation and Retaliation: Become "earned" in the eyes of the student.

It's as if the King and the Factory put together the perfect anti-teacher credibility machine—Core Irrational Belief II

> **Summary**
> ★ This belief is different because it doesn't just explain behaviour—it justifies retaliation.
> ★ It operates through a moral loop: unmet demand → condemnation → retaliation.
> ★ Students think the teacher isn't credible—and they act on that belief in ways that make the situation worse.
> ★ It spreads, turning isolated resentment into collective resistance.

From Belief to Behaviour: What Sets It Off?

Core Irrational Belief II doesn't come out of nowhere; it's often triggered by everyday events in the classroom. These activating events, a grade, a correction, classroom management decision—are all common classroom events.

But when filtered through an irrational belief like *"You must always treat me fairly, kindly, and competently,"* even small moments can feel like major issues of injustice. That's when distorted emotional begins—and defiance becomes justified.

Let's look at how common classroom events can activate this belief and spark the credibility-damaging behaviour that follows.

Core Irrational Belief II and Classroom Activating Events

Here are a few simple activating events that could trigger the irrational belief that a teacher must always treat students fairly and considerately, leading to defiance:

1. **Unfair Grading**: A student receives a grade they perceive as unfair or lower than expected. This can lead to feelings of resentment and the belief that you are not treating them fairly, justifying defiance.
2. **Classroom Discipline**: You discipline a student for behaviour they believe was not disruptive or deserving of punishment. The student may feel unjustly targeted and respond with defiance.
3. **Lack of Attention**: A student feels ignored or overlooked when they raise their hand or seek help. This can lead to the belief

that you're not considerate of their needs, prompting defiant behaviour.
4. **Perceived Favouritism**: A student perceives that you're favouring other students, giving them more attention or better opportunities. This can lead to feelings of unfair treatment and justify defiance.

These are just a few activating events that can lead to emotional responses like anger, frustration, or resentment—and to the irrational belief that defiance is justified. Emotional consequences trigger behavioural ones—and with this core irrational belief specifically, those behaviours often take the form of defiance or retaliation. These actions are supported by the student's internal logic. That's their cognitive environment—and it's where their inference-making is coming from.

How Irrational Beliefs Distort Credibility and Justify Defiance

Now that we've explored how common classroom moments—like grading, discipline, or perceived favouritism—can function as **activating events**, it's important to ask: *How do students interpret these events?*

When students operate under **Core Irrational Belief II**—that others *must* always treat them fairly, kindly, and competently—these activating events are often misread as personal violations. The result? Students begin to justify defiance by interpreting the teacher's behaviour as uncaring, incompetent, or untrustworthy.

The next table illustrates exactly how this irrational belief plays out in classrooms: how it distorts teacher credibility across all domains—**Care, Competence, and Trustworthiness**—and fuels defiant behaviour that feels rational to the student.

> **Quick Note**
> There are many examples here—maybe more than necessary. But I've experienced every one of them, consistently, in classrooms like Classroom A. These aren't random behaviours—they're driven by irrational beliefs that give students a logic for defiance. In my 25+ years of teaching, I've seen how these reactions often come in waves—and they can overwhelm even strong teachers.
> You don't need to read every row in one sitting, rather use this as a reference or scan for scenarios that feel familiar. Think of this table as a "pattern map" of how irrational beliefs can distort perception and damage teacher credibility.

Core Irrational Belief Applied to Teacher Credibility Perception: Classroom Impact

This table is an original educational synthesis, applying Core Irrational Belief II and derivative concepts from REBT (Ellis, 1994) to classroom scenarios and teacher credibility perceptions:

Student Irrational Belief	Classroom Interpretation	Credibility Consequence	Credibility Domain Affected	Justified Defiance Response
You must be nice and fair to me at all times.	Misinterprets feedback or discipline as personal attack	Sees teacher as uncaring	Caring	Talks back, ignores instruction, claims victimhood
You must teach in a way I enjoy or prefer.	Rejects legitimate instruction if it's not entertaining	Sees teacher as incompetent	Competence	Disengages, mocks lesson, undermines instruction
You must agree with me or validate my perspective.	Feels slighted when challenged or corrected	Sees teacher as untrustworthy	Trustworthiness	Accuses teacher of bias, refuses to listen
If you don't meet my expectations, you're a bad teacher.	I am not listening to anything you say.	Credibility collapses	All domains	Rallies peers, spreads rumors, refuses cooperation
You must never embarrass me or call me out.	Interprets gentle correction as humiliation	Sees teacher as hostile	Caring	Retaliates publicly, exaggerates harm, avoids accountability
You must always let me express myself without limits.	Reacts poorly to classroom structure or norms	Sees teacher as controlling	Trustworthiness	Interrupts, refuses turn-taking, tests limits
You must let me redo work or get exceptions.	Sees consistency as inflexibility	Sees teacher as unsupportive	Caring / Competence	Argues, pressures for special treatment, blames unfairness
You must make sure I never feel uncomfortable.	Experiences cognitive challenge as emotional harm	Sees teacher as unsafe	Caring	Complains, withdraws, weaponizes discomfort

Figure 12.5 Table applying Core Irrational Belief II to teacher credibility with simulated student beliefs, interpretations, affected domains, and defiance responses.

You must always believe my version of the story.	Takes neutrality as betrayal	Sees teacher as biased	**Trustworthiness**	Refuses resolution, discredits teacher to others
You must never side with other students against me.	Sees group correction as favoritism	Sees teacher as playing favorites	**Trustworthiness**	Accuses teacher of exclusion, escalates conflict
You must prioritize my needs over rules.	Rejects structure and consequences	Sees teacher as authoritarian	**Caring / Trustworthiness**	Defies rules, justifies noncompliance
You must always validate my emotions.	Sees neutral feedback as invalidation	Sees teacher as cold	**Caring**	Labels teacher dismissive, stops engaging emotionally
You must always explain things clearly the first time.	Expects perfect clarity without questions or repetition	Sees teacher as ineffective	**Competence**	Dismisses content, blames teacher for confusion
You must never make a mistake when grading.	Takes minor grading errors as proof of incompetence	Sees teacher as careless	**Competence**	Challenges grades, spreads doubt about teacher ability
You must give me high marks if I tried hard.	Confuses effort with outcome-based grading	Sees teacher as unfair or discouraging	**Competence**	Rejects feedback, disengages from future assessments
You must accept my explanation for missing work or doing poorly.	Sees accountability as lack of understanding	Sees teacher as unsupportive or unreasonable	**Competence / Caring**	Resents grade, stops seeking help

Figure 12.6 Continuation of Table 12.5.

You must praise my work publicly like others.	Feels ignored if not singled out for praise	Sees teacher as playing favorites or ignoring effort	**Competence / Trustworthiness**	Withdraws participation, challenges fairness of recognition
You must always give the same amount of help to every student.	Sees tailored instruction or support as favoritism	Sees teacher as inconsistent or biased	**Competence / Trustworthiness**	Complains of unfairness, disengages from support
You must teach the way I learn best.	Rejects different instructional methods or formats	Sees teacher as ineffective or unskilled	**Competence**	Refuses to adapt, blames teacher for poor performance
You must never say 'I don't know' or hesitate.	Views uncertainty as lack of knowledge	Sees teacher as unqualified	**Competence**	Mocks or doubts teacher authority
You must make sure assessments are always easy and predictable.	Interprets challenge as unfairness or trickery	Sees teacher as setting them up to fail	**Competence / Trustworthiness**	Avoids effort, complains about difficulty, disengages
You must never mark me wrong for interpretation or creativity.	Believes personal expression always warrants high marks	Sees teacher as stifling or narrow-minded	**Competence / Caring**	Rejects feedback, claims bias or rigidity
You must give full marks if I followed the instructions.	Equates procedural compliance with quality	Sees teacher as penalizing unfairly	**Competence**	Argues over grades, resists revision or deeper learning

Figure 12.7 Continuation of Table 12.5.

Core Irrational Belief II Doesn't Just Shape Perception—It Shapes Communication

In Classroom A, irrational thinking leads **to uncooperative communication**: students work against their teacher, not with them. Here's how these beliefs translate into two forms of communicative behaviour—**informatively** and **materially** uncooperative communication:

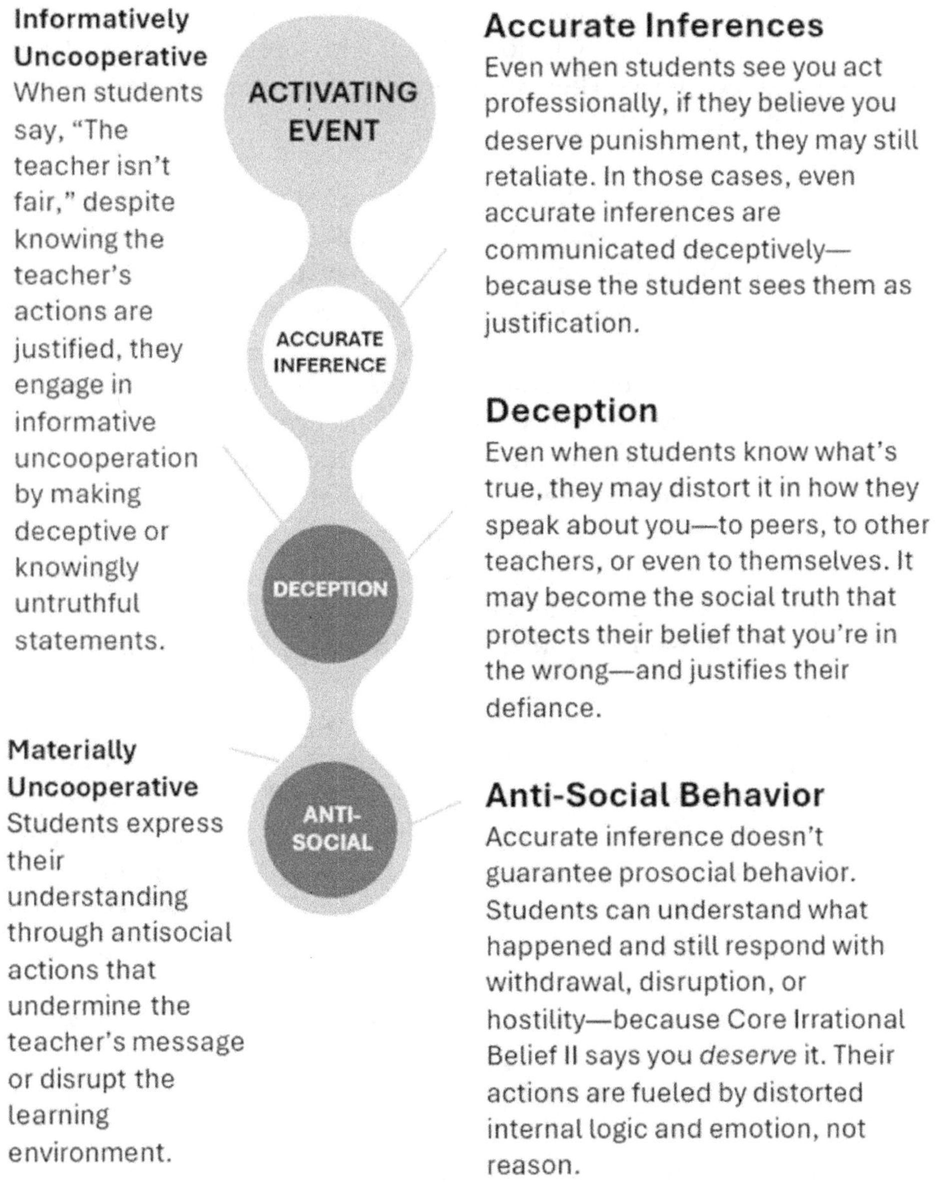
Informatively Uncooperative
When students say, "The teacher isn't fair," despite knowing the teacher's actions are justified, they engage in informative uncooperation by making deceptive or knowingly untruthful statements.
Materially Uncooperative
Students express their understanding through antisocial actions that undermine the teacher's message or disrupt the learning environment.
ACTIVATING EVENT
ACCURATE INFERENCE
DECEPTION
ANTI-SOCIAL
Accurate Inferences
Even when students see you act professionally, if they believe you deserve punishment, they may still retaliate. In those cases, even accurate inferences are communicated deceptively—because the student sees them as justification.
Deception
Even when students know what's true, they may distort it in how they speak about you—to peers, to other teachers, or even to themselves. It may become the social truth that protects their belief that you're in the wrong—and justifies their defiance.
Anti-Social Behavior
Accurate inference doesn't guarantee prosocial behavior. Students can understand what happened and still respond with withdrawal, disruption, or hostility—because Core Irrational Belief II says you *deserve* it. Their actions are fueled by distorted internal logic and emotion, not reason.

Figure 12.8 Infographic showing Core Irrational Belief II's impact on communicative cooperation through informative and material uncooperation.

Why Stress Dominates in Classroom A

One thing is clear: Classroom A produces a lot of stress—for your students, and for you.

I want you to think about this: the *Other Rating* that students apply to **you**, and all the trouble it causes. Well, when it's not directed at you, it's almost always directed **from one student to another**. You see where I'm going with this.

If a student believes that *others must treat me the right way—or they're bad and deserve punishment*, that logic doesn't stop with authority figures. It turns inward, toward their peers. They can apply a logic to retaliation and doing so treat each other badly, unfairly, even aggressively—because, in their minds, they're justified.

And when that happens, you get pulled in. You're constantly managing peer conflict, trying to keep the peace, and holding the emotional weight of everyone's irrational expectations. It's exhausting—for them, and for you. That's what makes this belief system so stressful when it dominates a classroom.

In a divergent Classroom A profile—where many students operate under irrational beliefs—disruptive, uncooperative, and even antisocial behaviours are also common. **But these behaviours aren't the result of poor teaching. The real issue lies in how students interpret what's happening.**

As REBT reminds us, it's not the events themselves that cause stress—it's the beliefs students attach to them. Rigid thoughts like "The teacher doesn't care," or "They should always let me do what I want" fuel emotional over-reactions: anxiety, frustration, anger, and ultimately, fight, flight, freeze, or dissociate.

In junior high, things can take a step for the worst, and Classroom A can become progressively more challenging. Dr. Stuart Shanker (2016) explains that adolescents experience a "dramatically increased sensitivity to stress," particularly in social situations. They often misinterpret neutral facial expressions or tone of voice as threatening, showing a "heightened bias for perceiving signals as negative—even when they're not." This means that even in the absence of dominant irrational beliefs, the classroom can still feel like a stressful environment for many students.

And when hidden attributes like past negative experiences, low self-regulated learning, and social contagion are in play, irrational beliefs can take over—creating a climate of persistent stress and distorted perceptions of your credibility.

That's where REBT and REE come in. These tools help us make sense of student behaviour—and serve as codes to help students interpret your behaviour, and each other's, more accurately. They guide both teachers and students in identifying and challenging irrational beliefs, replacing rigid "musts" with flexible preferences, and emotional reactivity with thoughtful reflection. The result? Less conflict and emotional drama—and more perceived care, trust, and cooperation.

Data-Informed Decision-Making: How Widespread Are the King and the Factory?

As we transition to the next two chapters—focused on implementing REE in your classroom—it's important to understand that irrational beliefs rarely form in isolation. Students don't leave their beliefs at the classroom door. Demandingness and its derivatives often follow them from one class to the next, from teacher to teacher, shaping how they interpret events throughout the school day.

So how common is Classroom A? Is it the exception—or the norm?

The more influence the King and the Factory have across a school's classrooms, the more difficult it becomes for any individual teacher to help students interpret intentions and behaviours accurately. This makes school-wide understanding and action critical.

That's why data matters.

Schools need consistent, meaningful data to help infer the presence of irrational student thinking patterns. Tools like student voice surveys, engagement metrics, school climate data, and even anecdotal reports can reveal patterns of misinterpretation, distrust, or uncooperative behaviour rooted in irrational beliefs.

When interpreted thoughtfully, this data can guide both classroom practice and school-wide initiatives. It can support strategies that promote accurate student inference-making, foster rational belief systems, and create a culture where teacher behaviour is understood—not distorted.

But here's the deeper risk: when irrational beliefs dominate, it's not just your credibility as a teacher that's affected. The school's credibility is on the line, too.

Students begin to interpret the school's rules, expectations, and even supportive structures through the same distorted lens. They may believe, "This school doesn't care," or "Everything here is against me." These interpretations aren't based on the actual policies or efforts of school staff—they're driven by irrational demands, emotional reasoning, and peer-reinforced narratives.

172 ◆ The Teacher Credibility Codebook

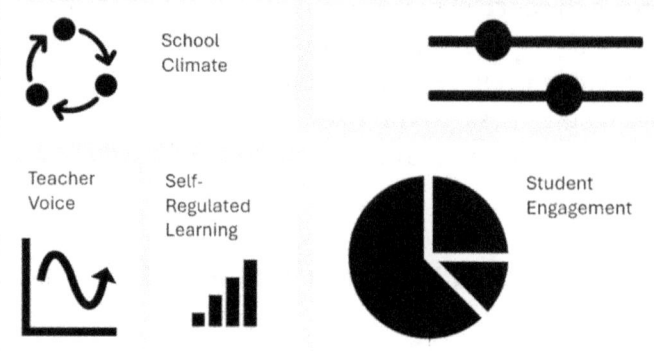

Figure 12.9 Data visualization showing the importance of data-informed decision-making to detect school-wide irrational thinking.

When this happens, the entire school environment can start to feel uncaring, and incompetent to students. Their cognitive environment no longer reflects the actual culture or values of the school—it reflects their unmet demands, emotional overreactions, and the influence of social contagion.

This distortion doesn't just affect students. It can take a real toll on teachers' emotional and psychological wellbeing—and erode their sense of collective efficacy.

That's why addressing irrational beliefs isn't just a classroom strategy—it's a school culture strategy. A rational-thinking school fosters shared credibility, reduces conflict, and creates an environment where students can make accurate inferences—not just about their teachers, but about learning itself.

> **Quick Note: Don't Forget the Hallway**
>
> Unstructured time—recess, lunch, the bus, the hallway—can quietly undo a lot of the work you're doing in the classroom. If students feel like no one's paying attention, that it's unsafe, unfair, or just plain boring, they start to form beliefs like "This school doesn't care" or "They should do more for us." And if those beliefs aren't corrected, they don't stay in the hallway; they walk into the classroom.
>
> Although those feelings might sound small because they're not really accurate, they can turn into big feelings—and those feelings show up in your classroom. That's why it matters how the school shows it cares, even when class isn't in session.

Chapter Summary

★ One of the most damaging irrational beliefs students hold **is Core Irrational Belief II,** the habit of making all-or-nothing judgements about others based on isolated moments. In this mindset, a late mark or neutral tone isn't just a mistake, it becomes "proof" that you're unfair or unworthy of respect. Your credibility isn't just doubted—it's attacked.

★ Classroom A is shaped not just by distorted perceptions, but by negative hidden attributes like past negative experiences, low self-regulated learning, and perceived teacher burnout. These student influences distort how they interpret your behaviour—and all tie back to a core irrational belief: Demandingness, along with its derivatives like Catastrophizing, Low Frustration Tolerance, and Self/Other Rating.

★ The result? Uncooperative communication. Students begin working against you, not with you. And it doesn't stop there: the same harsh judgements they place on teachers are often turned towards each other—leading to a logic of justification for pre-emptive attack, retaliation, peer conflict, and damages relationships.

★ Understanding these belief patterns helps you see the real source of resistance—not in your behaviour, but in how your actions are filtered through irrational thinking.

 Key Takeaway:

When students believe others must always treat them fairly—or else—they judge harshly, react defensively, and justify retaliation. This irrational mindset damages credibility, communication, and peer relationships across the entire classroom.

References

DiGiuseppe, R. *Distinctive features of cognitive behavioral therapy and REBT* [PowerPoint slides]. Albert Ellis Institute & St. John's University. https://www.numc.edu/wp-content/uploads/old/our-services/primary-care/Distinctive%20Features%20of%20cognitive%20behavioral%20therpay%20and%20REBT.pdf

Shanker, S., & Barker, T. (2016). *Self-Reg: How to help your child (and you) break the stress cycle and successfully engage with life.* Penguin Canada.

Will, Ross. (n.d.). Three Major Musts (REBT Network).

13

How Rational Thinking Transforms Your Classroom

Figure 13.1 Illustration: Removing demandingness and derivatives in the classroom.

Overview

Before we dig into how to apply REE, let's take a moment to imagine a classroom not shaped by irrational beliefs, especially Core Irrational Belief II, with its powerful "Other-Blaming" derivative. What does it look like when that belief isn't driving student behaviour?

Let's step into **Classroom B**, our history class where rational thinking supports a healthy learning environment—and see what it's like to teach there.

DOI: 10.4324/9781003644088-17

In this chapter, you'll observe how rational beliefs lead to emotional regulation and positive behaviour, create a noticeable shift in classroom dynamics. Students are more open to feedback, take greater ownership over their behaviour, and no longer default to blaming you when they feel frustrated or challenged.

You'll explore:

- How replacing irrational thinking improves academic risk-taking, emotional resilience, and student–teacher relationships

This chapter provides a model for what's possible when irrational thinking is replaced, not just with logic, but with a mindset of fairness, flexibility, and emotional growth. It sets the stage for Chapter 14, where you'll learn exactly how to foster this shift using REE in your classroom.

What Makes a Classroom a Rational Place to Learn and Work?

Let's flip the script.

In a classroom where most students interpret your behaviour—and their classmates' actions—through **rational beliefs**, everything changes. When your credibility is accurately decoded and Rational Emotive Behaviour Therapy (REBT) principles are at play, the emotional climate is more stable, and learning thrives.

Instead of...	We See...
Demandingness "I must succeed."	**Preference** Students stay calm when things don't go their way. They don't treat every challenge as a crisis.
Catastrophizing "This is awful—it's all ruined."	**Anti-Awfulizing** Students keep setbacks in perspective. They handle challenges without spiraling.
Low Frustration Tolerance "I can't deal with this."	**High Frustration Tolerance** Students tolerate discomfort, stay engaged, and bounce back from setbacks.
Self/Other Rating "I'm a failure" / "My teacher is terrible"	**Acceptance** They handle feedback well. They stay motivated and treat themselves and others with respect.

Figure 13.2 Table comparing demandingness and its derivatives with rational alternatives in a classroom context.

That's what it looks like in practice. Using REBT and REE as our model, the rational-thinking classroom has students who interpret activating events like this:

Now we have a clear example of rational thinking in action: History Classroom B—our Algebra group. These students perceive your credibility as high—and their perceptions align with both your own sense of effectiveness and that of a trained observer. So, what makes this class tick?

The answer lies in decoding and inference-making: in Classroom B, irrational beliefs have been replaced with rational ones.

How do we know? Because this classroom is shaped by four key *Hidden Attributes*—underlying student motivations that support rational interpretations and foster positive credibility:

1. **Upward-Mobile Orientation**
2. **Positive Past Classroom Experiences**
3. **High Self-Regulated Learning**
4. **Low Perceived Teacher Burnout**

We've also collected simulated student narratives based on these attributes. Now let's map those onto the REBT framework: what does a rational classroom mindset actually *look* like?

This isn't a rough morning—or an irrational hockey team.

This is Classroom B, where thinking patterns work *with* you, not *against* you:

These rational beliefs don't just shape perceptions—they shape behaviour.

In Classroom B, rational thinking leads to **cooperative communication**: students work with their teacher, not against them. Here's how these beliefs translate into two forms of positive classroom behaviour—**informative** and **material** cooperation:

Without the King or the Factory of Troubles at work, students in Classroom B are more likely to behave in ways that sustain a healthy, transparent, and supportive classroom culture.

Students with rational beliefs—Preference, Anti-Awfulizing, High Frustration Tolerance, and Self/Other Acceptance—are far more likely to engage in both informative and material cooperation. These internal beliefs don't stay internal; they show up in real social behaviours that reinforce teacher credibility and contribute to a positive classroom climate. They can take academic risks, and feel safe if they fall down.

Classroom B: Where Rational Thinking and Credibility Connect

	Preference	Anti-Awfulizing	HFT	Self/Other Acceptance
Upward Mobile	"This group project is huge, but I'm ready to put in the effort. I'm determined to get it done."	"Balancing this workload is tough, but it's teaching me valuable skills like prioritization and perseverance."	"Everyone's opinion matters in this class. That makes it easier to speak up."	"She treats everyone equally and holds us to the same standards. We feel respected."
Positive Past Experience	"Like all the teachers I've had, she sets high but achievable expectations."	"If something goes wrong, teachers at this school understand and handle it fairly—she always does."	"It feels like my ideas matter here, just like in my last class."	"I know she believes in me—it's the same feeling I've had with other good teachers."
Low Burnout Perception	"Strictness means my teacher wants us to learn."	"If I need help, I know she'll follow through—she doesn't just say it, she means it."	"We're all working together to make this a good class."	"She really listens—like she actually wants to know how we're doing."
High Self-Regulated Learning	"I respect the teacher's high expectations because they help me grow."	"My teacher's feedback helps me improve—her constructive criticism is a tool for growth rather than judgment."	"She gives me space to figure things out, but she's there when I need her."	"If I put in the effort, my teacher will recognize it. She values my hard work."

These rational belief types come from Rational Emotive Behavior Therapy (REBT), originally developed by psychologist Albert Ellis.

Figure 13.3 Table categorizing simulated student narratives within preferences and rational thinking that promote teacher credibility.

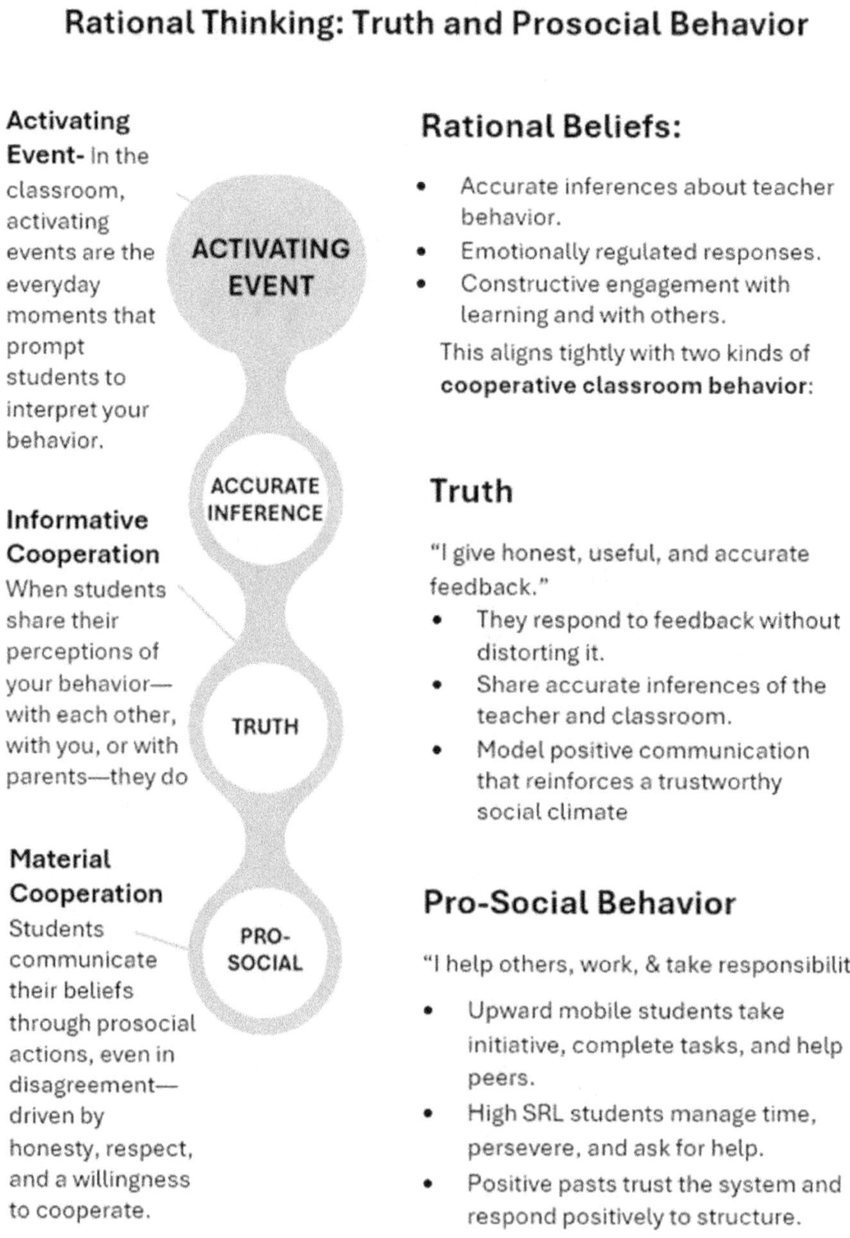

Rational Thinking: Truth and Prosocial Behavior

Activating Event- In the classroom, activating events are the everyday moments that prompt students to interpret your behavior.

Informative Cooperation When students share their perceptions of your behavior—with each other, with you, or with parents—they do

Material Cooperation Students communicate their beliefs through prosocial actions, even in disagreement—driven by honesty, respect, and a willingness to cooperate.

ACTIVATING EVENT

ACCURATE INFERENCE

TRUTH

PRO-SOCIAL

Rational Beliefs:

- Accurate inferences about teacher behavior.
- Emotionally regulated responses.
- Constructive engagement with learning and with others.

This aligns tightly with two kinds of **cooperative classroom behavior:**

Truth

"I give honest, useful, and accurate feedback."

- They respond to feedback without distorting it.
- Share accurate inferences of the teacher and classroom.
- Model positive communication that reinforces a trustworthy social climate

Pro-Social Behavior

"I help others, work, & take responsibility."

- Upward mobile students take initiative, complete tasks, and help peers.
- High SRL students manage time, persevere, and ask for help.
- Positive pasts trust the system and respond positively to structure.

Figure 13.4 Infographic illustrating rational thinking, truth, and prosocial behaviour in the classroom.

Stress Level

In a rational-thinking classroom like Classroom B, stress still exists—but it's regulated, not dominant. Students are more likely to self-regulate than burn out. Both students and teachers are less likely to operate in "survival mode."

Their brains are online—not hijacked by stress. Instead of reacting with fight, flight, or freeze, they stay grounded, reflect, and respond.

That's what allows learning—and credibility—to thrive.

Now, let's take a look at how REBT and REE can provide the codes that lead to more classrooms like Classroom B...

Chapter Review

- ★ When students replace irrational beliefs with rational ones, everything begins to shift. They become more open to feedback, take responsibility for their actions, and stop blaming the teacher when things don't go their way.
- ★ Rational thinking strengthens emotional regulation and encourages positive risk-taking. It also transforms student–teacher relationships—from conflict to cooperation.
- ★ Students who adopt rational beliefs like Preference over Demands, High Frustration Tolerance, and Self/Other Acceptance show this in their behaviour. They're more likely to Share information constructively (informative cooperation). They also Participate willingly in classroom routines (material cooperation).
- ★ In classrooms like **Classroom B**, stress doesn't disappear—but students manage it. Instead of reacting impulsively, they stay grounded and respond thoughtfully. This creates a healthier environment for both teaching and learning.

 Key Takeaway:

Rational student thinking leads to emotional regulation, prosocial behaviour, and stronger teacher–student relationships—shifting the classroom from survival mode to a space of cooperation and growth.

14

Code 1
Replacing Irrational Beliefs with Rational Ones

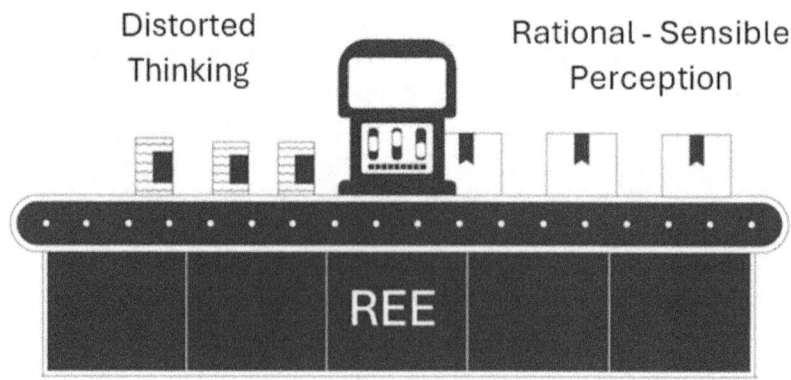

Figure 14.1 Illustration showing how REE replaces distorted thinking with rational perception.

Overview

Now that you've seen how rational thinking transforms a classroom, it's time to apply it—systematically, intentionally, and in ways students can use. **Code 1** gives you the tools to do just that.

Built on the principles of Rational Emotive Education (REE), Code 1 walks you through how to help students **recognize**, **challenge**, and **replace** irrational beliefs that undermine your credibility and sabotage their learning. These beliefs—especially those tied to blaming others, catastrophizing,

DOI: 10.4324/9781003644088-18

or low frustration tolerance (LFT)—can be powerful. But they're also teachable.

In this chapter, you'll learn:

- How to use the **ABCDE model** (Activating Event, Belief, Consequence, Disputation, Effect) to coach students through distorted thinking
- Why simply correcting behaviour isn't enough—and how changing beliefs changes behaviour
- How to facilitate brief, targeted discussions that move students from emotional reactivity to rational ownership
- Real classroom examples showing what Code 1 looks like in practice

There are many evidence-based models, modules, and lesson plans that implement Rational Emotive Behaviour Therapy (REBT) and REE in school settings. What I'm offering here is a teacher-adapted version of REE—designed for real classroom scenarios where irrational thinking undermines teacher credibility. This version draws on the foundational work of Dr. William Knaus and Dr. Raymond DiGiuseppe, while integrating practical strategies for everyday teaching. I'll also include supplemental resources you can explore for further reading and implementation at www.teachercredibilitycodebook.com.

A meta-analysis of multiple studies found that REE has a powerful impact on reducing irrational beliefs and dysfunctional behaviours. It also improves inference-making and emotional regulation, supporting its use as a viable approach in classrooms.
—Trip, S., Vernon, A., & McMahon, J. (2007). *Effectiveness of rational-emotive education: A quantitative meta-analytical study.*

"Can be self-taught without formal training or exposure."
"Even using general classroom problems as practice sessions for developing problem-solving skills."
—Dr. W. Knaus (1974), *Rational Emotive Education*, REBT Network.

"Non-mental health professionals produced REBT effects of greater magnitude than their mental health counterparts."
—Gonzalez, J. E., Nelson, J. R., Gutkin, T. B., Saunders, A., Galloway, A., & Shwery, C. S. (2004). *Rational Emotive Therapy with Children and Adolescents: A Meta-Analysis.*

182 ◆ The Teacher Credibility Codebook

Classroom A: Irrational Thinking and Distorted Perceptions of Teacher Credibility

This is your history class, made up of remedial math students. Their perception of your teacher credibility is significantly negative. Take a look at their caring scores, for instance. Since caring is the foundation of teacher credibility, this is deeply concerning:

Now think back to the seating incident from the previous chapter. After multiple rational and respectful prompts, you professionally addressed the disruption and eventually sent two students to reflection. In most classrooms, students would recognize these as the actions of a competent teacher who cares about maintaining a productive learning environment. And in your other classes, that's exactly what happened—students supported you.

But not here.

In Classroom A, students aren't evaluating your actions through a rational lens—they're reacting through the filter of irrational beliefs. Unless those beliefs—and the hidden attributes driving them—are addressed directly,

Figure 14.2 Illustration showing negative credibility balance in Classroom A (remedial math), contrasting strong negative perceptions with strong positive perceptions.

your credibility will continue to erode. Why? Because the real issue isn't your classroom management. It's the irrational thinking beneath the surface. That's the source.

The activating event, the one that led to the defiance, will return. Maybe not in the same form, maybe it'll escalate, but one thing is certain: the distorted perceptions will remain. Why? Because these students are operating in a separate cognitive environment, one that doesn't decode your actions rationally.

Instead, their interpretations are filtered through rigid demands. And when those demands aren't met, they spiral into catastrophizing, LFT, and self/other rating. The result? They believe *you* don't understand, *you* don't care, or *you* aren't competent.

The King and the Factory Are Hard at Work in Your Class

That's why you need a code, a shared framework to realign their cognitive environment with yours. A code that helps students think more rationally about you, the classroom, the school, and themselves.

The Scout Mindset, the Spectrum, and Being Kind First

Before we go any further, there are four critical conditions to establish before implementing the Code.

Start Before the Activating Event

Let's be clear: the ideal time to begin using the Code is not during an activating event. In fact, trying to implement REE in the heat of conflict often backfires—especially in Classroom A. Why? Because until your cognitive environments begin to align, activating events primarily harm your credibility. And, emotions are high, behaviours negative and resistance strong.

That doesn't mean it's useless to try. It can still be a powerful learning opportunity. But the best time to introduce the Code is outside the heat of conflict—when students are more open to reflection, and you're not seen as reacting to their behaviour.

Be Kind First

Why kindness? Because activating events, through the lens of irrational thinking, often lead students to feel hurt, angry, or misunderstood—emotions that drive defiance, deception, and disruption.

To engage the students farthest from you on the credibility spectrum—the ones whose views are most opposed to yours—you need them to feel safe

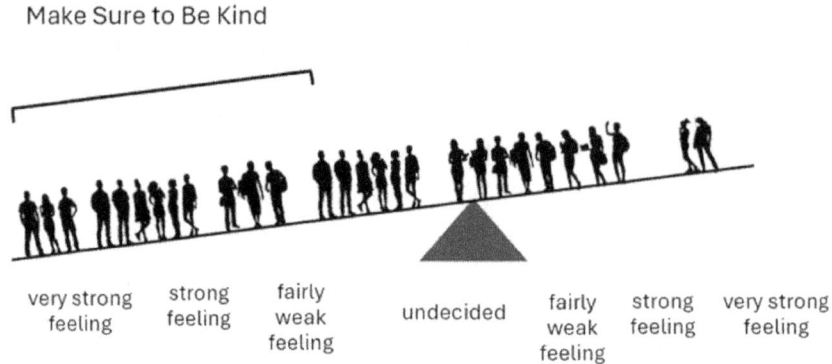

Figure 14.3 Illustration emphasizing kindness and patience for students with strong negative credibility perceptions.

using their voice. That means creating a classroom environment where your own emotions don't lead to reactivity, but to kindness, patience, and active listening.

Remember: your students are watching how you treat others just as much as how you treat them. Even if they're thinking irrationally, when they see you being patient, open, and respectful to their peers, especially in moments of tension, a seed of credibility is planted. This is a great time to show them you are listening, and you understand their perspective. They will, on their own, challenge the irrationality of their thinking and beliefs in time. So, support them now with acceptance of their irrational beliefs.

The Spectrum

Credibility doesn't shift overnight. You don't need to "win" every student over in a single conversation. Your goal is to move students' thinking incrementally, to shift their perception one rational step at a time.

Progress means that a student who once viewed you as uncaring might now see you as possibly fair. That's enough. Because when one student shifts, others notice, and many of your students are already somewhere in the middle of the spectrum. Their quiet adjustments are just as meaningful. Their justification for retaliation and defiance, because your bad, can start to shift.

Scout Mindset

To make this work, you must adopt a Scout Mindset. That means approaching student beliefs with curiosity, not defensiveness—and being willing to explore their thinking, even when it challenges you. It's the opportunity to build bridges for the future, when emotions most likely come into play.

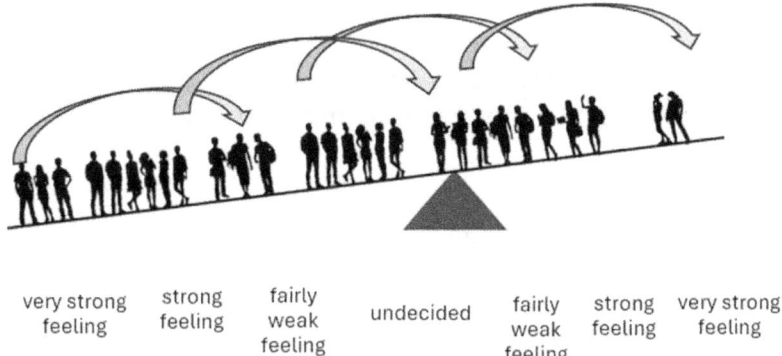

Figure 14.4 Illustration showing how small incremental steps can shift students along the credibility perception spectrum.

Here's the key: find a real-world application of the irrational belief you're targeting. Let students debate it. Dissect it. Replace it. This process—what we'll later call disputation, is essential.

Once students have accepted the rational alternative in a non-threatening, real-world context, you link it back to your own classroom. That way, when the activating event returns, as it will, students have a new lens for interpreting your actions. Not all will shift immediately. But one might say, "I get it now... you're actually trying to help us."

That's progress. That's credibility.

Starting with an Activating Event

What activating event is causing you the most trouble right now? Is it students ignoring instructions? Constant pushback? Deception? Defiance? Compulsive communicators? Maybe all of the above?

Start with the one that hits hardest—emotionally, psychologically, or professionally. Why? Because that's where the change matters most.

Keep this in mind: the goal of using REE isn't just to manage behaviour. It's to protect, promote, and maintain your *credibility* as a teacher. That means helping students change the way they interpret your behaviour in the classroom. We want to shift how they **interpret** those classroom events—so they respond based on reason, not irrational belief.

In the upcoming lesson, focus your REE teaching on the activating event that's currently damaging your credibility. To make it teachable, transform the event into a relatable real-world scenario. Start by identifying the student decision behind the event, then structure your scenario to show the consequences of that decision. This helps students see how irrational beliefs drive behaviour—and opens the door to rethinking those beliefs.

> **Key Idea**: We're not just managing misbehaviour—we're reshaping perception, so students see your authority, support, and instruction as credible, not uncaring, incompetent, or untrustworthy.
>
> REE is the *code* students can use to reinterpret—*decode*—your behaviour. Whether it's how you're managing misbehaviour, the teaching strategies you're using, the grades you're returning, or the group work you're assigning, you're introducing a way for students to make sense of your actions using rational thinking.
>
> Instead of jumping to distorted narratives—which often spread through social contagion—students learn to interpret your behaviour through a more accurate, evidence-based lens.

Code 1: REE Implementation

A Quick Note: There are many evidence-based models, modules, and lesson plans that implement REBT and REE in classrooms. What I'll show you here is how I've adapted REE to real classroom scenarios—specifically to respond to irrational thinking that distorts teacher credibility. I'll also share supplemental resources from well-supported approaches you can explore further.

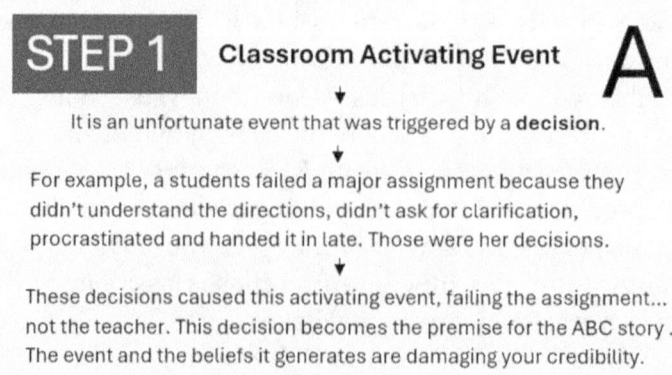

Figure 14.5 REE Step 1: Identifying the Activating Event.

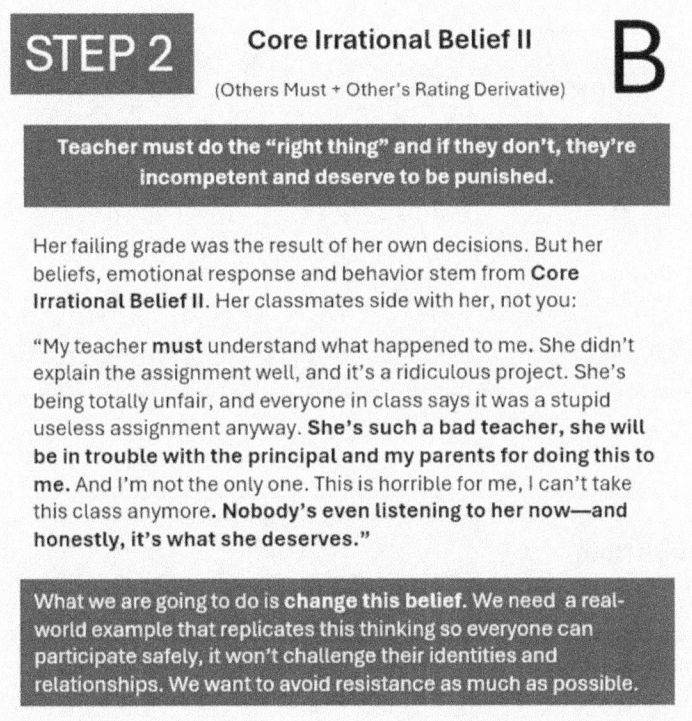

Figure 14.6 REE Step 2: Identifying Core Irrational Belief II ('Others Must' + Other's Rating Derivative) and its impact on teacher credibility.

Classroom Example: Steps 1 and 2—You Find Your Story

Teacher Created—A Safe Story for My Students

You've got a new job. You like it, and it pays pretty well. You've made a few friends at work, but there are also some coworkers you don't really get along with.

Your boss is okay, but lately, they've seemed a bit frustrated with you. It's not really your fault that some mistakes have happened, like missing a few deadlines. You asked for extensions, and that should've solved it. Some coworkers seem annoyed, though, because your delays mess with their schedules. Not your problem, they need to relax.

Decision Time (Remember: this REE activity includes a critical decision.)

You've got a team meeting this morning. You leave early to be on time—and plan to grab your favourite breakfast sandwich and coffee. You've got exactly 15 minutes before your bus arrives. If you miss it, you'll be 15 minutes late.

At the restaurant, the self-serve kiosks are down. The line doesn't look too bad, so you decide to wait. But it barely moves. Right as you reach near front, you see your bus pulling away—over 5 minutes early.

188 ◆ The Teacher Credibility Codebook

Tip: Little stick figure illustrations to share with students are very effective.

Figure 14.7 Example of a simple stick-figure illustration used to help students identify and challenge irrational thoughts.

> **Quick Note**
> The decision at the centre of this scenario was to stay at the restaurant—despite knowing the risk of being late for the team meeting.
> You can present the story in a number of ways: read it aloud, project it on a Smart Board, hand out printed copies, or use an approach that fits your classroom. You might even have your own version—like a movie clip, novel excerpt, your own crafted version, or a current event that mirrors the same pattern of thinking—and of course a decision.
> This can be an individual activity, a group task, or a whole-class discussion—whatever works best for you and your students. Your role is simply to share the story in a way that gets them thinking.
> Keep the lesson short and sweet. From beginning to end, it doesn't need to be long or complicated. Remember, **REE is a process**, not a one-time fix. Lessons like this are meant to be revisited and reinforced throughout the year—each one building on the last.
> As you move forward with the next steps of this activity, keep this in mind: implement, refine, modify, and adapt in whatever way works best for you. I'll share how I've implemented REE as a guide—but it's just that: a guide. Use it as a flexible framework to support your own style, your students' needs, and your classroom context. Create your own stories…

What?! You glare at the cashier and the customer ahead of you. **Total idiots.** Especially the cashier—what an incompetent employee. This isn't rocket science. Can someone please teach her how to take a simple order.

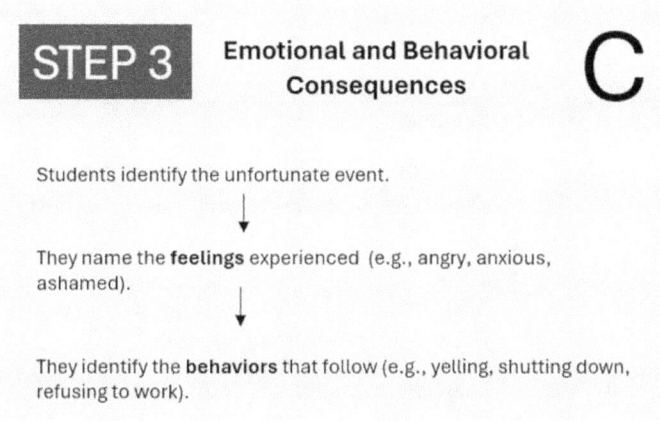

Figure 14.8 REE Step 3: Students identify the event, then name the feelings and behaviours that follow.

Honestly, she should get a formal reprimand, maybe a new job. Now because of her incompetence, I'm late for my meeting, and guess who's going to be all over my back at the office? (Ask students if they've ever seen adults lose their temper at fast-food restaurants?)

Classroom Example: Step 3

In this story, there are two possible unfortunate events—but stem from the same decision: staying at the restaurant for the breakfast sandwich. Some students might say the activating event was the delay at the counter that caused the missed bus. Others may say it was arriving late to the meeting. Either interpretation is fine—it's what feels most important to them that matters.

Student Task: Categorize the Consequences

Now, ask students to create two columns: (again could be a discussion, organizer graphic, group where one person is assigned a recorder, etc.)
 Emotions—What is the person feeling in this situation?
 Behaviours—What actions might they take as a result?
 You can apply this to either setting (the restaurant or the meeting) or even compare both. Let them brainstorm: individually, small groups, or as a full-class discussion (e.g., jotting ideas on the board or Smart Board).

Example:

At the meeting

Emotions	Behaviours
Anger	When they get to the office they might get into a conflict because they think everyone's against them.
Frustration	They might blame people for being unfair.
Worry	They might not have a very productive day, they're worried what everyone is saying.
	Snapping at coworkers or blaming others.
	Making excuses.
	Struggling to concentrate during the day.

Figure 14.9 Recording emotions and behaviours during Step 3.

At the restaurant

Emotions	Behaviours
Irritation	Muttering or complaining about the cashier
Anxiety	
	Being rude
Impatience	
	Blaming the cashier for ruining your day
Anger	

Figure 14.10 Continuation of emotions and behaviours log.

Wrapping up the Lesson

This might be a good place to conclude your first REE lesson—but you're the best judge of that. Keep the emotion and behaviour list visible or accessible so you can revisit it with the class when you're ready to move on to **Step 4**.

If engagement has been solid, and your students are following the flow, you can start revisiting the core beliefs behind those reactions. That's when we introduce the **King**, Demandingness, and his **Factory of Troubles**, the irrational derivatives like catastrophizing, LFT, and global ratings.

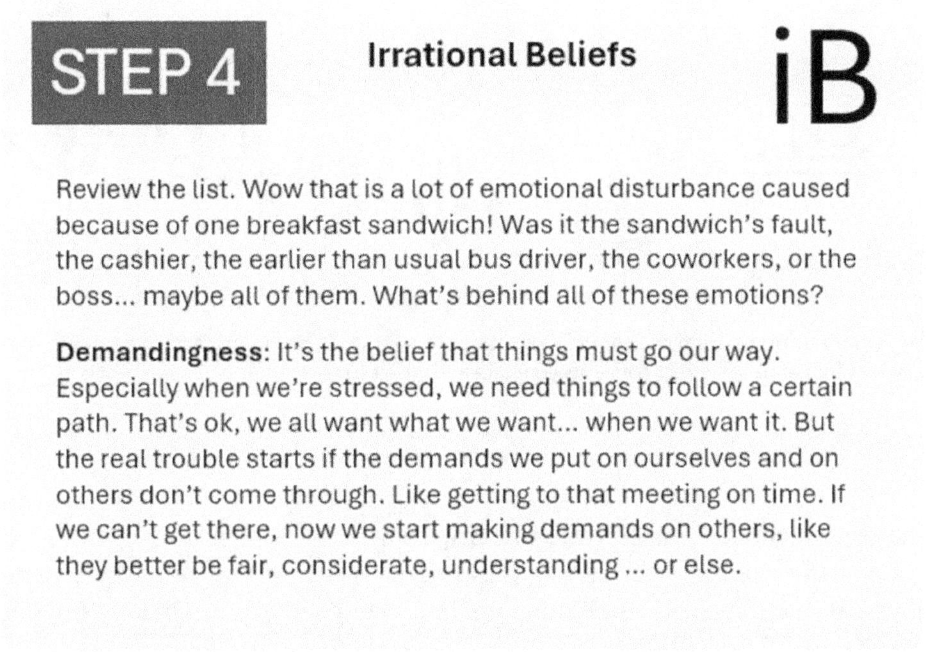

 **Irrational Beliefs**

Review the list. Wow that is a lot of emotional disturbance caused because of one breakfast sandwich! Was it the sandwich's fault, the cashier, the earlier than usual bus driver, the coworkers, or the boss... maybe all of them. What's behind all of these emotions?

Demandingness: It's the belief that things must go our way. Especially when we're stressed, we need things to follow a certain path. That's ok, we all want what we want... when we want it. But the real trouble starts if the demands we put on ourselves and on others don't come through. Like getting to that meeting on time. If we can't get there, now we start making demands on others, like they better be fair, considerate, understanding ... or else.

Figure 14.11 REE Step 4: Introduction to Irrational Thinking — Demandingness.

Classroom Example: Step 4

> **Quick Note**
> Step 4 offers a sample discussion or presentation on the concepts of Demandingness and its derivatives. You can use this example as a guide for your own class discussion, to build slides for a presentation, or as printed material for group activities. The purpose is to share an approach I've personally used to teach REE to students.
>
> For younger learners, Dr. Knaus' Rational Emotive Education Program remains the gold standard. It includes lessons and activities that you can implement as-is or adapt to suit your students' needs when teaching REE. This lesson is developed for older students, but REE is effective with all grade levels.

Ok, we've reviewed the emotions and behaviour list. Clearly, this breakfast sandwich caused a lot of trouble—or was it the cashier? Maybe it's your boss and coworkers who will actually cause the most stress when you show up late to work.

Figure 14.12 Example of using stick-figure illustrations to help students identify activating event —a visual tool that makes abstract concepts concrete and easier to recall.

Hmmm… who or what is really responsible for all the emotional and behavioural consequences you're facing today?

Let's say the most unfortunate moment—the one you're really worried about—is walking into that meeting late. That's the one sticking in your mind. In REBT, we call that:

A for Activating Event

Simple. It's the event you believe is causing your negative emotions and behaviours. It's the thing that's either happening or about to happen. But here's the twist—it's not actually the event itself that's causing all this stress.

It's not being late.

It's what you *believe* being late *means*.

That belief? That's where the real trouble starts.

Meet the King

The trouble starts when you're in a stressful or high-pressure situation, and your brain starts sounding like royalty:

Let's say you play sports and there's a big game coming up. The King might sound like this:

- "I **must** play my best game ever."
- "Coach, you **must** be smart and play me a lot."
- "Ref, you **must** call a perfect game and make zero mistakes."

Now, those don't *sound* terrible—until they don't happen.

You miss a few plays. Coach benches you. The ref makes a bad call. And suddenly…

Figure 14.13 Using the "King of Demandingness" illustration to introduce students to the concept of demands placed on themselves, others, and the world.

Figure 14.14 Factory illustration—introducing catastrophizing.

The King's demand gets sent to the **Factory**.

"This is awful. I blew it. I can't take this. My whole season is ruined."

That's the **belief** causing the emotional crash—not the bad pass, not the ref, not the bench.

It started with a **demand**, and when that demand wasn't met, the Factory produced a meltdown.

Now point it outward:

"Coach, you must play me… and if you don't, you're awful. You ruined my chance."

"Ref, you must call a good game… and if you blow it, the game's ruined. You're the worst."

That's the King's logic:

Unmet demands = catastrophe.

And that's how small setbacks turn into huge emotional outbursts— because the King's demands became law in your head. Even something like a slow line at the fast-food joint or a missed bus becomes a full-blown catastrophe—**a meltdown of kingly proportions.**

Catastrophizing Isn't the Only Product Coming out of the Factory

Here comes the King again—same demands, same game.

But this time, the Factory is churning out a different kind of irrational belief.

Same Activating Event:

You miss a few plays.
Coach benches you.
The ref makes a bad call.
You lose the game—maybe even the playoffs.
And suddenly...

The King's demand gets sent to the Factory.

But instead of Catastrophizing, this time it produces something else:
That's LFT.

Not the event itself—but your belief that you *shouldn't have to deal with it*—that it's **too much**, that you're **too overwhelmed**, that it's **intolerable**.

That belief causes the crash—not the ref, not the bench, not the scoreboard.

Now, watch how it plays out **towards others**:

"Coach, you must play me... and if you don't, I can't stand being part of this mess. It's too much, I can't take a whole season of this."

"Ref, you must be on your game... and if you're not, I'm done with this whole league. I'm out."

That's the King's logic again:

Unmet demands—I can't stand it—emotional shutdown or escape.

"I can't take this."
"This is unbearable."
"I'm done. I'm never playing for this team again."

Figure 14.15 Factory illustration—introducing Low Frustration Tolerance and Self/Other Rating.

> **Quick Note**
>
> I've found that this part can sometimes be confusing for students. When that happens, I occasionally insert a short mini lesson here to clarify things. It's not essential—but if you're getting blank stares or puzzled looks, this quick detour might come in handy.

Mini Lesson

The goal of this mini lesson is to help students practice identifying the King's demand and the Factory's two main products: **Catastrophizing** and **LFT**.

Activating Event (The Unfortunate Event)

You move your birthday party from Saturday to Sunday so your friend can attend. The party is outdoors—like a waterpark. Saturday's weather turns out to be perfect, but when you wake up Sunday… it's pouring rain.

Here's Where the Emotional and Behavioural Consequences Begin—Fuelled by a Demand

"This can't be happening. I must have a great party today—it's really important to me!"

That's the demand: The party must go perfectly, and the weather must cooperate—because I care about it deeply.

From there, the Factory kicks in:

Catastrophizing—The Self

I must, and if I do not, the outcome is horrible.

"I shouldn't have changed the date. I mess everything up. This is a complete disaster."

Can you think of a few more Catastrophizing beliefs directed at yourself? Try completing the list below.

> ★ Because of me, the day is ruined.
> ★ _____
> ★ _____

Catastrophizing—Others

Others must, and if they do not, it's awful

"My parents should have warned me—why didn't they check the weather? Now everything's completely ruined."

Can you think of a few more Catastrophizing beliefs directed at others? Try completing the list below.

> ★ My friend ruined everything by asking me to change the date.
> ★ _____
> ★ _____

Catastrophizing—the World
The World must, and if it does not, it's terrible.

"Nothing ever works out for me. The universe hates me."

Can you think of a few more Catastrophizing beliefs directed at the world? Try completing the list below.

> ★ Why does everything turn against me when it's important, can't I get one simple break? Now the day is ruined.
> ★ _____
> ★ _____

OK, enough catastrophizing, now we turn our attention to the next product manufactured out of the Factory: LFT

Low Frustration Tolerance—the Self
I must, and if I do not, I can't stand it!

"I can't stand this. I waited so long for today, and now it's all ruined. I just want to go back to bed and cancel everything."

Can you think of a few more LFT beliefs directed at yourself? Try completing the list below.

> ★ I shouldn't have made that decision… this is too much for me. I don't even want to go to my own party.
> ★ _____
> ★ _____

Low Frustration Tolerance—Others
You must, and if I you do not, I can't stand it!

"My parents should have planned better—I shouldn't have to deal with this mess."

Can you think of a few more LFT beliefs directed at others? Try completing the list below.

> ★ I can't handle it when I'm blamed for someone else's decisions.
> ★ _____
> ★ _____

Low Frustration Tolerance—the World
It must, and if it does not, I can't stand it!

"Why does the world seem to pick on me, on my birthday? This is too much. I can't take it anymore?"

Can you think of a few more LFT beliefs directed at the world? Try completing the list below.

> ★ "Why can she make it on the only day it rains! Why does this always happen to me? It's as if everything's against me. I don't want to have to deal with this on my birthday!"
> ★ _____
> ★ _____

> **Quick Note**
>
> I use **concept attainment** next to introduce *Others Rating*—the Core Irrational Belief II that causes some of the most damaging outcomes in the classroom, especially when it comes to teacher credibility.
>
> I want students to be able to clearly **distinguish this belief** from the others so we can examine it closely throughout the year. You can present this as part of the mini lesson or run it as a stand-alone activity.
>
> It's a good idea to revisit this belief periodically—it tends to resurface in different forms as students encounter new classroom situations.

Concept Attainment: Other Rating

There are several ways to implement a concept attainment activity. You could provide **yes** and **no** examples of the belief—in this case, *Others Rating*—without naming the concept up front. Then, give students some tester examples.

When students start to notice the difference, they can define it for themselves, create a working definition, and name the derivative. At that point, you can formally introduce the Factory's signature product: **Others Rating**.

At the end of the activity, students should be able to define the characteristics of Self/Other Rating as irrational beliefs that involve:

- a justification for punishment or retribution, and
- a devaluing of a person's worth when a demand is not met.

NO	YES
"I must always do well. If I fail at something, it means I'm no good."

"If something goes wrong, it's unbearable. I can't handle disappointment."

"Everything has to go exactly as planned, or the whole day is ruined."

"If I don't succeed, people won't like me, and I'll be worthless."

"I should never feel nervous or uncomfortable—something's wrong if I do."

"If I make a mistake, everyone will think less of me forever." | "Teachers must always treat me fairly, if they don't, they're bad and shouldn't be teaching."

"If someone messes up the group project, they're useless and deserve to fail."

"My friend should have remembered my birthday, if they didn't, they're selfish and fake."

"If someone criticizes me, they're just a bad person and don't deserve my respect."

"Adults should always be understanding, if they're not, they don't deserve my sympathy." |

Figure 14.16 Example of concept attainment activity for identifying Core Irrational Belief II (Other Rating).

"Things shouldn't be this hard. Life is too difficult and unfair."

"If I'm not the best, I've failed completely."

"There's no point trying if there's a chance I'll fail."

"I can't stand people judging me, I have to avoid it at all costs." | "The ref should never miss a call—if they do, they're completely incompetent and deserve to be fired."

"If someone lies to me once, they're a terrible person and can't ever be trusted again."

"Coaches must be fair with playing time—if they're not, they're biased and shouldn't be coaching."

"If someone makes a mistake that affects me, they deserve to be called out and humiliated."

"People should never make decisions that inconvenience me—if they do, they're inconsiderate and don't deserve kindness in return." |

Figure 14.17 Continuation of concept attainment activity.

> **"Others must treat me fairly, kindly, or competently. If they don't, they're bad, worthless, or deserve to be punished."**

Figure 14.18 Working definition from concept attainment: Others Rating as the foundation of Core Irrational Belief II.

You'll introduce this irrational belief during the mini lesson as Self–Other Rating, one of the Core Irrational Beliefs in REBT:

"Others must treat me fairly, kindly, or competently. If they don't, they're bad, worthless, or deserve to be punished."

Conclusion of the Mini Lesson
Recap: **Activating Event**

You move your birthday party from Saturday to Sunday so your friend can attend. The party is outdoors—like a waterpark. Saturday's weather turns out to be perfect, but when you wake up Sunday… it's pouring rain.

Demand
"This can't be happening. I must have a great party today—it's really important to me! The party must go perfectly, and the weather must cooperate—because I care about it deeply."

Now the Factory has one Last Product: Self/Others Rating. (This has been defined in the mini lesson) Let's now apply it to the birthday party.

Self/Others Rating—the Self
I must, and if I do not, I am no good!

"The rain is not my fault, but now everyone sees me as a loser. I can see why I don't have many friends, I'm an idiot."

Can you think of a few more Self/Other Rating beliefs directed at yourself? Try completing the list below.

> ★ I must plan the perfect party, and if I don't, I'm just a failure.
> ★ _____
> ★ _____

Self/Others Rating—Others
You must, and if you do not, you are no good!

Now this is where we focus on this specific product of the Factory. It's different from all the rest. As you discovered in the **concept attainment activity**, you already identified its key characteristics—and even gave it a name.

We now know this belief as **Self/Other Rating**. It causes so much emotional disturbance that the founder of REBT, **Dr. Albert Ellis**, elevated it to one of the **three core irrational beliefs**.

At the birthday party, **Others Rating** might sound like this:

"She asked me to move the party, and now that it's ruined, it's her fault. She doesn't deserve to be invited next time."

Can you think of a few more Self/Other Rating beliefs directed at others? Try completing the list below.

> ★ People who don't show up just because of a little rain are pathetic. If they were real friends, they'd come no matter what. Let's see who goes to any of their parties…no one."
> ★ _____
> ★ _____

Wrapping Up the Lesson

This is a good place to conclude the second part of the REE lesson. By now, students should understand what an *activating event* is—and that emotional and behavioural consequences do not stem from the event itself, but from the beliefs they attach to it. They should recognize that these beliefs drive strong emotions, which in turn influence behaviour.

Students should also be able to deconstruct irrational beliefs as demands placed on themselves, others, or the world. When these demands aren't met, derivative beliefs are produced—such as *catastrophizing* and *LFT*.

They should now have a solid grasp of these two derivatives. And when asked to explain how they differ from *self/other rating*, they should be able to identify a key distinction: **Core Irrational Belief II** (Self/Other Rating) includes a justification for punishment and retribution and devalues a person's worth based on their failure to meet the demand.

Consider reviewing these concepts before moving on to Step 5.

Step 5: Demands and Derivatives Applied

Now it's time to apply what we've learned to the *activating event* that poses a real risk to your teacher credibility. You might think, "This is just one student—why all the fuss?"

But here's the issue: this isn't just a moment of frustration. It's becoming a *shared narrative*—a kind of peer-approved "truth" that's spreading through the class. And once that happens, your credibility isn't being judged by your actual competence, care, or clarity anymore. It's being filtered through student beliefs that *justify* dismissal and defiance.

This is exactly the kind of irrational thinking that REE is designed to challenge.

When students hold beliefs like:

- "I don't have to listen unless I enjoy it."
- "You're not credible if I'm not entertained."

…it's not just misbehaviour—it's a full-blown *perceptual distortion* that erodes the learning environment.

That's why we start with the activating event. Not just to address behaviour—but to uncover and replace the beliefs behind it.

This brings us into the **Scout Mindset**—where we anticipate that the issue won't go away on its own. It will adapt, grow, and reappear in new forms. We're not just addressing what's happening but understanding *why* it's happening with our students and taking the lead.

Because at the heart of this resistance, you're not managing a single student—you're confronting a *contagious interpretation problem*. And your first move is helping students decode your behaviour rationally—before emotionally charged inferences spiral into defiance and damage your credibility as a caring, competent teacher.

Graphic Organizers

In Step 5, a highly effective and engaging way to apply what students have learned—particularly in the "Late for Meeting" scenario—is through a **graphic organizer**. This tool helps students visually break down irrational beliefs and make meaningful connections.

You can adapt the activity in a variety of ways depending on your students' needs. Scaffolding is key. Consider modifying the amount of information you provide, depending on the level of support required.

This activity can also be implemented in multiple formats:

- Individual or group work
- Poster presentations
- Illustrated or artistic responses
- Notebook graphic templates

The primary goal is for students to **identify the demand** and its **derivative beliefs**—especially the **core irrational belief** underlying the scenario.

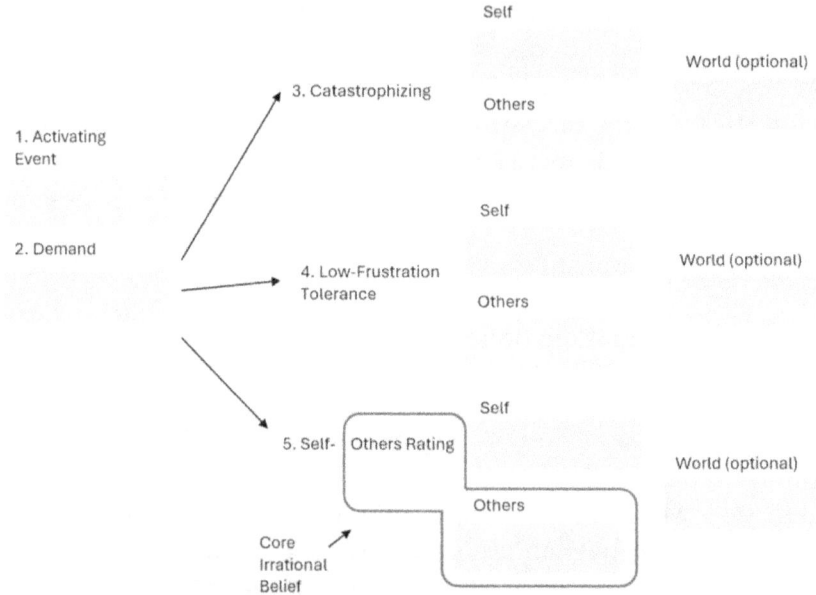

Figure 14.19 Graphic organizer for identifying the demand, derivatives, and Core Irrational Belief II.

This step is critical: when we move on to the consequences of irrational thinking, student understanding will depend heavily on how well they've grasped the **derivatives**. Translation: The better your students understand this, the more effective the tools and prompts will be in helping them change and maintain rational beliefs about your credibility.

The Deck

To support students in completing the graphic organizer, consider providing a deck of response statements. The way you introduce this resource depends on how much scaffolding your students need. You can:

- Withhold the deck completely (for advanced learners)
- Provide only the statements
- Include visual aids like the King and Factory icons
- Offer fully labelled cards showing the derivative and its associated belief statement

It's entirely up to you and your students' readiness.

For this activity, I recommend focusing especially on the "Others must" beliefs. These give students the clearest path towards recognizing how their thinking patterns drive emotional and behavioural responses—especially in relation to you, their peers, and the overall classroom climate.

For additional decks, templates, and classroom resources, visit https://teachercredibilitycodebook.com/

Demandingness of the Self:
I cannot be late for work because of this idiot cashier and the stupid bus.

And if I am...

Figure 14.20 Example of "Deck" scaffolding cards, used to help students recognize and label derivatives such as Demandingness of the Self and Catastrophizing when completing the graphic organizer.

Catastrophizing:
This is a disaster. Now I'll be humiliated at work, people will enjoy seeing me fail.

Figure 14.21 Continuation of "Deck".

Before We Look at the Evidence
(Technically, this part is called *Disputation*—the "D" in ABCD.)

Let's talk about how you're handling this situation. And it's okay, really. We all get into these moments when we've been hurt, when we're angry, or when we just need someone to have our back.

That's what friends are for, right? Support.

But that's exactly why we have to be careful. Because there's a trap here—and it's a harmful one. Once you fall into it, it's hard to climb out. It's the trap where your emotions start driving your behaviour, and your friends start agreeing with the belief that:

"If someone treats me unfairly—or just messes up—they deserve to be punished, disrespected, or written off."

When you buy into that, especially with others backing you up, the belief feels true. But it's still irrational.

Low Frustration Tolerance (LFT):
I don't know how much more I can take of being blamed for things I can't control—like the bus and that stupid restaurant.

Self-Rating:
If they blame me again, they'll think I'm useless… Maybe they're right. Maybe I'm just not good at my job.

Demandingness of Others:
My boss and coworkers must treat me with respect and give me the benefit of the doubt. I was late because of something I couldn't control—it's not my fault. They have no right to judge me or talk behind my back.

And if they don't…

Catastrophizing:
This is awful. Now everyone thinks I'm unreliable. My reputation's ruined. This could seriously mess up my future at work. They're going to hold this against me forever.

Figure 14.22 Continuation of "Deck".

Low Frustration Tolerance (LFT):
I'm sick of always being the one who gets blamed. I can't stand working with people who constantly assume the worst. I don't deserve this.

Others-Rating:
They're so fake. They act like they're better than me, but they don't even know the whole story. If they're going to treat me like garbage, then forget it. I'm not helping them ever again, I'm not showing them any respect—and I hope they get a taste of their own medicine soon. Honestly, I hope something makes them look bad next. I'll let my real friends here know what happened.

Figure 14.23 Continuation of "Deck".

And here's the real danger: The same belief system you use to judge others—"you must be 100% on my side or else"—will eventually be used on you. When you make harsh, irrational demands of others, you set a standard that comes back to you. The same logic that justifies *punishing them* for their mistakes will justify *others punishing and devaluing you* when you mess up. Yep, even your friends are susceptible, because those conditions and beliefs become accepted truths, like "snitches get stiches." Suddenly, you're in an alternate universe—one with irrational rules, enforced by a twisted logic that only applies if you're inside the group.

That's why we dispute it. That's why we challenge the belief—not just for the other person's sake, but for yours too.

What happens when this belief becomes the rule in your group?

STEP 6 — Invisible Damage

The most damaging consequences are often the ones students can't see—the ones hidden beneath their awareness.

That's the core purpose of Step 6: to reveal the invisible damage caused by irrational beliefs. These are the internal costs that shape how students relate to others, how they view themselves, and how they function in the classroom—even when they can't put it into words. This is especially true of Core Irrational Belief II:

"Others must treat me fairly and kindly—and if they don't, they're bad and deserve to be punished."

This belief doesn't just fuel conflict and retaliation—it quietly erodes relationships, trust, and mutual respect. And often, students don't even realize it's happening.

How to Lead Step 6

This step is **discussion-based**, and it's normal to encounter some resistance. That's not a problem—it's part of the process. Invite students into the conversation:

"What are your thoughts? Do you agree or disagree with this idea?"

Validate all viewpoints. The goal isn't to force agreement—it's to spark reflection. Use your visual illustrations as discussion anchors. Most importantly: Students need to reach their own conclusions, in their own time.

Step 7 will continue this journey by exposing the irrational foundations even more clearly.

Figure 14.24 REE Step 6: Hidden peer relationship damage from irrational beliefs.

Are You and Your Friends Right about This? Where's the Evidence that Someone Should be Devalued and Others Punished?

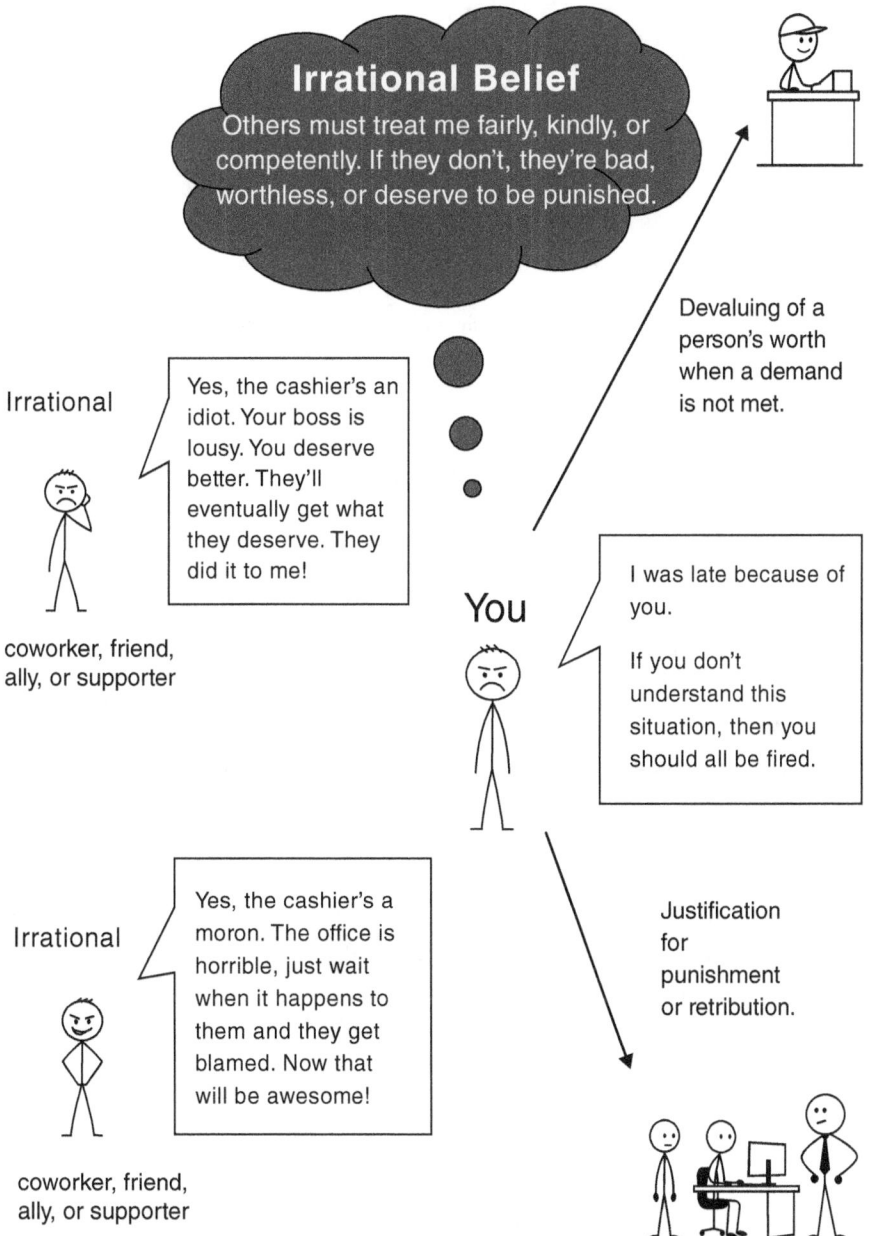

Figure 14.25 Example of a discussion prompt or student handout for disputing Core Irrational Belief II in peer-influenced scenarios.

Figure 14.26 Illustration showing the trap of applying Others Rating within peer groups, where the same punitive logic can be turned back on you.

Core Irrational Belief II is the Bait in this Trap

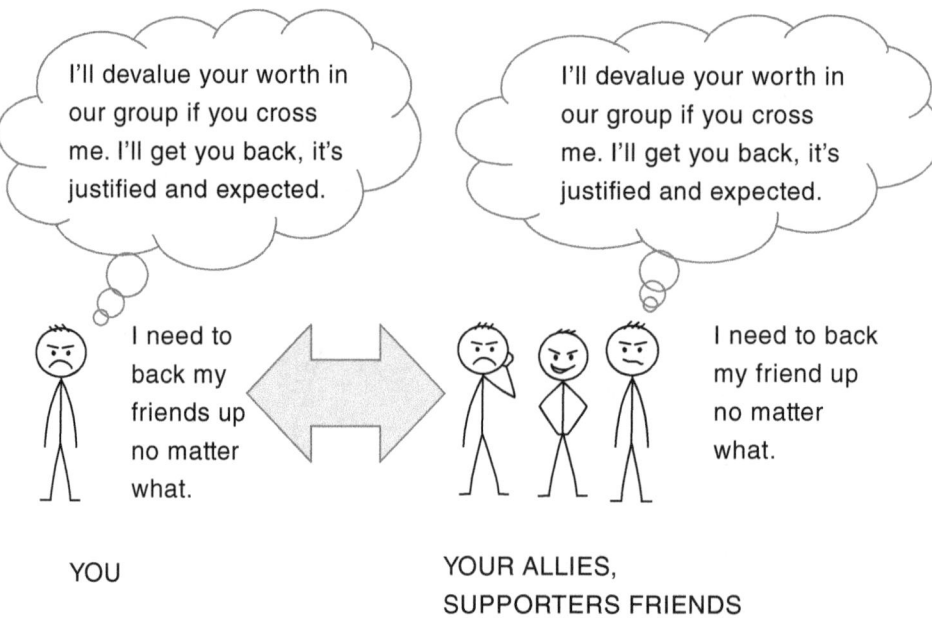

Figure 14.27 Illustration showing how Core Irrational Belief II can become a group norm, creating a "trap" where mutual loyalty reinforces retribution and devaluing others' worth.

> **Quick Note**
>
> Irrational beliefs often fuel social hierarchies. We'll explore hierarchies, social contagion, and misinformation in the next chapter—but here's a key connection:
>
> When irrational beliefs are supported without evidence, they function like falsehoods. Over time, that lie can become a kind of "social truth"—reinforced not by facts, but by peer approval, echo chambers, and group loyalty.
>
> In this environment, beliefs don't need to be true to be powerful. And in my experience, when this takes hold in a classroom, students begin launching preemptive strikes—unprovoked attacks—because their internal logic is distorted by irrational thinking that feels justified.

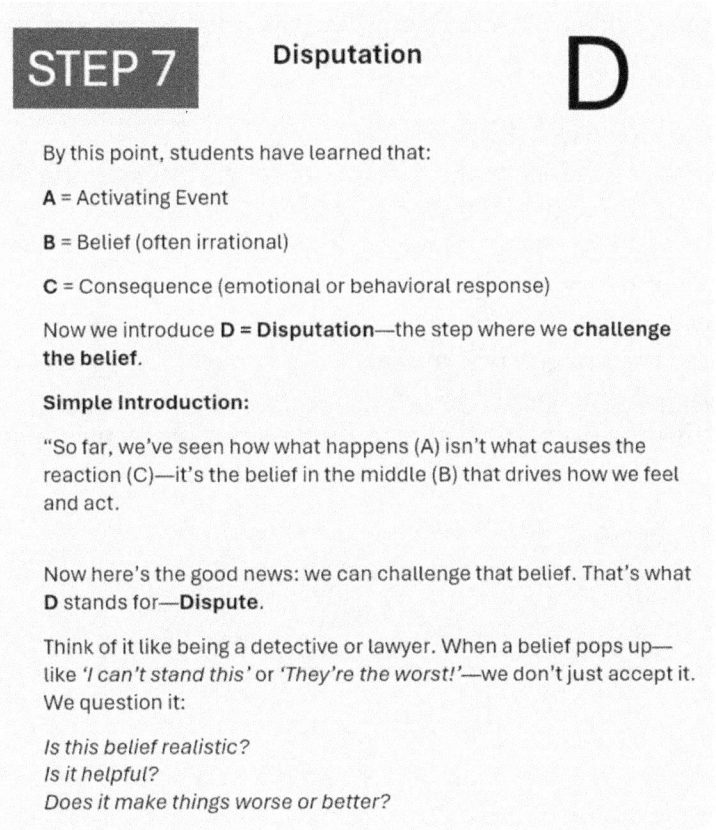

Figure 14.28 REE Step 7: Introduction to Disputation—challenging irrational beliefs by questioning their evidence, helpfulness, and impact.

> **Quick Note: Make it Your Own**
>
> Feel free to modify, improvise, or adapt everything here to fit your classroom. These activities work great as quick mini-lessons—students can simply listen to the stories and reflect, without needing to write anything down, or role-play every time.
>
> Also, keep in mind that the example with the cashier might not click with all students. If it doesn't resonate, swap in an activating event that better matches their interests, routines, or school experiences. The goal is to help students *see themselves* in the situation so they can better challenge their beliefs and responses.

Where's the Evidence?—REBT Disputation Activity

Students have to divide their paper into two columns to compare rational and irrational beliefs. This builds on the previous lesson and their graphic organizer work.

Role-Play and Interview Activity

Students examine the accuracy of irrational beliefs by exploring different perspectives. Use one of the following formats:

- Partner interviews
- Small group simulations
- Class front role-play (hot seat)
- Scripted character handouts
- Activating event info cards (with missing/supplemental info)

Belief Comparison Chart

Rational Beliefs (Established during disputation)	Irrational Beliefs (From previous graphic organizer)

Figure 14.29 Example of a student organizer for categorizing rational and irrational beliefs during the disputation process.

Essentially it looks like this:

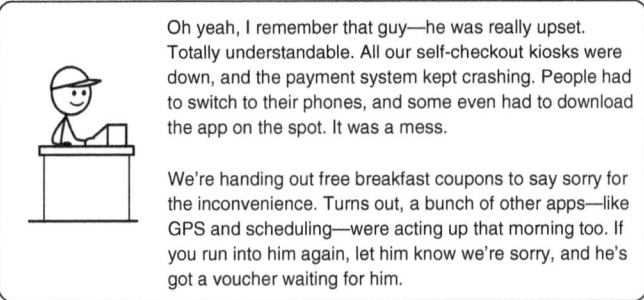

Figure 14.30 Example of a role-play activity for exploring and comparing alternative perspectives in the disputation process.

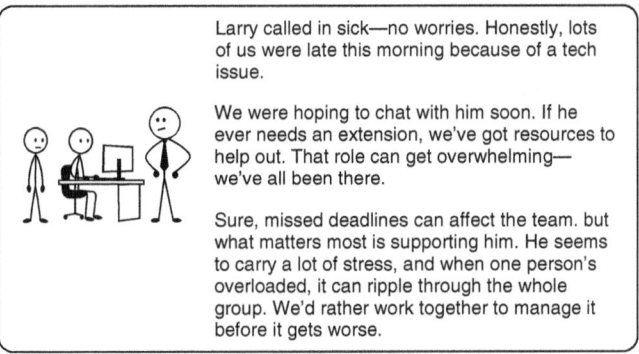

Figure 14.31 Second role-play activity for practicing perspective-taking in REBT disputation.

Example irrational beliefs to investigate:

- "Everyone at work will laugh at me."
- "The boss is an idiot—he'll get the bare minimum from me."
- "The cashier is an idiot, he's responsible for me being late. Get a new job buddy!"

Students should ask:

- What facts support this belief?
- What else could explain this situation
- What might you learn by asking questions or hearing the other side?

After the activity, students return to their chart and revise or add to their Rational Beliefs. Discuss how emotions can distort thinking and how gaining new information can change perspective.

The Real Consequence of Core Irrational Belief II

Ask students to reflect of these two visuals.

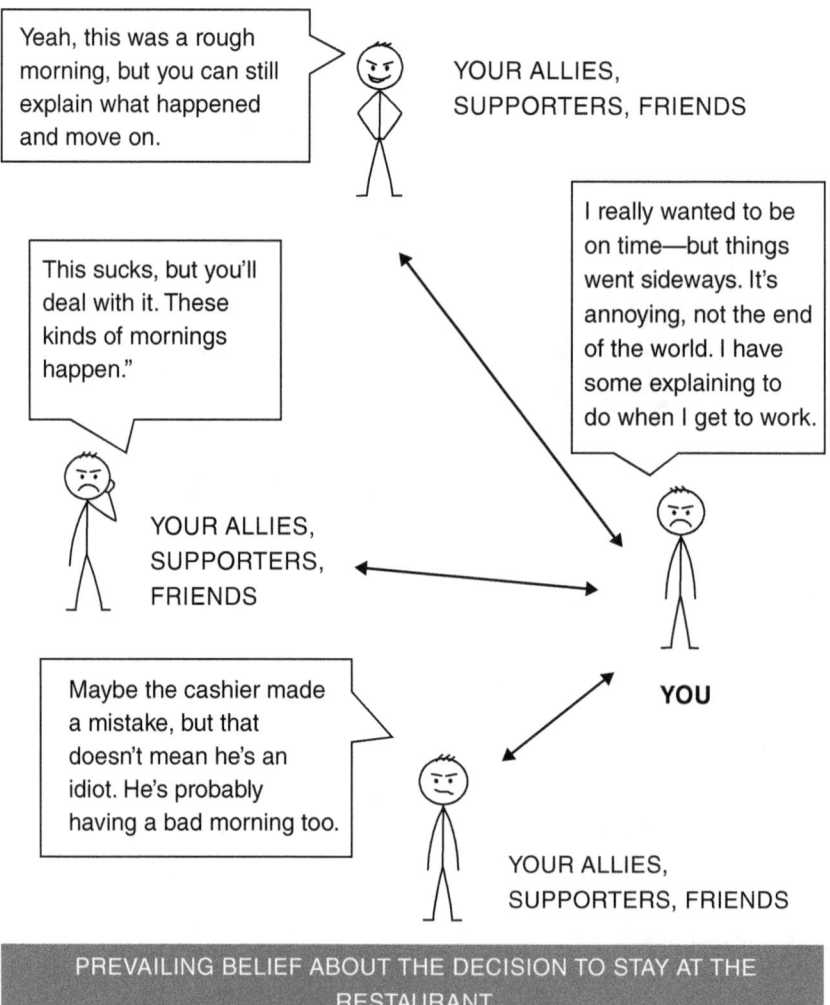

Figure 14.32 Example of a student graphic organizer or discussion prompt for evaluating the benefits of rational thinking reinforced through peer feedback.

Code 1: Replacing Irrational Beliefs with Rational Ones ◆ 213

Irrational: Harmful, Unrealistic Thinking

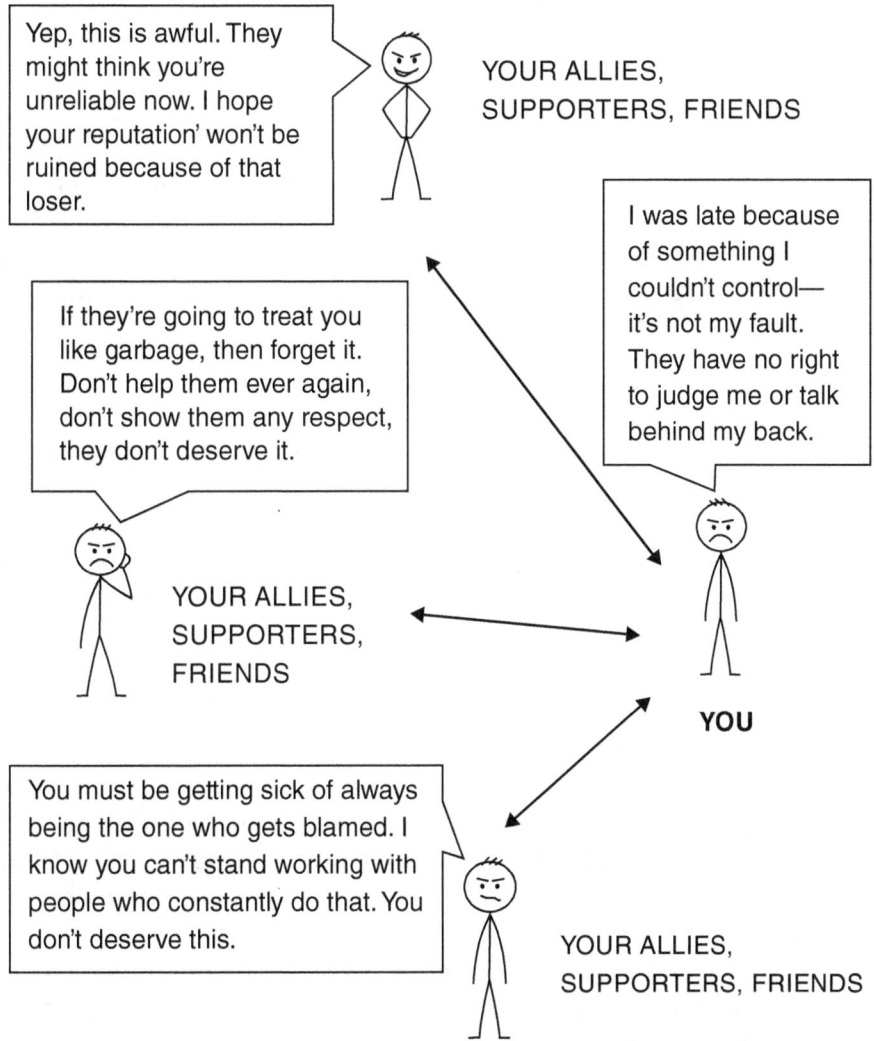

PREVAILING BELIEF ABOUT THE DECISION TO STAY AT THE RESTAURANT

It's not my fault that other people are such losers. I *should* be able to get a breakfast sandwich on time—and not be blamed for every problem in the world. And honestly, my friends agree: people need to get a life. Especially my boss.

Figure 14.33 Example of a student graphic organizer or discussion prompt for evaluating the consequences of irrational thinking reinforced through peer feedback.

What's Going On?

This is another chance to genuinely listen to student perspectives. Some students may still be holding onto or defending an unpopular position—or even resisting the activity entirely. That's okay. Record their contributions without evaluating or judging their opinions.

Remember: the goal isn't to get students at the far end of the spectrum to immediately adopt a rational belief. What you *don't* want is to argue with them or only validate the opinions that align with the lesson. Doing so can unintentionally push those students further into their position and entrench those who are influenced. Instead, keep the space open. The real shift happens when students are allowed to see, hear, and reflect on the consequences of irrational beliefs on their own terms.

Some Discussion Questions:

- Does the cashier deserve to be called an "idiot" because his mistake made you late?
- Is your boss really out to get you, or are you filling in the blanks?
- Are your friends, who validated your anger, given you good advice?
- What happens when a peer group uses Core Irrational Belief II as a badge of loyalty?

In what situation are you able to learn? What are the short- and long-term consequences of not learning the right decision? What are the consequences of being supported and validated for making poor decisions and not learning?

In my experience, these steps are powerful tools for building student understanding, encouraging cooperation, and—most importantly—creating a shared cognitive environment where your credibility is more accurately understood.

The final step involves introducing students to a simple but powerful table. It's the same mental framework that many elite performers, including professional athletes, already know:

You can ask them to identify the differences between the two columns, which of these do they feel is the most important. Do they agree replacing a demand with a preference helps lower the temperature of emotions and the resulting behaviours?

Once you've shared this, invite students to examine both columns. Ask:

- What's the difference between the two ways of thinking?
- Which belief shift do you think would be hardest?
- Do you think replacing a demand with a preference actually lowers the emotional temperature?

 **Replacing the Irrational Belief**

By this point, students have learned that:

A = Activating Event

B = Belief (often unhelpful or unrealistic)

C = Consequence (emotional or behavioral response)

D = Disputation — the step where we challenge the belief

E = Effect — the new, more constructive emotion or behavior that results from adopting a more rational belief

In this final step, we swap out the unhelpful belief for one that's realistic, balanced, and more effective. This new belief helps shape emotions and behavior in ways that allow us to **learn, accept,** and **grow** from the experience.

This is exactly why REBT works so well in sports. It gives athletes the tools to respond with perspective, accept themselves and others, and focus on improvement.

Take the quarterback who fumbled the ball. Instead of blaming the offensive line or the coach's play call, they reflect: *How can I improve in practice? How can I support my teammates? How can we grow together?*

That's far more productive than blaming themselves or seeking revenge on teammates or coaches—because in the end, that mindset teaches nothing. It blocks progress.

This is what successful athletes do. It's what strong leaders do. And it's the same mindset that helps students and friends grow into their best selves.

This is also immensely more helpful to you—and to your credibility as a teacher—when students face classroom challenges with rational beliefs and a mindset shaped by REBT. "By learning to challenge their thinking, students become more self-aware, more resilient, and more responsible for how they respond—both in the classroom and beyond.

Figure 14.34 REE Final Step: Replacing the Irrational Belief—adopting a realistic belief that shapes constructive emotions, behaviours, and outcomes.

In my experience, the most transformative shift—for individuals and peer groups alike—is Acceptance. This is the belief that replaces Core Irrational Belief II. If students can develop acceptance towards themselves and others, they unlock their capacity to learn and grow. They can forgive, recover, take risks, and persevere.

Instead of...	We See...
Demandingness Things must go my way. Others must treat me fairly. I must not be inconvenienced. And if I am, then their no good and should be punished.	**Preference** I'd prefer things to go my way—but I can handle it when they don't.
Catastrophizing This is a disaster. I'm going to get in trouble, and it's not even my fault!	**Anti-Awfulizing.** "This is frustrating, but not the end of the world."
Low Frustration Tolerance "I can't take this anymore—why does this always happen to me?	**High Frustration Tolerance** "It's not ideal, but I'll deal with it and bounce back."
Self/Other Rating That cashier is an idiot. My boss is unfair. People suck. I hope they get what they deserve."	**Acceptance** People make mistakes. That doesn't mean they're bad people, they deserve to be punished and devalued, or that I'm helpless."

Figure 14.35 Example of a student activity table comparing irrational beliefs with rational alternatives, illustrating the improved emotional and behavioural outcomes from adopting more rational thinking.

And in a classroom built on that mindset—where students feel safe to stumble and supported to rise again—you create the conditions for real learning.

Just like Maslow taught us: once safety and belonging are in place, higher-level learning becomes possible.

Transition to the Next Chapter

Now, when you present that next assignment to students, you have powerful tools at your disposal. Those at the extreme end of the spectrum may not have changed—but you now face a new audience, shaped by a new cognitive environment. One that's better equipped to decode assignments and deadlines as reasonable and justified. A classroom more likely to interpret your behaviour as caring, trustworthy, and competent.

This shift didn't happen by chance—it's the result of surfacing irrational beliefs, replacing them with rational ones, and helping students build a healthier mental framework.

This is where you can implement what we'll call a booster shot.

Now, you can frame deadlines not as rigid rules, but as shared responsibilities. You can remind students that asking for help is a smart, strong decision. That having teammates who support positive choices truly matters. That no one is to blame for the assignment—events like this are part of life.

And that the decisions they make are their own—so own them. Don't assign blame. Don't play the victim.

And if they feel they're being treated unfairly, say:

"Come and see me. We'll work through it together."
You're here for them.
And now—they're more ready to believe it.

Chapter Review

- ★ Code 1 helps students recognize, challenge, and replace the irrational beliefs that quietly damage your credibility and their own learning. These beliefs—like blaming others, exaggerating problems, or giving up easily—can be powerful. But they're also teachable.
- ★ In Classroom A, students aren't always reacting to your actions rationally. They're reacting through distorted beliefs. That's why discipline alone won't fix the problem. The issue isn't just behaviour—it's the thought underneath.
- ★ The goal of Code 1 is to help students identify these irrational beliefs, especially the **core belief driving the reaction**. Once they understand that root belief, they can better understand its emotional and behavioural consequences—and begin to shift their thinking.
- ★ One belief to watch for is this: *"Others must treat me fairly and kindly—and if they don't, they're bad and deserve to be punished."* This belief causes real damage. It breaks down trust, increases conflict, and harms relationships—even when students can't fully explain why they feel the way they do.
- ★ By helping students name these beliefs and replace them with more rational thinking, you protect your credibility and build a healthier classroom culture.

> **Key Takeaway:**
>
> Students don't lose respect for you because of a single action—they lose it when their irrational beliefs distort your behaviour into something unfair, unkind, or threatening. Until those beliefs are identified and replaced, your credibility will keep eroding—no matter how effective your classroom management seems.

Suggested REE Resources

Vernon, A. (1980). *Help yourself to a healthier you: A handbook of emotional education exercises for children*. University Press of America.

Vernon, A. (2006). *Thinking, feeling, behaving: An emotional education curriculum for children (Grades 1–6) (2nd ed.)*. Research Press.

Vernon, A. (2006). *Thinking, feeling, behaving: An emotional education curriculum for adolescents (Grades 7–12) (2nd ed.)*. Research Press

15

Code 2
Replacing Peer Coercion and Misinformation with Critical Thinking and Prosocial Behaviour

Social Inoculation Overview

By now, you've learned how to identify irrational, distorted beliefs that harm your credibility and how to replace them with rational, constructive ones. These changes reduce emotional intensity, minimize disruptive behaviour, and critically decrease the tendency to devalue or punish those who are seen to interfere with distorted demands.

In this chapter, you'll be introduced to **Code 2**, a new tool designed to further strengthen your credibility by addressing how misinformation and peer influence shape student beliefs. **Code 2 is grounded in the research-backed strategies outlined in** *A Practical Guide to Prebunking Misinformation* **(Harjani et al., 2022)**.

You can use Code 2 on its own or combine it with the Rational Emotive Education (REE) work you've already implemented through **Code 1**. For example, if you've addressed an activating event and used REE to surface irrational beliefs, Code 2 helps reinforce those gains—preventing the return of harmful narratives and protecting students against new ones.

At the same time, you may find Code 2 works well as a standalone approach within your teaching practice. That's great too. Its purpose is to help students detect and resist misinformation—especially the kind that undermines your credibility—and to understand how social hierarchies and peer dynamics can be used to manipulate their thinking.

DOI: 10.4324/9781003644088-19

Prebunking Works Much Like the ABC Model

It strengthens your students' mental filters so they can resist irrational groupthink and recognize when their beliefs are being manipulated.

Key concepts like the **Scout Mindset**, the **Spectrum of Beliefs**, and **Be Kind First** are all part of effective deployment.

Code 2 Includes Two Targeted Prebunking Methods

- **Issue-Based Prebunking**: Helps students resist broad, recurring false narratives (e.g., "school is pointless," "authority is always unfair").
- **Technique-Based Prebunking**: Teaches students to recognize specific tactics used to spread misinformation (e.g., false dilemmas, scapegoating, social proof).

Used together, these tools strengthen student reasoning and social awareness—resulting in a more stable, trusting, and credible classroom.

Inoculation Theory

Prebunking is built on inoculation theory, which was developed in the 1960s by social psychologist William McGuire, and designed to be used as a psychological "vaccine for brainwash." Much like how medical vaccines confer physiological resistance against future infection, psychological inoculations confer resistance against future attempts of attitudinal manipulation (akin to the immunity provided by antibodies).

(Harjani et al., 2022)

Prebunking Involves Three Key Components

In *A Practical Guide to Prebunking*, the authors explain that inoculation interventions can build students' **"mental antibodies"** to encountering false beliefs in the future, in the same way vaccines create antibodies that fight against further infection. For an intervention to successfully qualify as a prebunk, you need three key components:

Warning

Alert students to attempts to manipulate them. Inform them that they are likely to encounter classroom activating events in the near future that may lead to inaccurate inferences (misunderstandings) and false beliefs about teaching (assessment, rules, classroom management, authority, etc.), subjects (usefulness, necessity, work requirements, etc.), and school (purpose, value, etc.). These events can result in powerful motivations and persuasion to participate in deception and antisocial behaviour.

Preemptive Refutation

Expose students to effective rebuttals. Rather than directly challenging or telling students what to believe, this technique focuses on how people are commonly manipulated and misled. This approach resonates because it is generally educational, non-judgemental, and non-accusatory in tone. As the authors in *A Practical Guide to Prebunking Misinformation* explain:

> *It often focuses on higher-order techniques and narratives being shared, seeking to empower individuals to spot **how** they are being manipulated. Prebunking assumes no prior capabilities or knowledge of a topic, making it widely usable across age groups and settings.*

Preemptive refutation can take the form of discussions, group activities, book/movie responses, etc., where all viewpoints can be considered. The teacher can facilitate the refutation before conflict arises, making it easier to demonstrate caring, trust, and competence. This approach allows all students to be listened to non-judgementally (considering student identity and social connection) and affirms that their voices have been heard and valued. As Clear advocates, this intervention emphasizes being kind first and right later. This is the time.

Microdose

In addition to equipping students with counterarguments, introduce weakened or practical examples of false inferences that are harmless (e.g., will not distress your students or cause them to repeat the false belief). This "microdose" or weakened example of the misinformation helps students more easily recognize it in the future.

Be Kind First, Be Right Later: Spectrum of Beliefs

It is very important to consider the degree to which students already believe the misinformation you are aiming to debunk, as well as the current school climate and culture. Ideally, the intervention will reach these students before they are fully bought into the misinformation.

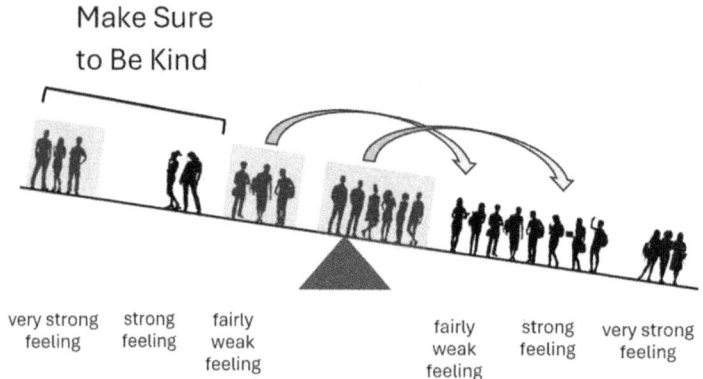

Figure 15.1 Illustration revisiting the spectrum of teacher credibility, emphasizing the importance of showing kindness towards students with the most negative perceptions of your credibility.

Keep the classroom climate open and engaging during the intervention, ensuring that students with hardened viewpoints feel recognized and reaffirmed that their voices have been heard. Avoid speaking down to them or making them feel patronized. This is essential in the process of pulling students closer to you using codes. Very strong feelings need your support.

According to *A Practical Guide* audience receptivity is key to the microdose in particular and the prebunking intervention in general. Recommended is to always maintain intellectual humility and a non-judgemental tone. They stress that refutation and microdosing should not be a one-way conversation. As the guide makes evident, it is important to maintain humility and engage in dialogue with your students after sharing messages that tackle misinformation. (before it becomes widespread.)

Prebunk an Issue or a Technique

In *A Practical Guide to Prebunking*, the authors break prebunking down into two forms: issue-based prebunking and technique-based prebunking. They both address different types of misinformation:

Code 2.1—Issue-Based Approach

Misinformation encountered in your classroom often comes in the form of opinions or beliefs about a particular activating event. However, individual activating events and the associated beliefs can often feed into broader narratives. Issue-based prebunking tackles these broader, persistent narratives of false beliefs beyond the specific activating event.

As *A Practical Guide to Prebunking Misinformation* explains, instead of addressing individual beliefs associated with a specific activating event—which is time-consuming and reactive—prebunking broader student narratives can dismantle the foundations of multiple inaccurate inferences and beliefs at once. This approach can be much more effective at building resilience to new beliefs that share this false foundation. Additionally, the mutual cognitive environment necessary for successful communication between students and teacher can include these broader narratives.

> **EXAMPLE: CLASSROOM AND SCHOOL JUSTICE**
>
> Consider the following student statement in open class:
>
> *Why should I tell you? Nothing will happen. And I'm not a snitch. Do you know what happens to rats? I'll take care of this on my own. No one really cares anyway. It's not fair that I'm being blamed, he said a lot worse than I did.*
>
> This belief is one of many falsehoods that are part of the broader, misleading classroom/school narrative that it is morally justified to take authority into your own hands, to vilify those who cooperate with justice (stigma of snitching), and to distrust school authorities. Prebunking can address this broader narrative by warning students of the consequences of believing in this narrative and interpreting teachers' intentions through this lens. It encourages students to be sceptical of those who advocate these beliefs and to understand the consequences of acting on them, without necessarily debating the specifics of the activating event.

Inaccurate Inferences

Inaccurate Inferences

Deployed as a code, issue-based prebunking targets future inaccurate inference making. Teachers with a "scout mindset" may anticipate how certain activating events can lead to broader, misleading narratives and inaccurate perceptions of teacher credibility. By providing pre-emptive refutation and microdoses, teachers expose students to more accurate interpretations. When an activating event is imminent, prompting students with the pre-exposed code (booster shot) helps constrain and limit possible student inferences about what caring, trustworthiness, and competence look like in this situation. This approach also reduces the spread and" catching" of inaccurate beliefs via contagion.

Figure 15.2 Diagram illustrating issue-based prebunking as a proactive 'scout mindset' strategy—helping students preemptively form accurate inferences about teacher credibility before activating events occur.

> **Quick Note**
>
> Much of the misinformation in your classroom can be traced back to irrational beliefs— the demands and their derivatives. Take this common narrative:
>
> "Most classes are useless. School isn't necessary to live a productive life."
>
> At its core, this reflects a rigid demand:
>
> **"If this class isn't meaningful to me, it better not inconvenience me. And if the teacher makes us work anyway, they're incompetent—and we're justified in checking out."**
>
> This belief combines low frustration tolerance and others-rating—both of which quietly erode your perceived credibility if left unchallenged. Recognizing these narratives gives you a chance to intervene early. You can counter them using Code 1 (REE) to help students dispute the belief, or Code 2 (Prebunking) to warn students about misleading thinking before it spreads.
>
> Unaddressed, these issue-based narratives can grant students social permission to disengage. You'll hear:
>
> "This class is a waste of time.
> "None of this matters in real life."
> "No offense, but this is pointless."
>
> Whether you respond through Rational Emotive Behaviour Therapy (REBT), inoculation, or both, the goal is the same: protect credibility by making irrational thinking visible and replace it with something stronger.

Code 2.2—Technique-Based Approach

Deployed as a Code, technique-based prebunking focuses on the **tactics** used to spread misinformation—not the content itself. This approach shows students how they're being manipulated, without needing to argue over the issue. As explained in A Practical Guide to Prebunking Misinformation, this method builds "broad resistance across multiple encounters of misinformation."

In classrooms, we often see similar techniques across very different narratives:

"Teachers can't tell us what to do."
"Grading is unfair."
"It's morally okay to disrespect authority if it feels unjust."
"School is useless."
"Cooperating with teachers makes you a sellout."

When your students use these kinds of narratives repeatedly, teaching them the underlying manipulation tactics—like false dichotomies, emotional manipulation, or us-vs.-them framing—helps them recognize when they're being influenced, no matter the topic. Because this approach targets techniques (not specific events), it's also:

- Less judgemental: Students don't feel attacked.
- More apolitical: It avoids debates about right or wrong.
- Stronger for group-based misinformation: If the belief is tied to identity or peer loyalty, you're addressing it as a general tactic—not singling anyone out.

Finally, this method helps shape a shared cognitive environment in your classroom. It encourages open thinking and inquiry, rather than reaction and resistance—all essential for your credibility.

Communicative Cooperation

Technique-based interventions can target students' communicative behaviour, specifically informatively and/or materially uncooperative behaviour. Many classroom/school techniques and tactics used to spread misinformation narratives about a teacher's credibility leverage social hierarchies and status to:

1. Manipulate others into believing teacher credibility misinformation.

2. Manipulate others into communicating teacher credibility misinformation deceptively.

3. Manipulate others into acting in antisocial ways with teacher credibility misinformation.

Figure 15.3 Diagram illustrating technique-based prebunking as an effective strategy that proactively fosters both informative and material cooperative behaviour in students.

By introducing technique-based prebunking interventions, you provide your students with a code that helps them understand when and how they are being misled or manipulated. When an activating event is imminent, prompting students with the pre-exposed code provides a framework for interpreting manipulation and its incentives. This can help students recognize why, in a given activating event, positive teacher credibility is perceived negatively and communicated deceptively in order to mislead others and additionally understand the antisocial objectives this tactic serves.

Social Hierarchies and Technique-Based Prebunking

In their article *Classroom Social Dynamics Management: Why the Invisible Hand of the Teacher Matters for Special Education*, Farmer et al. (2017) offer a powerful, real-world look at how peer groups shape classroom culture. They show how social hierarchies—whether across the whole class or within small peer groups—can reinforce exclusion, bullying, or disengagement if left unchecked. Their research gives us a clear picture of what happens when classrooms are organized around social status.

Building on this work, we introduce **Code 2.2: Technique-Based Prebunking** as a strategy for managing social hierarchies and promoting teacher credibility. In these classrooms:

1. **Code 2.2 helps students recognize how they're being manipulated**—especially by peers who use status, ridicule, or false narratives to control group behaviour. When students can name the tactic, they're less likely to fall for it.
2. **It helps shift status towards prosocial behaviour.** By managing peer dynamics and reducing harmful hierarchies, you can tie influence to cooperation and credibility—not conflict or misinformation.

"By viewing the teacher as an invisible hand, we do not need to leave moment-to-moment social factors to chance, but instead can leverage a probabilistic knowledge base to unobtrusively shape the classroom social system."

Farmer et al. (2017) *"Classroom Social Dynamics Management: Why the Invisible Hand of the Teacher Matters for Special Education"*.

As Farmer et al. (2018) explain, students can establish their own rules, expectations, and beliefs that do not necessarily align with broader societal norms. In classrooms like this, students may create peer norms that promote antisocial behaviour and diminish the value of prosocial actions. Understanding classroom social dynamics, therefore, requires attention to how these norms are enacted and reinforced within the peer system.

Hierarchically Organized Classrooms

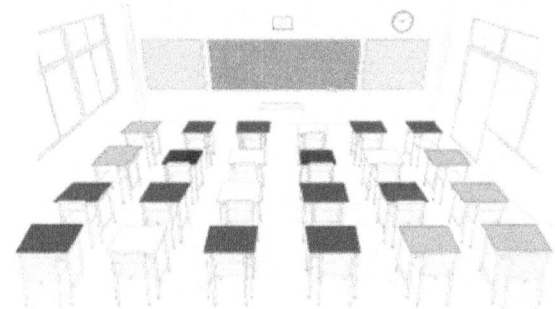

High Status, High Salience Students:

A few students or groups are socially dominant and set the tone for the classroom culture. Everyone knows who they are. Their actions and words influence others. They may not always be well-liked, but other students watch them, talk about them, and respond to what they say and do.

Lower Status, Lower Salience Students:

Socially peripheral or isolated. Mostly unnoticed. Their actions have little effect on group behavior. They are secondary or peripheral in their peer groups, and a few students tend to be isolated and are not members of a peer group.

> Importance of hierarchical social structures is that, depending on the High Status, High Salience Students:

Classroom social dynamics may contribute to a **coercive climate** that supports bullying, social exclusion, **decreased instructional engagement**, and noninclusive roles for socially vulnerable youth. In other words, if left unchallenged, these dynamics can significantly **undermine your teacher credibility**.

Graphic created based on: Farmer, T. W., et al. (2018). Classroom Social Dynamics Management: Why the Invisible Hand of the Teacher Matters for Special Education. *Remedial and Special Education, 39*(3), 177–192. https://doi.org/10.1177/0741932517718359

Figure 15.4 Infographic illustrating how high-status, high-salience students can shape classroom culture and influence teacher credibility in hierarchical social structure.

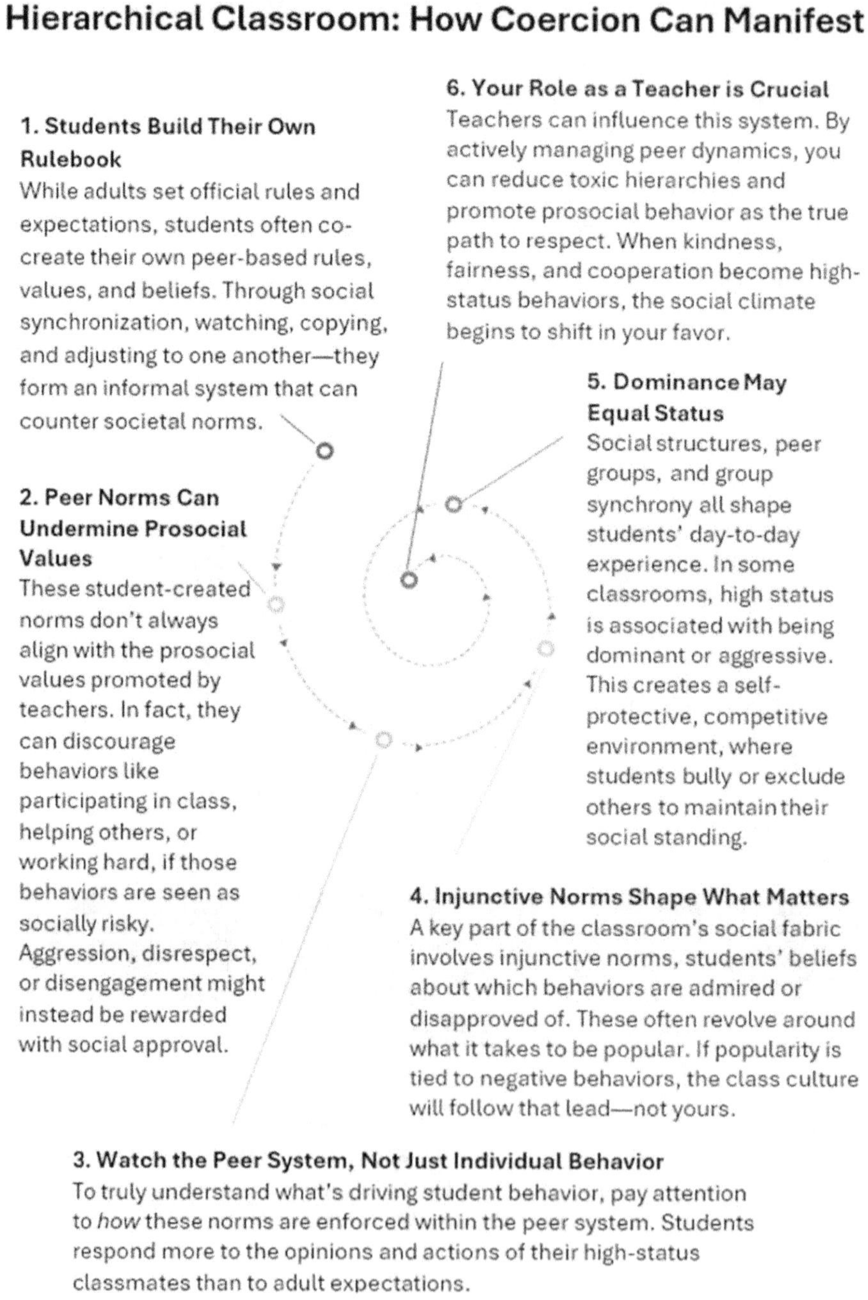

Hierarchical Classroom: How Coercion Can Manifest

1. Students Build Their Own Rulebook
While adults set official rules and expectations, students often co-create their own peer-based rules, values, and beliefs. Through social synchronization, watching, copying, and adjusting to one another—they form an informal system that can counter societal norms.

2. Peer Norms Can Undermine Prosocial Values
These student-created norms don't always align with the prosocial values promoted by teachers. In fact, they can discourage behaviors like participating in class, helping others, or working hard, if those behaviors are seen as socially risky. Aggression, disrespect, or disengagement might instead be rewarded with social approval.

3. Watch the Peer System, Not Just Individual Behavior
To truly understand what's driving student behavior, pay attention to *how* these norms are enforced within the peer system. Students respond more to the opinions and actions of their high-status classmates than to adult expectations.

4. Injunctive Norms Shape What Matters
A key part of the classroom's social fabric involves injunctive norms, students' beliefs about which behaviors are admired or disapproved of. These often revolve around what it takes to be popular. If popularity is tied to negative behaviors, the class culture will follow that lead—not yours.

5. Dominance May Equal Status
Social structures, peer groups, and group synchrony all shape students' day-to-day experience. In some classrooms, high status is associated with being dominant or aggressive. This creates a self-protective, competitive environment, where students bully or exclude others to maintain their social standing.

6. Your Role as a Teacher is Crucial
Teachers can influence this system. By actively managing peer dynamics, you can reduce toxic hierarchies and promote prosocial behavior as the true path to respect. When kindness, fairness, and cooperation become high-status behaviors, the social climate begins to shift in your favor.

Graphic created based on: Farmer, T. W., et al. (2018). Classroom Social Dynamics Management: Why the Invisible Hand of the Teacher Matters for Special Education. *Remedial and Special Education, 39*(3), 177–192.

Figure 15.5 Infographic illustrating the mechanisms by which coercion can emerge and persist in hierarchically structured classrooms, highlighting peer rule-making, status norms, and the critical role of teacher influence.

When it comes to your credibility, this becomes especially important. Norms may be shaped by a group of socially dominant students whose views hold high value among peers. If those views run counter to the behaviours that build teacher credibility—such as fairness, caring, and competence—you face a significant challenge.

Farmer et al. (2018) also describe how coercion can emerge in hierarchical classrooms, where dominant students transmit and enforce these peer norms. This is where Code 2 becomes useful: it helps disrupt not just the false beliefs themselves, but also the *techniques* students use to spread those beliefs through social pressure and coercive dynamics.

Does This Peer System Operate in Your Classroom?

If you answered yes, you're attuned to the social dynamics of material and informative noncooperation, then it's probably time to activate Code 2.2 Remember, the sooner the better, considering the degree to which students already subscribe to norms that undermine your teacher credibility. Once beliefs are solidified or polarized, it can be more challenging to debunk them.

In hierarchically organized classrooms, where dynamics contribute to a coercive climate, a few students or groups can leverage social hierarchies and status to manipulate others into believing misinformation, communicating deception, and/or acting in antisocial ways.

Code 2 (technique-based prebunking) focuses on the tactics used by others in a hierarchical ecosystem. It helps students understand how they are being manipulated, rather than disputing the content of the manipulation.

It is necessary to understand both the overall social hierarchy of the classroom and in distinct peer groups. So, Code 2 is more about managing the peer system in ways that reduce hierarchies and also as a means to link status with prosocial student behaviour.

In that way, it resembles the 'invisible hand' that Farmer advocates in his article, described as a metaphor referring to "teachers' impact on the classroom peer ecology." The invisible hand, in this context, has the potential to "unobtrusively manage the classroom social environment in ways that promote a positive culture for all students." Additionally, it can be used as a social intervention to help prevent the undermining of teacher credibility:

230 ◆ The Teacher Credibility Codebook

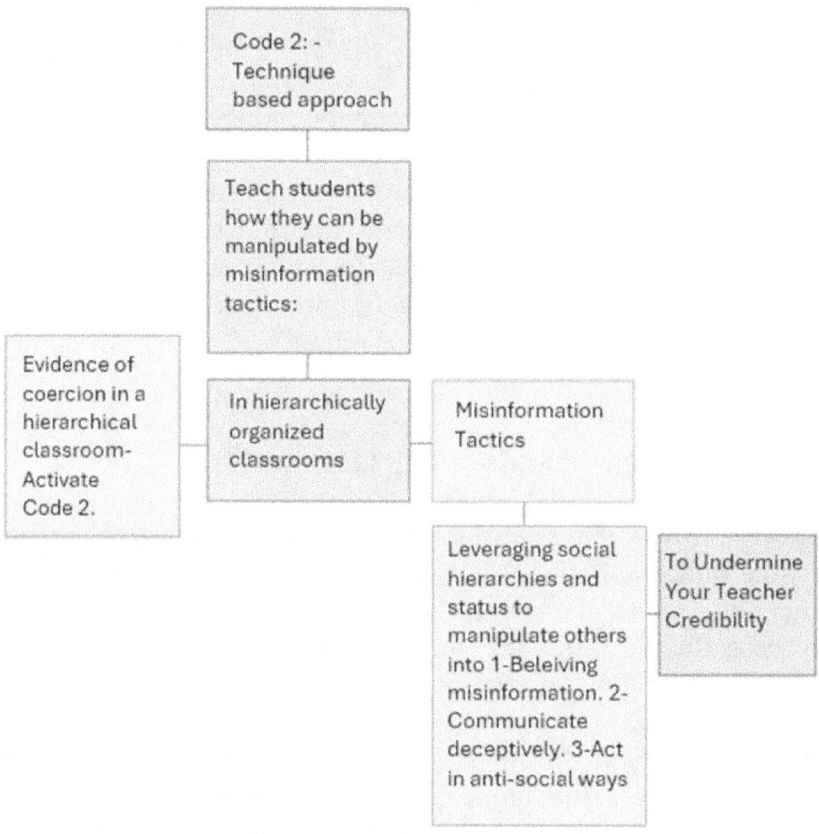

Figure 15.6 Infographic for identifying whether a peer system operates within a hierarchical classroom group, where coercive social contagion may be influencing student behaviour and undermining teacher credibility.

Prebunking: Manipulation through Extortion

Prebunking gives students the tools and knowledge to recognize and resist manipulation *before* it happens. In this lesson, we apply prebunking to a specific classroom dynamic: manipulation and coercion through extortion within peer hierarchies.

Using insights from *A Practical Guide to Prebunking Misinformation*, we will define the purpose of this intervention. In this case, our goal is to protect, enhance, and maintain your teacher credibility by linking prosocial behaviour with respect—and by challenging toxic narratives that reinforce harmful social hierarchies.

Learning Objectives

After completing this prebunking lesson, students will develop:

1. **Knowledge and Skills**
   Students will learn:
   a. What social hierarchies, coercion, and extortion look like in peer settings?
   b. The difference between justice, snitching, and vigilantism.
   c. How to identify when they're part of a hierarchical group—and when someone is using social leverage to manipulate others.
   d. How to counter narratives like:

"Snitches deserve punishment."
   "Loyalty to the group matters more than protecting victims."
   They will build resilience to these coercive messages and practice strategies to resist future manipulation.

2. **Attitudes**
   Students will shift how they:
   a. See themselves—as capable of defending against manipulation and coercion.
   b. View their peers who spread harmful misinformation or use extortion to gain power.
   c. Think about loyalty and silence—not as strength, but as **tools of control** that hurt others.

3. **Behaviours**
   We aim to:
   a. Change how students respond to misinformation like:
      "If you tell, you're a snitch. You're disloyal. You're not a true friend. You'll be excluded. So shut up and follow along… or else."
   b. Promote prosocial behaviour that actively resists coercive hierarchies.
   c. Encourage students to become allies rather than bystanders, and to recognize that true respect comes from protecting others—not from silence or compliance.

These behaviours don't just support peer safety—they reinforce your credibility as a caring, fair, and competent authority figure.

Designing the Intervention Using the Guide

Following the structure from *A Practical Guide to Prebunking Misinformation*, the lesson includes three key components:

Warning
Alert students that manipulation is coming. Set the stage.

"In groups—especially social groups with status and power—manipulation often shows up as *extortion*. It may sound like loyalty, but it's really about control. You'll hear things like:

"Don't rat,"
"Stay loyal,"

or

"If you say something, you're done."

This is not strength—it's fear disguised as leadership.

Preemptive Refutation
Explain the Technique and How It's Manipulative
Preemptive refutation is where you introduce the manipulation technique—in this case, coercion through extortion—and explain why it's misleading, harmful, or false. Just like in Rational Emotive Behaviour Therapy (REBT) or REE, the goal is not to mock or shame, but to equip students with tools to dispute false beliefs before they take hold. Always maintain a non-judgemental tone.

This part of the lesson must be delivered with humility and respect. Avoid being patronizing or preachy. Students may feel vulnerable, and some may have previously participated in the very behaviours you're describing. That's why it's critical to protect their identity, not expose it. Think of this as building "mental antibodies" (as the Guide puts it)—the internal strength to resist manipulation in the future.

The Guide also wisely reminds us to acknowledge the limits of your counterarguments. Some students may already have deeply entrenched views. If you're tackling a narrative they strongly identify with (like "snitching makes you disloyal"), be aware: direct refutation might not work. In fact, it could backfire if students feel personally attacked.

A practical and powerful solution?
Bring in an outside voice—someone students respect and relate to.

For example, when a pro football team visited our school, some players went classroom to classroom speaking with students. They didn't preach. They told real stories—about social hierarchies, loyalty, silence, and regret. And it landed. Some of my students connected to *them* in ways I never could. They issued the warning. They delivered the preemptive refutation.

My role was to keep that message alive—to reinforce it, support it, and guide it forwards in our classroom.

So, if your students are especially attached to the false narrative you're challenging, consider who else might speak to them—not instead of you, but alongside you.

Student Package: A Time-Saving Option for Busy Teachers

If you're a busy teacher with a packed curriculum and limited time, here's a practical strategy I've used before—especially during the refutation stage of prebunking.

Instead of delivering a full lesson, I give students a simple handout that explains the manipulation technique we're addressing (e.g., coercion through extortion). You don't need to overhaul your period or lose instructional time.

This works in any subject area—even if you're teaching chemistry, math, or geography. Just:

1. Distribute the handout.
2. Walk students through the key points with a brief discussion.
3. Collect the handouts afterwards (you can bring them back for follow-up later).

That's it. It's short, simple, and effective—and it doesn't derail your core lesson.

In fact, it often enhances your teaching, because you're showing students that you care about more than just the content—you care about how they're treated, how they think, and how they resist toxic group dynamics. That builds trust. That builds credibility.

> **Quick Note**
> The package doesn't need to be a worksheet. It could be a short film clip, a scene from a novel, a piece of news media—*whatever resonates with you, your students, and your teaching style.*

Sample Student Package

On a school team, a small group of players quietly controls the social hierarchy. They roast others, spread inside jokes, and publicly embarrass teammates during practice and in the locker room. It's not extreme, but it's constant—and accepted as part of the team culture.

One lower-status member of this group starts getting targeted. Even though he's part of the inner circle, he's mocked, excluded, and blamed. He considers speaking up, but he's taken part in the same behaviour. Reporting it would mean exposing the group—and himself. The social fallout—being cut off, losing status—feels worse than the low-level harassment. So, he stays quiet.

He doesn't want to be labelled a snitch. He doesn't want to be kicked out of the group. So, he continues participating, even though he knows it's wrong. Now, someone else on the team—a good teammate—is becoming the focus of harassment by this veteran leadership group.

Background Information

In subcultures where loyalty to the group and a code of silence are highly valued, individuals who refuse to "snitch" or cooperate with authorities may be rewarded with social status and recognition. This can create a hierarchy where those seen as the most loyal—and most willing to protect the group's interests—are elevated in status and granted greater privileges or responsibilities.

This promotion of unethical behaviour acts as a form of **social control**, where the group enforces its norms through rewards and punishments. Loyal members are rewarded; those perceived as disloyal or untrustworthy may be punished or ostracized.

However, rewarding unethical behaviour can harm both individuals and the group. In the short term, it normalizes dishonesty and manipulation. Over time, it can erode trust, weaken group cohesion, and lead to serious consequences—including legal or disciplinary trouble.

In these subcultures, high-status members may exploit or harm less powerful peers without fear of consequences. Victims often hesitate to appeal to formal authorities like teachers or coaches, fearing it will be seen as betrayal and result in retaliation or social exile.

There may also be broader cultural or social barriers to seeking outside help. Some groups distrust authority or believe problems should be solved internally. Victims may also fear retaliation—not just from the original aggressor but from other group members.

In some cases, victims fear reaching out because they've engaged in unethical behaviour themselves. They worry that involving adults could lead to punishment for their own actions. This fear can create a **culture of**

vigilantism, where conflicts are handled informally rather than through legitimate channels of justice.

In such environments, students may feel they *can't* rely on formal authority to help them. Instead, they take matters into their own hands. This often leads to a **cycle of retaliation**, where acts of revenge escalate and students resort to increasingly harmful behaviour in pursuit of control, status, or self-protection.

Example of Student Activities

Think About:

- ★ What does *justice* look like in a situation like this? Who is protected? Who is held accountable?
- ★ What is *vigilantism* in this context? Who decides what's right? Who enforces it?
- ★ When someone *snitches*, what assumptions are being made about loyalty, fairness, and group betrayal?
- ★ When someone *authentically appeals to authority*, how is that different? What might make it feel safer, or more just?

Your Task:

In small groups, create two Venn diagrams:

1. **Justice vs. Vigilantism**
2. **Snitching vs. Authentic Appeals to Authority**

Identify where they **overlap**, and where they are clearly **different**—especially in terms of motivation, consequences, fairness, and who holds power.

Use examples from the team story, the background info, and your own experiences or insights.

3. **Microdose**

A weakened or practical example of misinformation

Use the Learning Objectives for Microdose Discussion

When reviewing the microdose, touch on these key outcomes:

1. Knowledge & Skills
   ☐ Recognize social hierarchies, coercion, and peer-based manipulation.

☐ Understand the difference between justice, snitching, and vigilantism.
☐ Learn how to resist group narratives like "snitches deserve punishment."

2. Attitudes
   ☐ See themselves as capable of resisting manipulation.
   ☐ Rethink loyalty and silence as forms of control—not strength.
   ☐ Recognize harmful group behaviours for what they are.

3. Behaviours
   ☐ Challenge threats like "stay quiet or be excluded."
   ☐ Practice prosocial responses.
   ☐ Act as allies, not bystanders—protecting others builds real respect.

Microdose Scenario One

There's a private group chat where some students joke about classmates, post embarrassing pictures, and spread rumours. Everyone in the chat knows it's messed up, but no one says anything, because that's just "how the group works."

One student starts to feel sick about it. It's not funny anymore. They try to back out but someone in the group says, "Don't even think about leaving. We've got your screenshots too. You don't want those to get out."

Now they feel trapped. If they stay, they're part of the damage. If they speak up, they'll get exposed or kicked out. So, they stay quiet….

Link to Key Outcomes

Knowledge: They now recognize coercion, group control, and how silence protects the powerful.

Attitudes: They begin to question loyalty and see that resisting manipulation takes strength.

Behaviours: They are encouraged to speak up, act as an ally, and understand that protecting others earns real respect—not staying silent.

Microdose Scenario Two

Some of the older players on the team think they run things. They skip drills, mess around during practice, and haze the younger kids. The coach kind of knows something's up, but no one ever says anything.

Then at a team event, a younger player gets completely humiliated in front of everyone. One of the quieter teammates sees it and knows it crossed the line.

Later, they mention it to another player, but get shut down fast: "Don't bring the coach into this. You'll screw it up for everyone. If the team gets in trouble, it's on you." Now they're stuck.

Speak up, and risk losing their spot, their friends, and their rep.

Stay silent, and pretend it never happened. Next practice, they're forced to laugh like it was all just another joke.

Why This Scenario Works

Knowledge: Makes social hierarchy, silence, and coercive group loyalty crystal clear.

Attitudes: Students confront fear, complicity, and the pressure to "protect the group."

Behaviours: Promotes critical thinking about when loyalty becomes harmful and the courage to protect others.

Microdose Scenario Three

Someone in the group gets called out for spreading rumours about another kid. Instead of talking to a teacher, the group decides to "get even." They post embarrassing pics, spread lies online, and tell people not to trust that student.

One person in the group feels like it's gone way too far. They say, "Maybe we should tell a teacher or counsellor—this isn't okay." But the group shuts it down quick: "What, you're going to snitch now? We don't need adults getting involved. They'd just mess it up."

Now that student is stuck. If they speak up, the group turns on them.

If they stay quiet, they're part of the damage. So, they say nothing—and watch it keep going.

Why This Scenario Works

Knowledge: Highlights the difference between vigilantism ("we'll handle it ourselves") and justice (asking for help through proper channels).

Attitudes: Challenges the belief that group loyalty is more important than doing what's right.

Behaviours: Encourages students to question mob-style retaliation, reject coercive silence, and choose prosocial accountability.

Booster Shots for Your Credibility

Now you've got tools you didn't have before. You have a rationale and a structure students can use to recognize, promote, and even reward prosocial behaviour.

Remember: your classroom is shaped by coercive social hierarchies. Students decode your behaviour through the lens of their peer norms. And when those norms are set by high-status, high-salience students, they can directly undermine your credibility with others.

That's why, when you know something like group work will be socially risky or difficult, you can use a microdose ahead of time. Present it to students and open the discussion:

- What do you think about this situation?
- What should a responsible adult do if they overhear students using social power to pressure or control others?
- Would the teacher be justified in stepping in? What does that look like?
- What would a prosocial response from the group look like?

Now, students have the code—the knowledge, attitudes, and behaviours—to interpret your actions accurately, not as threatening their social status within their group... but as caring, trustworthy, and competent.

Misinformation Techniques in the Classroom: Leveraging Social Hierarchy and Status

There are many classroom scenarios where misinformation spreads—often reinforced by social hierarchies and peer status. To explore more real-world examples and practical techniques, visit www.teachercredibility codebook.com.

There, you'll find new contributions from myself and fellow educators, including accessible lesson plans, student-facing strategies, and expanded breakdowns of misinformation techniques that may best resonate with you and your students.

Student Subcultures

Some student subcultures form around values and behaviours that directly oppose the academic goals and expectations of a teacher or school.

These groups often reward status for defiance—skipping homework, mocking assignments, or undermining authority. Loyalty to the group is enforced through tactics like peer pressure and the idea that "ratting" is worse than the behaviour itself.

Classroom Example
A group of students treats academic effort as a joke. They brag about skipping homework, mock assignments, and use sarcasm to discredit the teacher when corrected. Their behaviour is seen as cool, and their popularity gives them influence. Over time, their attitude spreads—making it harder for other students to stay motivated or take school seriously.

Why This Matters
This is an example of an **anti-school subculture** leveraging **social hierarchy** to spread **misinformation**—about school, effort, and even the teacher's credibility. When high-status students reject classroom values, they shape peer norms around disengagement. This damages not just the learning environment, but how students perceive and respond to **you** as a teacher.

Karpman's Drama Triangle
In some classrooms, students use the roles in **Karpman's Drama Triangle** (Karpman, 1968) to manipulate social dynamics and discredit teacher authority:

1. **Victim**—A student claims unfair treatment (whether true or exaggerated).
2. **Persecutor**—The teacher is cast as the villain enforcing rules.
3. **Rescuers**—Peers are recruited to defend the "victim," often based on incomplete or false information.

Classroom Example
A student receives a poor grade, crumples their assignment, and throws it in the trash in front of the class. Some students cheer. When the teacher addresses it, the student claims they're being unfairly targeted. Peers step in to defend them, arguing the teacher plays favourites or didn't offer equal support. The student accepts no responsibility—blaming the teacher entirely. The class begins to adopt that narrative.

Why This Matters
Whether it's one student or part of an anti-school subculture, the **Drama Triangle** can be used to spread **misinformation** about fairness, grading, and

your credibility. When these roles are accepted by peers, they create a distorted story: teacher = unfair persecutor; student = helpless victim. This dynamic damages the classroom culture and makes it harder to uphold standards or maintain trust.

Peer Orientation (Neufeld, 2004)
This isn't a misinformation technique—it's an instinct. According to Gordon Neufeld, peer orientation happens when students form stronger attachment bonds with peers than with adults. The more their identity depends on peers, the more peer approval—and peer rejection—matter.

In his book *Hold On to Your Kids*, Neufeld explains that when peer bonds replace adult relationships, students may become secretive, hostile, or dismissive towards teachers. Their cues come from friends, not authority figures. This peer loyalty can cause students to resist adult guidance—not out of rebellion, but because it feels disloyal to their group.

Classroom Example
You've separated a group of four students who constantly ask to sit together. One is absent, and the other three invite someone new into their group. Before class starts, you ask everyone to sit in their assigned seats. The three original students reluctantly comply, but the new student refuses—choosing peer closeness over following directions.

After a warning, they move—but spend the entire class acting out while the group cheers them on. The defiance isn't random—it's reinforced, even rewarded, by peer approval.

Why This Matters
Peer-oriented students will often resist adult expectations if they conflict with peer loyalty. In this case, the teacher becomes the outsider, withholding proximity. The group doesn't just break rules—they reinterpret the teacher's actions as unfair, spreading misinformation about intent and authority.

Neufeld calls this counterwill—the instinct to push back when control comes from someone the student isn't emotionally attached to. When peer relationships dominate, counterwill protects the bond with peers and undermines the bond with you.

Social Media Apps
Social media strengthens classroom social hierarchies by running 24/7 and connecting students with peers far beyond the classroom. It amplifies the gap

between high- and low-status students, making group norms harder to challenge and peer pressure harder to escape. Constant visibility, group chats, and the permanence of posts can reduce collaboration and increase student anxiety about social image.

Why This Matters

In any of the previous scenarios—peer orientation, anti-school subcultures, or victim-persecutor-rescuer dynamics—**social media acts as an amplifier**. It extends peer influence beyond your reach, reinforcing status-based norms that can contradict classroom values.

Students may resist rules, avoid participation, or reject teacher authority—not because of what's happening in the room, but because of pressure or narratives playing out online. Even if teachers aren't aware of the source, they'll feel the effects through shifts in student behaviour, morale, and engagement.

When credibility is on the line, social media can quietly shape how students interpret your decisions—and how far they're willing to go to stay in good standing with their peer group.

And for more Code 1 and 2 and teacher resources visit www.teachercredibilitycodebook.com

Chapter Review

- ★ Code 2 helps students resist false beliefs **before** they take hold. Like the ABC Model, it strengthens their mental filters—making them less vulnerable to **peer pressure, social contagion**, and **groupthink**.
- ★ Prebunking works by giving students **small, pre-emptive examples** ("microdoses") of how beliefs can be distorted. These are used ahead of activating events—like a test, correction, or peer conflict—as "booster shots" to shape how students interpret your credibility: your caring, trustworthiness, and competence.
- ★ You can use Code 2 on its own or combine it with **Rational Emotive Education (Code 1)** to build stronger resistance to irrational thinking.
- ★ Research from **Farmer et al. (2018)** shows that students often build peer norms that clash with school values—especially in hierarchical classrooms. Prebunking disrupts not only the false beliefs, but also the **social pressure to adopt them**.

> **Key Takeaway:**
>
> Prebunking equips students to resist distorted beliefs and peer pressure—**before** credibility is lost. It prepares them to interpret your actions fairly, even in challenging moments.

Looking Back

We've covered a lot:

Part I explored how student perceptions form—from inference-making to cognitive environments and social contagion.

Part II examined the forces behind aligned and divergent classrooms, and how hidden attributes shape collective narratives.

Part III introduced practical tools—REE and Prebunking Codes—to challenge distorted beliefs and protect your credibility.

Now, before we move into the **Quick-Start Study Guide**, let's take one last look at Classroom A, but from a new perspective.

What happens when a classroom is composed primarily of students with influences that, according to Hattie's research, have effect sizes likely to negatively impact achievement? (Visible Learning MetaX, 2024)

These influences, such as anxiety, frustration, or procrastination—don't just affect how students learn. They shape how they perceive your credibility, interpret your behaviour, and respond to your teaching—even when you're doing everything right.

So now, with the tools you've gained, what does it look like to lead, teach, and thrive in a classroom like this? In my experience, classrooms like these are never easy—but when your credibility holds, they're the most rewarding of all. Use the study guide to prepare a lesson plan for a divergent group like Class A, with your credibility not just intact, but strengthened.

Student Influences in Classroom A

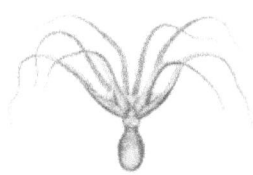 Likely to have a negative impact on achievement       Potential to considerably accelerate achievement

Negative Student Influences

- Anger
- Boredom
- Lack of Attendance
- Procrastination
- Depression
- Anxiety
- Frustration
- Stereotype Threat
- Lack of sleep
- Aggression/Violence

Positive Student Influences

- Emotional Intelligence
- Executive functioning
- Working memory strength
- Self control
- Self-efficacy
- Intelligence & Achievement
- Critical Thinking
- Relating Creativity to Achievement
- Happiness, Motivation, Enjoyment

Based on data from Visible Learning MetaX (2024)

Figure 15.7 Infographic comparing negative and positive student influences in Classroom A, based on Hattie's Visible Learning MetaX (2024). Shows how hidden attributes, both harmful and beneficial, affect teacher credibility perception.

As We Move into the Quick-Start Study Guide, Ask Yourself This

Would you approach teaching **Classroom A** any differently now that you better understand student inference-making, cognitive environments, and how perceptual variance can persist—even in the presence of high-credibility teaching?

Consider how the **student influences** in Classroom A shape your planning. What changes might you make before formally launching your lesson, your learning intentions, norms, or feedback strategies now that you see the room through this lens? Do you look at lesson planning any different?

References

Farmer, T. W., et al. (2018). Classroom social dynamics management: Why the invisible hand of the teacher matters for special education. *Remedial and Special Education, 39*(3), 177–192.

Harjani, T., Roozenbeek, J., Biddlestone, M., van der Linden, S., Stuart, A., Iwahara, M., Piri, B., Xu, R., Goldberg, B., & Graham, M. (2022). *A practical guide to prebunking misinformation*. https://prebunking.withgoogle.com/docs/A_Practical_Guide_to_Prebunking_Misinformation.pdf

Karpman, S. (1968). Fairy tale drama triangle. *Transactional Analysis Bulletin, 7*(26), 39–43.

Neufeld, G., & Maté, G. (2004). *Hold on to your kids: Why parents need to matter more than peers*. Vintage Canada.

Visible Learning MetaX. (2024). *Visible learning MetaX: Research database of influences on student achievement*. Retrieved from https://www.visiblelearningmetax.com

16

Quick-Start Study Guide
Turning Codes into Classroom Practice

Overview

Whether you're using the Codebook on your own, with a colleague or as a Professional Learning Community (PLC), most teachers start with lesson planning. That's because planning—*before any activating events occur*—is the ideal moment when student beliefs are most open to influence. It's through your choices about learning intentions, classroom norms, and feedback that those beliefs begin to take shape.

This is where your **scout mindset** comes into play: *How will the behaviours I'm about to communicate be interpreted by my students?* For example, when you return graded assignments or correct behaviour in a group, ask yourself:

- **What beliefs will students form about me?** Will those inferences be accurate or distorted? Rational or irrational?
- **Will students communicate their beliefs truthfully or deceptively?** Will they respond with prosocial or antisocial behaviours based on their perception of my credibility?
- **Will my actions be read as caring, trustworthy, and competent**—or something else entirely?
- **How might these interpretations spread among peers and shape a collective narrative** about my credibility or the lesson itself?

DOI: 10.4324/9781003644088-20

By proactively considering how your actions will be perceived, you create opportunities for **rational inferences** and **prosocial behaviour**—the core outcomes of using the Codebook.

This short chapter offers a five-step quick-start study guide to help you, and your colleagues apply the Codebook directly to your lesson planning, a practical, collaborative path to begin applying the Codebook to your own personal lesson design. It's simple enough for busy teachers to use immediately, and powerful enough to reshape how your students interpret, respond to, and communicate about your credibility.

Lesson Planning through the Lens of Student Belief

Use whatever lesson planning format you and your colleagues are most familiar with and comfortable with. Here's a simple example:

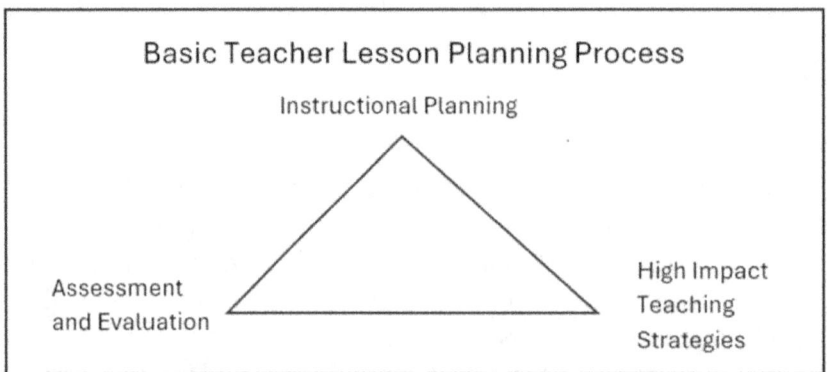

Figure 16.1 Diagram of the Basic Teacher Lesson Planning Process, showing three interconnected components: Instructional Planning, High-Impact Teaching Strategies, and Assessment and Evaluation.

This study guide doesn't ask you to change what already works. Instead, it invites you to add just one powerful element to your existing process: **student belief about your behaviour during this lesson that maintains, builds, and protects your credibility.**

Why? Because how students interpret your actions directly shapes their motivation and behaviour. Everything else in your lesson planning stays exactly the same.

Ask yourself: "What do I want students to believe about me by the end of this lesson?"

```
                Instructional Planning
                         /\
                        /  \
                       / Student \
                      /  Belief   \
                     /              \
   Assessment       /_____\      High Impact
   and Evaluation                           Teaching
                                            Strategies
```

Figure 16.2 Diagram illustrating a conventional lesson plan enhanced with one key innovation: adding "Student Belief" as a central consideration alongside instructional planning, assessment, and high-impact strategies.

Quick-Start Credibility Study Guide

This five-step study guide is designed to help you apply the Codebook directly to your lesson planning—whether you're working independently, with a colleague, or in a PLC. It offers a simple, structured process that integrates student belief into your planning to build, maintain, and protect your credibility in the classroom.

Step 1: Discuss the Checklist

Review the checklist at the end of Part II with your colleague or PLG. Discuss whether the listed criteria are present in your classroom. Use this as an opportunity to revisit earlier chapters and begin talking about student belief data.

Step 2: Data and Mutual Cognitive Environments

Gather teaching and student perceptual data. Use video recordings, observations, and student surveys (like the McCroskey Scale). Collect writing prompts and classroom behaviour evidence to determine how your intentions are being interpreted. Ask: Do student beliefs align with your behaviour—or are they distorted by motivation, past experiences, or peer influence?

> **Step 3: Apply the Core Irrational Belief Table**
>
> Review your lesson plan through the lens of Core Irrational Belief II ("Other Rating"). Discuss which lesson components (group work, homework, deadlines) could trigger justified defiance. Refer to the Chapter 12 table to predict and plan for misinterpretations.
>
> **Step 4: Discussion—What's Driving the Credibility Threat?**
>
> Ask: Is the threat to credibility coming from teaching behaviour, a perception, a belief, or a motivation? If it's a behaviour, adjust your classroom strategies. If it's a belief, use Code 1 or 2. Discuss whether social contagion or peer dynamics are driving false narratives.
>
> **Step 5: Build Your REE or Prebunking Plan**
>
> Use your insights to develop a rational thinking (REE) or prebunking mini-lesson. Design a collaborative activity that helps students challenge irrational beliefs or inoculate against misinformation. Reinforce these strategies before and during the lesson using booster shots to sustain prosocial interpretations.

Step 1: Discuss the Checklist

Yes, it really is that simple. With your colleague or PLC, take a look at the Checklist for Understanding Hidden Attributes at the end of Part II. Go through the list together and ask: Do these criteria apply to our classrooms?

Start with the first item: **You're consistently demonstrating credible, supportive teaching:**

That's your foundation. If you're already doing that—and still seeing student resistance, defiance, or disengagement—this checklist helps uncover why. This is also a good moment to start thinking and talking about **data**—student voice, classroom behaviour trends, or even your own reflections. Feel free to revisit earlier chapters as needed. This checklist pulls together the key ideas, so you can begin applying them where it matters most: in real classrooms.

Checklist for Understanding Hidden Attributes

How do I know if hidden motivations and social contagion are at work in my classroom—and what do I do about it?

You likely need the Codebook if:

1. ☑ You're consistently demonstrating credible, supportive teaching.

2. ☑ Yet a significant number of students still interpret your behavior negatively, even when your actions clearly demonstrate caring, trustworthiness and competence.

This suggests:

3. ☑ Student interpretations are being shaped by hidden attributes, irrational thinking and peer influence, not by your actual behavior.

4. ☑ That's why perception varies across students, and why some develop persistently inaccurate inferences, a pattern I call the *Divergent Profile*.

5. ☑ These inaccurate inferences aren't just misunderstandings. They're emotionally charged, rigid beliefs, central to the ABC Model, that distort how students interpret your actions (A) and lead to negative emotional or behavioral responses (C).

6. ☑ Hidden attributes and social contagion explain how distorted beliefs can take root, and how they can erode your credibility, even when your teaching is strong.

So what do you about it?

7. ☑ At the root of informatively and materially uncooperative behavior are distorted beliefs, shaped by internal student motivations like social contagion and other hidden attributes. These beliefs distort how students interpret your behavior (A) and lead to the negative consequences you see (C).

Change the belief to change the perception.

8. ☑ To shift student perception, you must target not just the belief—but the motivation behind it. These motivations shape how students interpret everything you do.

A   B   C

So how do you do that?

9. ☑ Use the **Credibility Codebook** to target *B*—students' beliefs—through practical, research-informed strategies. These are organized into *codes*: tools designed to help students form more accurate inferences, resist peer-driven distortions, and adopt healthier, more rational beliefs about your behavior.

Figure 16.3 Excerpt of the "Checklist for Understanding Hidden Attributes," designed for use in PLGs to guide lesson planning discussions.

Step 2: Data and Mutual Cognitive Environments

Now that you've reviewed the checklist, it's time to gather data that helps you interpret and respond to student beliefs. This is where the concept of **mutual cognitive environments** becomes practical: What are you intending to communicate and what are students actually perceiving?

One of the best ways to explore this gap is by working with a trusted colleague or coach. Start by observing your teaching, or even better—**video a lesson.** This gives you clear, observable data about your communication, classroom behaviours, and teacher credibility. If you're trying to develop more credible behaviours (or clarify the ones you already use), this is the ideal moment to collaborate. Before you move further down the checklist, consider checking off this crucial step.

A—Collect Credibility Data from Your Students

Discuss with your colleague or PLC: How would we go about collecting authentic feedback about what students believe about us as teachers? As John Hattie notes:

> *This is a call for more about the **students' conceptions** of what it means to be a learner, whether the class is an inviting place to come and learn, and students' conceptions of their learning. Such feedback to teachers could be among the more powerful to improve teaching quality.*

So, here are a few ways to collect perceptual data. They can be used not only to measure and develop a better understanding of your students' present credibility beliefs, but also to measure the effectiveness of your credibility intervention (code) at the end of your lesson.

Tools to Collect Student Belief Data

- **Exit Tickets or Surveys**
  Use the *McCroskey Teacher Credibility Scale* to gather student ratings of your *care, trustworthiness*, and *competence*. You can use the full 16-item version or select 1–2 questions per dimension for a quick pulse check.
- **Writing Prompts:**
  Try reflective questions like: "When you get a disappointing grade, what do you assume? That I don't care? That I didn't teach it well? That the assignment was unfair?" Collect these responses and review

them with a colleague. **Ask**: Are these perceptions grounded in observed classroom reality, or distorted by emotions, past experiences, or peer influence. Do these responses signal an instructional issue—or a motivational one?
- **Behaviour and Work Sample Review**
  Examine student work and engagement after a lesson where **you know** your teaching was strong. If your lesson was clear, engaging, and aligned with curriculum—and student responses are still negative, disengaged, or incomplete—that's a key indicator of motivation influencing student perception as it diverges from observed classroom reality.

B—Collect Data from Your Own Teaching

Record and analyse your own teaching with a colleague. Use a coaching approach to examine, for example:

- Time on task
- Teacher talk vs. student talk
- Respectful interactions
- Disruptions

Jim Knight's (2017) Impact Cycle is a great resource for collaborative coaching tools to observe teaching behaviours, gather feedback, and reflect on credibility alignment. **Ask**: Does the way I appear to teach match the way students are perceiving me? If there's a disconnect, is it rooted in your instructional behaviour—or in how students are interpreting that behaviour?

Tie It Back to the Codebook

As you gather data, keep Parts 1 and 2 of the Codebook close at hand. These chapters help interpret your findings through concepts like:

- Inference-making
- Communicative cooperation
- Social contagion
- Echo chambers
- Divergent profiles
- Hidden attributes

Use these tools to determine whether the perception problem is driven by irrational beliefs, uncooperative communicative behaviour, peer influence, or gaps in instructional behaviour.

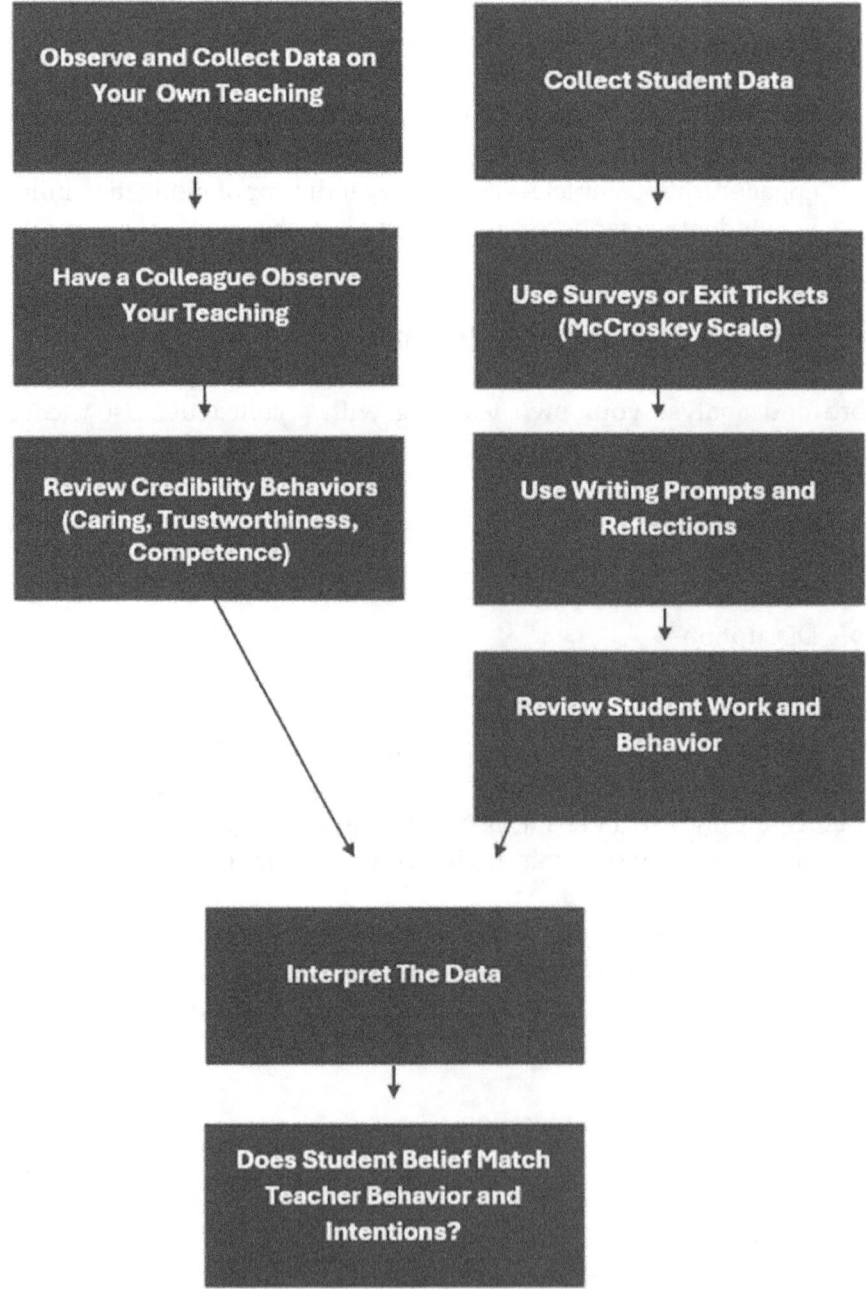

Figure 16.4 Flowchart: Gathering and Interpreting Teacher Credibility Data.

Step 3: Use the Core Irrational Belief Table

Now it's time to apply what you've gathered.

With your colleague or PLC, take a closer look at your developing lesson plan. Ask yourselves:

- Is the lesson structured around formative vs. summative assessments?
- Will students present their work in front of peers?
- Does it involve group work and collaborative teams?
- Will it include homework or independent assignments?
- Is the lesson scaffolded in stages, where falling behind is a real risk?

Each of these examples, and others, can act as an activating event—a moment in the lesson where students form beliefs about your behaviour and intentions.

Why This Matters

Use your scout mindset here: Are any of these lesson elements likely to activate Core Irrational Belief II in students? This belief—what we call the "Other Rating"—distorts your behaviour through a lens of justified defiance:

Student Irrational Belief	Classroom Interpretation	Credibility Consequence	Credibility Domain Affected	Justified Defiance Response
You must be nice and fair to me at all times.	Misinterprets feedback or discipline as personal attack	Sees teacher as uncaring	Caring	Talks back, ignores instruction, claims victimhood
You must teach in a way I enjoy or prefer.	Rejects legitimate instruction if it's not entertaining	Sees teacher as incompetent	Competence	Disengages, mocks lesson, undermines instruction
You must agree with me or validate my perspective.	Feels slighted when challenged or corrected	Sees teacher as untrustworthy	Trustworthiness	Accuses teacher of bias, refuses to listen
If you **don't meet my expectations**, you're a bad teacher.	I am not listening to anything you say.	Credibility collapses	All domains	Rallies peers, spreads rumors, refuses cooperation

Figure 16.5 Excerpt of the Core Irrational Belief II designed for designed for use in PLGs to guide lesson planning discussions.

"The teacher does not care, is unfair, or disrespectful, so I'm justified in defiance, pushing back and disrespect."

If your student or teacher data already suggests that this belief is present in your classroom, now is the time to plan for it:

Refer to the Table

Use the **Core Irrational Belief Applied to Teacher Credibility Table** from Chapter 12: "The One Core Irrational Belief That Destroys Your Credibility."

Together with your partner, use the table to:

- Identify lesson elements that may trigger Core Irrational Belief II.
- Predict potential misinterpretations of your teaching behaviours.
- Spot consequences like resistance, disengagement, or peer-aligned defiance.
- Strategize credibility-building responses in advance (Code 1 or Code 2).

Goal of This Step

By anticipating student misinterpretations before the lesson, you avoid being blindsided by them during the lesson. Discuss how you might use the Core Irrational Belief Applied to Teacher Credibility Table to review your developing lesson. How will you avoid activating events and student beliefs that lead to the dreaded justified defiance… the King and the Factory's most unpleasant product.

Step 4: Discussion—What's Driving the Credibility Threat?

Now that you've collected and analysed your data, it's time to act. **Ask**: Based on what we now understand, what's the best next move to protect or restore credibility?

- If it's a **teacher behaviour issue**, use classroom management, instructional clarity, or climate-building strategies to shift student response.
- If it's a **belief issue**, use **Code 1** (REE) or **Code 2** (Prebunking) to realign perceptions and disrupt distorted narratives.

Also consider: If it's a **belief issue**, then motivation is likely **shaping perception**. In that case, discuss:

- Which Code (Code 1: Rational Belief Replacement or Code 2: Prebunking Misinformation) or a combination of both, will best protect your credibility?
- What strategies will help students revise irrational interpretations, social contagion and misinformation?

Review your data for signs of **social contagion** or **hierarchical peer dynamics** that may be fuelling or sustaining false narratives:
- Are high-status students modelling defiant beliefs?
- Are inaccurate perceptions spreading among peers before you even begin the lesson?

Identifying the source of the threat is the key to planning your lesson effectively.

Step 5: Build Your REE or Prebunking Approach

This is where your credibility-building plan becomes real. With your lesson plan in hand and your understanding of student belief in focus, work collaboratively to: **Design a Rational Emotive Education (REE) Mini-Lesson**

Revisit **Part 3: Activating the Codebook**, and choose the REE Code that fits your situation.

- What irrational belief are you helping students confront?
- How will you help them replace it with a rational alternative?
- How can all students—regardless of where they fall on the belief spectrum—participate with your support?

Use scaffolding, modelling, and discussion to make this safe, collaborative, and empowering learning experience for your students.

AND/OR: Plan a Prebunking Strategy

If you've identified **manipulation**, **social contagion**, or **false narratives**, consider an **issue-based** or **technique-based prebunking approach**:

- Issue-based: Tackle a common false belief head-on (e.g., "School is useless, no one here cares.").
- Technique-based: Reveal and neutralize the manipulation tactic itself (e.g., peer coercion, exaggeration, victimization).

Use **booster shots** to reinforce the strategy before the lesson begins, and revisit as needed. These are great, low-emotional levers to get students back on track.

Final Reminder

With this quick-start process, you're not just building lessons—you're building credibility in a way that protects learning and empowers students. You're showing them how to think clearly, interpret fairly, and behave respectfully, even in challenging situations. For more teacher created resources, please visit www.teachercredibilitycodebook.com

Discussion Prompts for the Five-Step Quick-Start Guide

Step 1: Discuss the Checklist
You're consistently demonstrating credible, supportive teaching
- ★ Are there any items where we're uncertain or inconsistent? What makes us say that?
- ★ Have we ever been surprised by a student reaction—even when we believed we were being clear, fair, or supportive?
- ★ What past experiences (ours or students') might be influencing how credibility is built or eroded in our classrooms?

Step 2: Data and Mutual Cognitive Environments
How are our intentions being interpreted?
- ★ What does our student data tell us about how students currently perceive us?
- ★ Have we seen a gap between what we believe we're communicating and how students interpret it?
- ★ Based on classroom behaviour or feedback, what inferences do we think students are making about our credibility?
- ★ What data could help us clarify whether this is a **teaching** issue or a **student interpretation** issue?

Step 3: Use the Core Irrational Belief Table
Is this lesson vulnerable to distorted beliefs?
- ★ Are here any parts of this lesson that might trigger Core Irrational Belief II (Other-Blaming)?

- ★ Which parts of our plan might feel unfair, confusing, or judgemental—even if they're well-designed?
- ★ What irrational interpretations might students form—and what would those sound like?
- ★ How can we adjust the lesson, or prepare students, to minimize these risks?

Step 4: Discussion—What's Driving the Credibility Threat?
Is the issue a behaviour, a belief, a perception, or a motivation?
- ★ If students respond poorly, what's most likely driving it?
- ★ A gap in our instruction?
- ★ A misperception of our intent?
- ★ A motivational belief (e.g., Karpman's Drama Triangle, Low Self-Regulated Learning)?
- ★ Peer influence or social contagion?
- ★ What behaviours or structures could we change immediately to strengthen credibility?
- ★ What supports or conversations could we offer to students who may be misinterpreting us?

Step 5: Build Your REE or Prebunking Plan
How can we shift beliefs before they distort learning?
- ★ Which irrational beliefs or narratives do we want to address head-on?
- ★ Are we focusing more on internal beliefs (Code 1: REE) or external social pressure (Code 2: Prebunking)?
- ★ How can we structure this as a collaborative, safe discussion—not a correction?
- ★ How will we know if our REE or prebunking strategy is working?
- ★ What "booster shots" can we use throughout the unit to keep credibility strong?

Final Prompt (Post-Planning Reflection)

This guide doesn't ask you to change what already works. Instead, it adds one key question to your planning:

"If this lesson goes as planned, what do we hope students will believe about us by the end?"

That one shift—focusing on how students interpret your behaviour—can help protect and build your credibility. Why does it matter? Because what students believe about your caring, trustworthiness, and competence directly impacts how they behave and engage.

Everything else in your planning stays the same. This guide just helps you make student belief a more intentional part of the process.

The five-step approach can be used on your own, with a colleague, or in a PLC. And it emphasizes one often-overlooked element: **data**. To strengthen your credibility, you need feedback on two things:

1. What students believe about you
2. What you believe about your own teaching

Together, these insights help you plan more purposefully—and protect what matters most: your credibility in the eyes of your students.

Chapter Review

★ Whether you're working on your own, with a colleague, or in a PLG, lesson planning is the most effective place to start using the Codebook. That's because planning—*before* any activating events occur—is when student beliefs are most open to influence.

★ This study guide doesn't ask you to change what's already working. Instead, it adds one powerful layer: considering how students are likely to interpret your behaviour during the lesson, and how that perception affects their motivation, cooperation, and engagement.

★ The process starts with data collection—not just from your students, but from your own teaching. Ask: *Does how I appear to teach match how students experience me?*

★ As you gather this data, connect it back to Parts I and II of the Codebook. Use tools like inference-making, communicative cooperation, echo chambers, social contagion, and hidden attributes to better understand what's driving any disconnect.

 Key Takeaway:

Planning isn't just about what you'll teach—it's about how students will interpret you while you teach it. When you plan with credibility in mind, you shape beliefs that drive motivation, cooperation, and trust.

References

Knight, J. (2017). *The impact cycle: What instructional coaches should do to foster powerful improvements in teaching*. Corwin.

McCroskey, J. C., & Teven, J. J. (1999). Goodwill: A reexamination of the construct and its measurement. *Communication Monographs, 66*(1), 90–103. https://www.jamescmccroskey.com/publications/180.pdf

For Product Safety Concerns and Information please contact our EU representative GPSR@taylorandfrancis.com
Taylor & Francis Verlag GmbH, Kaufingerstraße 24, 80331 München, Germany

www.ingramcontent.com/pod-product-compliance
Lightning Source LLC
Chambersburg PA
CBHW081145230426
43664CB00018B/2815